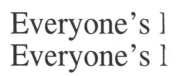

Everyone's]
Everyone's]

A Trip of a Lifetime.....Literally

By: Joei Carlton Hossack

Skeena Press
P.O. Box 19071
Sarasota, Florida 34276-2071

September 16, 2007.

To Heather Herd.

Enjoy the journey

Joei Carlton Hossack

Published by: Skeena Press
                  P.O. Box 19071
                  Sarasota, Florida 34276-2071

Copyright © 1998 Joei Carlton Hossack

Cover Design: Jeffrey Stephen Rafuse
                  Copico Inc.
                  Mississauga, Ontario, Canada

ISBN Number: 0-9657509-1-4

Library of Congress Catalogue Card Number: 98-90573

Printed in USA
Printing 10 9 8 7 6 5 4 3 2

For Paul

Dedicated to the wonderful people who helped me when I could not help myself.

Special thanks to Joe Burke, Joan Dressler, Elizabeth Pace and Peter Teigrob for their editing skills.

By the Same Author:

Restless From The Start
By: Joei Carlton Hossack

ISBN Number: 0-9657509-0-6

Library of Congress Number: 97-91654

Available from: Skeena Press
                     P.O. Box 19071
                     Sarasota, Florida 34276-2071

U.S. Funds: $10.95
Postage and Handling: $3.50
Florida Sales Tax: 7%

Chapter 1

"Where the hell are you going?" demanded Anna, my favorite customer, slamming the door of my wool shop.

"Paul and I are going traveling," I answered as nonchalantly as I could.

"What do you mean, you're going traveling?" "When are you leaving?" "Where are you going?" "When are you coming back?" all her questions starting to run together.

"We're going to Europe." "We're leaving when we sell everything and I have no idea when we're coming back," I answered, hoping I hadn't left out any of her questions.

"You can't travel forever," Anna whined, her lower lip starting to quiver. "Why don't you sublet the store and reopen it when you come back?" she volunteered.

"No, I need a change." "When, or should I say if, Paul and I come back, we'll do something together." "I don't know what yet," I said confidently. "He needs a change too."

This conversation would be repeated over and over, day after day, until all my customers knew, I would be leaving. They believed none of it. Perhaps I didn't either, however, I went along explaining all of our plans to everyone who asked.

Although I had been talking about going traveling for the five years that I had owned my store, putting a "Business For Sale" sign in my window, took my customers completely by surprise. The date was April 1, 1989.

I signed a new two year lease, with a two year option,

for the nine hundred square foot store that was located in the heart of the Italian/Greek area on the Danforth in Toronto, Canada. The owner of the building was pleased that I renewed the lease; but, it was signed with the understanding that I could sublet the store if I could not sell the business. The same day that I signed the papers, I put the business up for sale, advertising it in several Toronto newspapers.

If I was not able to sell the business, I did not want another wool store to move in the day I closed my doors. I had worked hard creating a business where there was none. I did not want anyone to take advantage of my hard work.

When the business did not sell by the end of the first month, I put all the stock on a 'fifty percent off' sale. I called my customers to let them know about the bargains and by the end of the day they were arriving in carloads. They brought their friends and bought the yarns, wools and needlepoints by large, black, garbage bags full.

Thankfully, my customers supported me right to my last day. Some customers even brought potential buyers for the business to the store. Everyone I did business with, suppliers and customers alike, knew my little shop was a going concern. No one believed that I would walk away from such a profitable business, but my husband had been dreaming about traveling for ten years or more and I would have followed him to the ends of the earth. Besides, we had to do it now. We were still young and were both in good health. We had put away the money for our adventure and we needed an exciting change in our lives. Before I could leave the country, however, I had one problem to correct. I needed knee surgery.

It was a disastrous cross country skiing accident in 1974 that precipitated major surgery to pin and staple my knee back together. The initial surgery had lasted, without complications, until the mid 1980's. By 1989, however, several times a year, floating debris would get caught in the knee joint, causing severe pain. I would limp noticeably until it dislodged. With the help of orthoscopic surgery, I was promised relief. "A piece of cake" the doctor had called it. My surgery was scheduled for the twenty third of June. In preparation, I would close my store on the first of June.

In the end, after much advertising and spreading the

news by word of mouth through friends and customers, there were no buyers for the business and most of the stock had been sold. I sublet the store to an acquaintance from the flea markets who was a distributor of bathing suits. On the last day of May, Paul and I moved boxes crammed full of unsold craft supplies and a dozen metal shelving units into the basement of our home in the Beach area of Toronto. My customers were devastated.

My days became unstructured. I continued to visit the nursing homes, hospitals and flea markets in an effort to get rid of my excess stock. Also, since I could arrange to be home any day I chose and could keep the place neat and tidy, we listed the house with a real estate agent. Toronto was still at the peak of the housing market and we hoped to take advantage of it. Initially, as with the store, many looked, no one offered.

The surgery, on that Friday in June, was a disaster. From the moment I opened my eyes, I knew I was in trouble. I awoke gagging and immediately started vomiting on the sip of water I had been given. Hoisting myself up on one elbow, I looked down at my knee and saw rivulets of blood running down my right leg. The layer of bandages that covered the three small holes was soaked. The nursing staff had been watching me and as soon as I opened my eyes a nurse came and stood at my side. She put a layer of fresh bandages over the bloody ones and applied light pressure She sent an aide for a cold cloth for my forehead, that had beads of prespiration forming from the slight exertion. My head was throbbing.

The "piece of cake" that was supposed to have taken forty-five to fifty minutes, according to the doctor, had taken over three hours. Sedatives relaxed my stomach while I waited for Paul to come get me.   When I left the hospital that evening, four hours later than expected, I was woozy and giggly on relaxants. We stopped only once on the way home and filled the prescription for pain killers. It was a long and painful night. Not too graceful, the next morning, I hobbled around.

I rested and recuperated over the weekend trying not to move too much for fear of opening the stitches. On Monday, a nurse from the hospital called to advise that the operation had not been successful and my doctor wanted to schedule more surgery. I refused. By the end of the week, my thigh muscle atrophied. The same had occurred after the 1974 surgery. I would have to endure the same painful procedure as before. I needed physiotherapy.

Paul was an investment dealer. In early July he gave his company two months notice. Merrill Lynch spent the months trying to convince Paul to take a leave of absence for as long as he wanted. They could not believe they were losing "The Hoss." So many people talk about "packing it in and no one ever really does it," they argued. They were positive we would go traveling for a couple of months and return home sick to death of camping, foreigners and, possibly, each other. Paul promised his company that he would give them the right of first refusal, if he came back. They had no choice. They accepted his resignation.

The phrase we heard most often, from our friends and family, in those months of preparation was "we were living their dream." Everyone talks about getting out of the rat race. No one ever does it. Why would we be any different, we wondered. But we were different. Of that, we were sure. We were really leaving.

It took time, energy and a persistent real estate agent, but we eventually sold the house and at the price we wanted. We wanted to close the deal quickly and since the buyers paid us forty percent in cash, we held the mortgage. The mortgage payment would be our traveling money and our friend and lawyer, Pat Thomas, agreed to make the monthly deposit and pay our bills for us.

We spent mid August to mid September getting rid of everything we could. We had yard sales every week. Although I still called on the nursing homes and hospitals trying to sell my stock, I had overloaded them with supplies and the wool sold better in the yard sales. We sold our books, furniture, kitchen gadgets and all of the odds and sods that we had hidden in cupboards and closets that we had not used or even looked at in years. Everything that we could sell, we sold. What didn't sell, was given to friends or donated to charity. What we wanted to keep, and there was still too much, eventually went into storage.

It was all going smoothly and right on schedule, except, of course, for my knee. A month before our house closing and departure date, I could no longer walk without great pain and a severe limp. I desperately needed help in rebuilding my thigh muscle.

The hospital sent me a prescription and I applied for physiotherapy. Over the telephone, I explained my problem to the therapist and an appointment was arranged for later that same day. Since I would be leaving in one month, the therapist suggested that I go for therapy every day. I took his advise. Not only did I submit to the daily torture; but I walked the mile to the clinic in an effort to speed up my recovery.

There had been many advances in physiotherapy between 1974 and 1989. Although I was still required to lift leg weights hour after hour, electrodes were attached to the muscle and the muscle puffed up with each impulse. The mile walk home was considerably less painful each day than the walk there. The therapy progressed well, but when all was sold and we were ready to go, I still needed help. I was fitted with a leg brace of heavy rubber with steel hinges and long velcro straps so my knee would not give out at an inappropriate moment. I wore it constantly.

On the fifteenth of September, 1989 we deposited the cheque, from the down payment on the house, into an investment account. From the bank, luggage in hand, we trudged straight to the train station in downtown Toronto. Paul boosted me up the stairs and he hopped on a train. We headed to Montreal, Quebec, arriving early evening. We spent that night and the next day visiting with our families and trying to arrange a flight to Britain. The cheapest flight we could get left that night. We took it.

There were sixteen people at the airport that night. Friends and family stayed with us for an hour or so before saying goodbye. Once on the plane, we looked at each other. Did we really know what we were doing?

Everyone's dream......and we were living it.

Chapter 2

Phil Webb was not difficult to spot in the crowd waiting at Gatwick Airport, south of London. At six feet, six inches he towered over most of the awaiting throng and the fact that two year old Cameron sat on his shoulders, made seeing him even easier.

Phil was from London, Ontario, Canada. Before transferring to Nassau in the Bahamas and then London, England, he had been a client of my husband's and had always considered Paul his mentor. They were good friends as well.

We were greeted with a big, toothy grin, hugs, kisses and handshakes and laughter from Cameron, who was much bigger and more grown up than his two years would indicate. With our salutations over, Phil led us through the airport to the luggage area.

I was almost totally ignored and decided to pick up our luggage while "the men" caught up on the investment business. The business conversation stopped only long enough for me to enquire about Andrea.

"Big as a house, she's due in about a month and can't stand it much longer," Phil volunteered before returning to the previous conversation with Paul. I retrieved our two pieces of luggage. We breezed through customs and made our way to Phil's car.

The highway drive back to Otford was unimpressive or perhaps I was just too tired to concentrate. It was about forty minutes later when we arrived in Sevenoaks that Phil started on a little sightseeing monologue.

"In 1987 a horrendous tornado-style storm blasted through this area and they are still cleaning up from the destruction," Phil explained. "That was when Sevenoaks became One Oak." "Six gorgeous, thousand year old, oak trees blew down in the storm." "Terrible loss for this area," he continued.

Once in the town, we discovered a lovely small community dating back to the tenth century. I could hardly concentrate on St. Bartholomeow's church on the left, before seeing a large modern supermarket, Tesco's, on the right. Sevenoaks was the home of dress shops, children's clothing stores, shoe stores, a wool and yarn store, a hardware store at each end of town, and a couple of book stores. All were housed in buildings hundreds of years old. It was hard for my mind to comprehend all of it on just a couple of hours of interrupted sleep.

Once through Sevenoaks, the countryside reverted to open fields. Again we were in an area of rolling hills for a short distance before turning off the main road and onto a one and a half lane road and into the town of Otford with a total of about a dozen shops, a roundabout and the ruins of Otford Palace on the right. We drove up the main street, past the train station and turned right onto Coombe Road. A gentle grade preceded a right turn onto a driveway so steep only a mountain goat could maneuver and we were there. Standing in the doorway, filling it out almost entirely, was Andrea. Phil was right, she did look ungainly; however, she had no trouble throwing her arms around me for a high energy hug and a welcoming kiss on the cheek.

Although Paul and I tried to sleep in the afternoon, it was useless. We talked, we rested, we tossed and turned and finally got out of bed. We spent the remainder of the afternoon talking with the Webbs and planning an evening at the pub. The Webbs had friends who would be coming over.

Paul and I were sitting on the couch in the den until around seven o'clock and just before the door bell rang, I fell over and could not for the life of me open my eyes. I could hear everything happening and the voices sounded eerily distant, but I could not move. I slept for about fifteen minutes and felt Paul shaking me for a long time before I could rouse myself.

At the pub we were treated to a beer and the much anticipated English fish and chip dinner. I tried the mushy peas that came included with the meal. Leave it to the English to spoil a perfectly good vegetable and one of my favorites. We were not the greatest of company at that point and the evening did not last long. Thanks to Andrea's delicate condition, we were home by nine thirty. Paul and I stayed awake another ten or twenty seconds. So ended our first day in Jolly Old.

Chapter 3

There is always a moment in the life of a traveler when he knows that he is somewhere totally foreign. England, for us, was just such a country. Not just because they drive on a different side of the road or eat food that is greasy and devoid of flavor or serve their national dish wrapped in newspaper or speak English in such a manner as not to be understood even by their own countrymen from another district. I am speaking in ways not only foreign but basically unsavory.

The buying of our motorhome was just such a transaction and the dealings started before we left our home in America. Through a British car hiring company doing business in Canada, we were put in touch with a small, family run, motorhome company in Staines, just west of London. We were told that they rented their motorhomes for two years only, then sold them off. The vehicles, supposedly, were in excellent shape externally and very well maintained mechanically.

By mail, we advised the dealer in England when we would be arriving, approximately how much we wanted to spend and the size of vehicle we preferred. Paul called Bob Stokley the day after we arrived and was advised that he had received our letter and had exactly what we were looking for in stock. Although suffering from jet lag, we were excited about our upcoming quest and set up an appointment to see the vehicle the next day.

After spending several hours on the train from Otford to

London to Staines, finding the bus station located on a side street, dragging ourselves onto the correct bus for a couple of miles and walking the remainder of the distance, Mr. Stokley, a short stocky man, in his mid thirties, advised us that he had rented out our potential purchase that morning. "It'll be back in a fortnight," he said. Stunned into silence, we glared at him, not quite comprehending or believing. We then stared at each other, our mouths agape, before reverting our gaze back to Mr. Stokley, who finished talking like nothing was amiss. He then showed us pictures of our potential treasure, told us the price, which was within our range and advised us to return in two weeks if we were still interested. We left for our return to Otford still shaking our heads, our energy sapped.

Since Andrea was not her usual runabout self these days, she loaned us her car on a few occasions. We drove around the countryside answering ads for motorhomes for sale and visiting various dealerships. Unfortunately we found little that interested us. We certainly would have pounced on an opportunity not to have to deal with the greedy, diminutive, unscrupulous troll in Staines.

Two weeks later and nothing to show for our efforts, we went back to Staines and really liked the two tone beige/brown van we saw. It was perfect. After inspecting it, inside and out, we gave him a five hundred ($750.00 U.S.) pound sterling deposit. That left a balance owing on the vehicle of six thousand, five hundred pounds. Stokley promised in writing to clean up, inspect, grease and oil, certify (Management of Capabilities.....MOT for short) and fix a few things on the Renault Trafic high top that we had just agreed to purchase. We would be back at the end of the week to pick it up. All the way back to Otford we planned excitedly. This was just the beginning of our adventure.

We arrived at the end of the week to discover he had increased the price by an additional five hundred pounds. It seems that in those few days he had advertised the van and received another bid on it. He told us if we didn't come up with the additional money, he would return our deposit and sell it elsewhere.

Paul, before taking early retirement, had been an investment dealer. Habitually, hundreds of thousands of dollars worth of business was conducted on the strength of one telephone call or a handshake. I, too had been in business for years without any unpleasant incidents. This form of shabby business transaction was completely unfamiliar and degrading to us. If we refused, we would be back to square one. We would have to waste more precious weeks looking for a replacement. We had already spent two weeks, finding nothing that was gently used and we certainly could not afford a new vehicle. We paid the money, left with our vehicle and the sour taste of shady dealings in our mouths.

We drove the M25 back to Otford, not saying much and trying to concentrate on the unfamiliar roads and equally unfamiliar vehicle. Fortunately British maps are very precise and even the smallest of country roads is identified. Paul did all the driving, at my insistence. I was not prepared emotionally, or otherwise, to drive on the wrong side of the road, shift with the wrong hand and try to maneuver through those narrow lanes and hellish roundabouts.

We returned to the Webb's residence without getting lost and as soon as we had their full attention, we blurted out the story. They were not the least bit surprised. Phil advised us that our unpleasant experience was standard practice in Britain and he apologized for not warning us about it. The conversation continued with Phil telling us his most recent horror stories in the buying and selling of homes.

He recounted several stories of acquaintances who had sold their homes, packed up and were ready to go out the door, possessions in a truck or, in one case on board ship, and the buyers backed out. No explanation need be given. Nothing could be done and, of course, that usually started a chain reaction. We promised Phil that we would be more careful in all future dealings; however, all future dealings would be minor compared to the purchasing of our motorhome.

The next day, we were off to Argosy, a discount department store in the heart of downtown Croydon. Croydon was a city just large enough for us to go round in circles each time we visited. We managed, even with precise directions and street names, to get lost. It was, however, home of the closest Argosy store and we eventually found it. There we purchased most of the supplies we needed for our new little home on wheels.....linen, pillows, sleeping bags, pots, pans, cutlery, a two cup kettle, dishes, glasses, two coffee mugs. When all the boxes and bags were piled up in front of me on the counter, I came across a cute little cardboard box without markings and could not image what it contained. With my husband nattering at me, I decided to open it. To my surprise and delight, it contained the two cup kettle we had ordered. It looked so small. I pulled the gray-and-white kettle out of the box and the inch thick round cord trailed out behind it. Just as Paul asked, "What the hell are you doing?" the entire cord fell out of the box. At the end of the cord were four little wires pointing straight up in the air, like asparagus sprigs demanding its share of sunshine. I stood transfixed, staring at this strange looking and somewhat incomplete cord. I looked at the clerk bewildered, who was now staring back at me. I looked again at the cord, not having a clue as to what to make of it. I could almost see the light bulb go on over the head of the clerk....."ow" she said, "did you want a plug with that?"

"No," I answered in total amazement, "I'll just stick it up my ass and see if I can get it going that way."

While Paul and I shook our heads in disbelief, the clerk went off to find us a prefused plug, if she could find one or a regular plug if she couldn't. Surely Phil would help with the fuse and the plug and have the tools necessary to complete the task.

That evening while Phil instructed Paul as to how to attach the enormous plug, with its three huge prongs, onto the end of the cord of our tiny two cup kettle, Phil told us the true story of a neighbor who was having marital problems. After much fighting and back biting the husband decided to leave the wife. His plan was to leave his wife stranded with their three children. He decided that he had to do it quickly or she would become suspicious. He couldn't empty the house of all belongings, so like a thief in the night, he removed all the plugs from all the appliances and took them away with him.

Early the next morning, when the wife realized what her husband had done, she called Phil, crying uncontrollably.

"I picked her and the children up and brought them over here for Andrea to calm down." "I went back and checked the appliances," he continued. "I made a list of what she needed, scrambled around to several hardware stores and spent the rest of that day and the entire next day, putting plugs back on all the appliances," Phil said. "Up to that point, I had really liked her husband," he went on. "I couldn't believe he would turn into such an asshole."

I know that most appliances come from different parts of the world. In every part of the world that I have been in, except England of course, plugs come included on all products. "What do the manufacturers do," I asked Phil with as poker faced an expression as I could manage, "cut off the plugs of the appliances coming into Britain?"

There are times when you know that you are in a really different country. These two incidents proved how really different England is; but we did not leave England until we had seen and experienced much of the joys of the country. And there were many.

Chapter 4

With such a poor beginning in this strange country, we tried not to become too disenchanted. While all the nonsense was going on with our van, we spent two weeks in and around London. We recovered slowly from jet lag.

The first day we had a bit more energy, we took the train into the city "to visit the Queen," my diary said. We walked Trafalgar Square with its millions of pigeons and stopped at each of the craft stalls in Covenant Gardens inspecting handmade sweaters, carved candles, beaded necklaces, handmade soaps and everything else displayed. We stopped in a basement pub for a beer and sandwich. By mid afternoon, having ran out of steam temporarily, we hopped onto a double decker bus and scurried upstairs to see the world from a loftier perch. We went off in some direction to see what turned out to be the shabbier parts of town. At the end of the line we got onto another bus for the return trip to London's center, via an alternate route.

"Bored, yet?" I asked, watching Paul's eyes darting around, not wanting to miss a thing. I was rewarded for my comment with a hug, a kiss on the nose and a lick across my glasses.

On another jaunt into the city, we walked Piccadilly Circus before heading to St. Paul's cathedral. With much of the interior of St Paul's cordoned off, we suddenly found ourselves in the room with the brass rubbings and watched in fascination as tourists, working with white paper and gold crayons, brought

14

the rubbings to life. We decided to wait until another time before we tried our hand at the craft, since we had no idea where we would store such a treasure in our van.

On one of our day trips into London we purchased last minute tickets to our first play and after a light dinner, we saw Blood Brothers at the Royal Adelphi Theater. We were as thrilled with the theater as we were with the play. Each visit held new sights, sounds, tastes and smells.

Before acquiring our van, on the twenty ninth of September, we had one more treat in store. Thanks to Phil's company, we enjoyed an unforgettable day of War Games.

Early Saturday morning, after Phil picked up a couple of his coworkers, he drove us to the designated area out in the country. Without a good sense of direction or knowledge of the countryside, your guess is as good as mine as to where we were. The jungly-looking place where we finally stopped was filled with enormous trees and dense scrub brush and after tramping through the area marked with flags stuck in the ground, we discovered a command post had been set up in the middle of a well worn clearing.

Few introductions were made, although everyone acknowledged each other with a brief nod and half a smile. We realized that because of the size of both companies involved, many employees in the same company did not know each other.

We were handed uniforms that appeared similar to a complete set of overalls that protected our clothing. We were each given a rifle that held balls of paint in either fire engine red or brilliant canary yellow, depending on which team you were on. The "rules of the road" were explained in infinite detail.

What worried me somewhat, was the fact that some of the men arrived in their own camouflage uniforms, carrying their own rifles. These were serious participants, whom I was sure, would not take likely to losing. To them, this was war.....without the games.

Since two financial institutions were involved, we were on Phil's company team, and given the dark blue overalls along with a helmet, goggles and ten red paint balls to start. If more ammunition was needed, you bought a ten pack from the commander running the base camp. We were told that hitting in the face was illegal and you were "not dead" if struck there.

Anywhere else on the body constituted a hit and you were out of the game.

Once the strategy was underway, it was every man or woman for themselves. It was truly a fun filled day until close to the end. Some of the men from each company, who had a particular dislike for some of the people on either their own team or the "enemy team" decided that it was time to aim for the face. When those little paint balls hit, they struck with force enough to cause severe bruising and the game immediately turned nasty. Since Paul, Phil and myself were long out of the game, we chose to stay well out of the line of fire.

We arrived at the Webb's late afternoon totally exhausted, voraciously hungry and splattered from head to toe with red and yellow paint. To Andrea we must have looked like a litter of Dalmatian puppies that had collided with the NBC peacock. We were ushered to the showers before we were allowed to sit down. We talked about the experience for days. We stopped talking about it when most of the bruising had either stopped hurting or disappeared.

*   *   *   *   *

It was a few days after the War Games that we acquired our motorhome and decided that it was time for us to tour the adjacent countryside. We stayed in the vicinity of Otford, taking a few day trips. We armed ourselves with local maps and pamphlets from the Tourist Information Center in Sevenoaks. Some ideas we gleaned from Phil and Andrea about their favorite spots. We were well equipped each day to do some serious looking and learning.

It was also important that we check out our van, making sure that everything worked and that we had all the correct gear. Should the van need any repair work or added bits and pieces, we wanted to make sure we were in a country where we understood (and I use the term loosely) the language. Also, before crossing the English Channel into France, we had a wedding to attend on the fourteenth of October. We decided we would stay close to home and get our feet wet or, at least, damp.

It did not take us long to become enamored with our lot in life. My husband was falling in love with every inch of this history filled country and what was built on it, while I was still wrestling with a kitchen, living room, dining room, bedroom all rolled into what was the size of our bathroom back home. A "back home" that no longer existed. We had been in this strange country two weeks and although we still felt like it was just a vacation, we were not ready for the adventure to end.

We toured the south and visited Bateman House, home to Rudyard Kipling until his death in 1936. Much of the house and his book-lined study remains exactly as he left it. His 1928 Rolls Royce was still parked in the garage awaiting his next joy ride. Since his scouting days, Paul had loved Kipling and would read his books under the blankets at night, thanks to a trusty flashlight. He could still quote from the Jungle Book. Each room held some treasured memory for my husband.

A tour of medieval Bodiam Castle followed and the sight of the castle mirrored in the water-lilied moat was breathtaking. When we arrived in Hastings and I discovered that the Battle of Hastings in 1066, actually took place in the town of Battle, five miles from where we were standing, my British history days sprang to life. I was hooked.

Hastings was the site of our virgin camping experience. There was a minor struggle getting everything set up. We seemed to be in each other's way every time we moved. Paul plugged in our power source and discovered that it didn't work. We were sure it would be some minor problem because everything had worked at the dealer. We found no switch and when I plugged the two cup kettle directly into the outside source, it worked. We would figure it out another time and set about making dinner for the first time. Since our stove was propane generated and we had a newly filled propane tank, we knew that dinner was not going to be a problem. We had a refrigerator full of perishables and cupboards full of cans, bottles and bags. We also purchased a small barbecue so Paul was happy as a clam, doing "man's" work. He worked outside. I worked inside.

Setting up the bed for the first time was another nuisance. The driver seat and the passenger seat folded back. The two back seats made into benches which we left as bench seats. The two tables slid down the center, making two single beds into a large double bed. All the pillows and bolsters had to be used in a sequence that we had not been shown. That night we had one lumpy night's sleep, but it was a start.

After breakfast and cleanup the following morning, we headed for a motorhome dealer and asked him to check our electricity. He flipped the tiniest "S" shaped switch on what he referred to as "the zig" located on the wall above the refrigerator and presto, Edison would have been so proud. The salesman laughed heartily, wished us pleasant traveling and we left, feeling sheepish, with our tails between our legs. Paul headed for the closest golf course to heal his wounds. I walked nine holes with him and went back to our house to have a cup of tea and read the guidebook.

For the next two weeks, we wandered the living history book. We walked the Palace Pier at Brighton. We visited Arundel Castle, still inhabited by the Earl of Norfolk. We enjoyed our first dock lunch of cockles and Scottish salmon. We drove through the hills and dales of Devon and Dorset and got lost in Exeter. The resort towns of Torquay and Paignton charmed us and driving the Moors, even in daylight, intimidated us a bit.

The Moors were cold, uninviting, and covered with forest green prickly bushes called gorse. Only the wee, bright yellow flowers that dotted the gorse gave the tiniest indication of something other than a severely harsh life. The road, snaking over the forbidding landscape, was so narrow that two small cars could not pass each other. One car had to pull over into a lay by and stop. We left the Moors just before nightfall. A blanket of fog was just beginning to cover the ground, hiding the monsters that waited to pounce on any unsuspecting intruder that did not have the good sense to leave the Moors before dark.

We found a campground in the village of Okehampton, parked our vehicle on a bit of level ground and went for a walk to stretch our legs. We treated ourselves to a pint of ale at the local pub. Since we had survived the Moors and had kept The Hound at bay another night, we celebrated and enjoyed a fish and chip dinner as well.

We spent a day cliff walking in Bude and actually had to pay to get into the town of Cloveley. The entire town is built on a steep cliff heading down towards the water. Wheeled vehicles were not permitted on their roads for fear of damaging the cobblestones. Cars were parked in a large, flat lot at the entrance to the town. A person residing in Cloveley, must have all items brought down by sledge and, I must assume, received a pass of some sort so they did not have to pay each time they headed for home.

We stopped at Minehead for some grocery shopping and then at the sheepskin factory in Glastonbury. We discovered, to our dismay, that purchasing a sheepskin from the factory, was almost twice the price of purchasing the same in a department store. We left empty handed. From Gastonbury it was an easy drive to the ancient town of Bath. Everything is available in Bath, except of course, a bath. The mineral waters were no longer open to the public. Much of the town had been turned into a pedestrian area and hanging flower baskets were everywhere. We explored the Roman Baths, watched over by the magnificent statues that surrounded the second story, and we visited the elegant Pump Room. The Pump Room had been totally restored, renovated and turned into a coffee and afternoon tea room. We did not stop for tea. We visited the Bath Abbey, which had been rebuilt over the years, before heading to a pub for a bite to eat.

After touring Bath for several hours, we found a campground on the outskirts and walked back into the town to see a movie. That year Lethal Weapon ll, with Mel Gibson and Danny Glover, was hot. We enjoyed the movie, a bite to eat afterwards and the long walk back to the campground.

Heading north, we walked through the Manor House at Castle Coombe. We visited Woodhenge, which was not terribly impressive. We stopped at Stonehenge and watched as the sun set, casting long eerie shadows on the ground. We visited Old Sarum because Paul had just finished reading the book by Edward Rutherford and later that afternoon spent some time at Salisbury. Our last stop of that day was Winchester, visiting both the cathedral and the museum.

Our two weeks of roaming the English countryside were almost over. We returned to the Webb's, filled with stories of successes, minor failures, lots of jokes and tales of interesting people, places and food. We cleaned up substantially, bid our friends a fond farewell and headed into London for the wedding.

Since we had an extra day to visit London, we asked our friend, Maria Venczel, the mother of the bride, to meet us for lunch. We all ended up wanting to see Herrod's. Maria wanted to go because it was one of her favorite spots in the world. We wanted to go because we had never seen it. She took us to her favorite part of the store.....the food section. We wandered the venison area, the snake area and the frozen alligator section. The cheese section was better stocked than anything we had ever seen, as was the prepared food section. It was a feast for the eyes but it was our mouths that were drooling. We bought samplings of several of the prepared foods, a bread stick, a bottle of wine, found a table and dined.

The next day we attended the wedding of Christina and Peter at the Brompton Oratory. We were more impressed with the church than we had been at St. Paul's. The organ music resounded through the church that was meant to hold over a thousand people and there were less than a hundred present. The reception was held at the Le Meridan Hotel in Piccadilly and as with every party we have ever attended where Maria was in charge, she spared no expense. The food was extravagant. The flowers brilliant. The wine superb.

We slept late the next morning and just before heading south, called the Webbs to tell them about the wedding. Phil gave us the news that while we were enjoying the wonderful formal British wedding, he became the proud papa of a bouncing baby boy. They planned on naming him Graeme. Andrea was thrilled that it was over. Everyone was well and exhausted.

Chapter 5

We were now seasoned travelers. We were about as seasoned as two people can be after living in the close confines of a small motorhome for two weeks and not yet having the urge to kill each other or anyone else. Although we were still in the habit of counting off the weeks, we were starting to relax a bit and were eager to explore new worlds.

The weather, although never really good in England for long periods of time, had turned nasty. The never ending drizzle, now chilled us to the bone, since it was accompanied by strong winds. It was mid October and many Britishers, with their campers, were heading south for the winter. There was a steady stream of well stocked vans, motorhomes of all shapes, sizes and descriptions and tuggers, as the Brits liked to call trailers, traveling with us on our route to Newhaven. We drove straight down to the dock, parked in one of the few vacant spots and went into the office to purchase a ticket for ourselves and our van. We booked passage on the last ferry of the day to Dieppe, even though there would be two ferries leaving before our eleven o'clock departure time. Although it was only late afternoon, we decided the savings of over a hundred dollars for taking the last ferry, was worth the wait.

We parked in the queue line early and took off for a little hike. We did not have to go far for conversation. Paul always enjoyed hanging around the water's edge and talking to the fishermen. When we (or should I say "I") had enough talking (or should I say "listening") we went for a beer, a fish and chip dinner and a walk around town in the dark. The hours passed quickly. We returned to the van after eight, I brewed some tea and we settled down to read our books. A knock on the window by a man in uniform told us to "start our engines." We were moving on board.

Our Puddle Jumper, the endearing name for our van, was sandwiched below deck and we wandered the length and breadth of the ferry hoping to find a friendly face or two. No luck.

It was pitch black outside with a distinctly nasty chill in the air, so we did not spend much time walking the outside deck. One quick tour, seeing nothing of interest or otherwise, was enough. We went into the bar with our books, sat on a well-padded bench seat and set our belongings down on the large round table in front of us. We each nursed a beer.

It was less than a five hour crossing and at some point, while revisiting the English countryside on the inside of my eyelids, I dozed off. I had no idea what time it was or how long I had been asleep, but I felt a large hand shaking my shoulder roughly and my husband's deep voice insisting "wake up, come on, Joei, wake up." My eyes refused to focus. With clenched fists, I rubbed them in the hopes of seeing more clearly.

"Are we there yet?" I asked groggily, running my tongue over teeth desperately in need of brushing.

"No," said Paul, "remember that cruise I promised you, well wake up and enjoy it. You're on it."

Obviously he couldn't sleep and wanted some company. When I finally understood his problem, I laughed and snuggled up close to him, kissing his neck just under his stubbly chin. With his arm around my shoulders, we both dozed off.

It was in the middle of a deep sleep that the fog horn blasted and a disembodied voice announced that we had arrived in Dieppe. We gathered our belongings that lay sprawled around the table, stuffed them into the pink and black knapsack that I had purchased at the flea market in Sevenoaks and stumbled down the stairs to retrieve our van. We drove our English Renault Trafic motorhome up to the border, passports in hand. The booth stood empty. We drove straight out onto the streets of France.

It was still black as a witch's heart and a heavy mist hung in the air. The roads were unfamiliar and we were now driving on the right with a vehicle that preferred the left. We did not go far. Our few minutes of interrupted sleep had not been sufficient to cope with these monumental changes in our lives. Exhausted, we pulled into the first vacant lot that we felt we could spend what little remained of the night. It happened to be a empty gambling casino parking lot. With no one around, we made up two single beds and slept, undisturbed, until eight thirty in the morning.

Once awake, we did not linger. We needed to find a washroom. We had a portipotty in our van but we had already decided that it would be used for the middle of the night emergency only. We drove into the heart of Dieppe and found a public washroom almost immediately.

With the engine still running, I jumped out of the van, walked briskly to the bathroom, opened the door and .....horrors. There, on the floor, were two porcelain footprints on a porcelain platform with a hole and a chain and what the hell was I supposed to do with that. I slammed the door, stomped back to the van, glared at my husband and spat "you get me back to civilization." "I want to go back to England.....I'll use the bathroom there." Paul stared back at me in mock horror, not saying a word. Only when I realized what I had just said, did we both start laughing. Even I knew, that under no circumstances, would it be possible to wait until England before using a bathroom. I emptied my pockets so as not to lose everything down the dreaded hole and returned to the French-style torture chamber, clutching a roll of England's finest toilet paper.

This would be a good time to remind you about the unsuccessful knee surgery that I had on the twenty third of June from which I had not yet fully recovered.

Thus started what would become a love affair with France.

*　　*　　*　　*　　*

I know that old joke. There were so few tourists in France, the waiters had to insult each other. That, however, was not our impression of the country. Since we were not staying in hotels, nor eating in restaurants much, nor taking taxi cabs, we found France, right from the beginning, to be one of our favorite countries, people and all.

We spent the first few days just trying to adjust to the driving. Again at my insistence, Paul did all the driving as he had done in England, but I was now an vitally important part of the procedure. Since Paul sat behind the steering wheel located on the right side of the van, he needed my sharp eye in trying to pass other cars. He could not see oncoming traffic. It was a tricky maneuver. He did, however, enjoyed the challenge and occasionally pulled out into the oncoming lane just to test his reflexes and my vocal cords, as I screeched "NOOOOOO" at the top of my lungs.

On day one in France we walked the cliffs of Entretat with its fabulous rock formations, then stopped at Caen for a city stroll. We drove on to Bayeaux to tour the city and spent the afternoon studying the fabulous and intricate tapestry. We ended our first day in St. Aubin Sur Mer.

We visited the Normandy Beaches early the next day to see where the Americans landed and died during World War II. We spent some time at the cemetery before walking down to the beach. Two of Paul's uncles, on his mother's side of the family, died on these beaches. We paid our respects by quietly walking the area trying to understand the enormity and senselessness of it all.

The previous evening I lost two hands playing the card game, cribbage. My punishment was that I had to drive the van. When we left the Normandy Beaches I was behind the wheel. The entire incident bordered on nightmarish. It was bad enough that I was sitting in the ditch with a tendency to drift over the center line, but when I had to stop and fill up the gas tank, I misjudged and ran over the corner stone, supporting the gas tanks. That did it. I filled the tank, paid the bill, opened the passenger door and pulled Paul out of his seat. My driving days were over. I promised that since I wouldn't be driving, I wouldn't complain about his driving. That promise lasted less than an hour.

Once into the Mont St. Michel, St. Malo area we were awestruck. During high tide Mont St. Michel can be visited only by boat. At low tide, the parking lot is cleared of mud and debris and cars are parked, between the white lines painted on the ground, exactly like every other parking lot. Leaving our vehicle, we walked towards the gate to the city. Our guidebook warned that around the back of Le Mont was quicksand, so the tour around the base of the city that we wanted, was out of the question. We walked up the long, winding, narrow street lined with gift and souvenir shops, to the top for the view from the abbey. The abbey was balanced precariously on the jutting rock. Magnificent. We spent most of the day walking to the end of each short side street just to admire the view of the calm water and the fishermen with their catch.

The campground in St. Malo was built around an old bunker and we explored many of the bombed out areas. It had become a playground for children. There was so much World War II history in the area that Paul was in his glory. He regaled me with war stories. We stayed several days.

By the time we moved on, it was late in October and we were beginning to have trouble finding open campgrounds. I had not been on the road long enough to be comfortable camping in town squares, out in the countryside, under trees or at the water's edge, as Paul always threatened to do. Every camper we had come across up to this point had told us we would be perfectly safe doing it; however, I wanted campgrounds.....safe, convenient, and with other campers around. That kind of campground. I wanted clean, warm, indoor facilities.

One particular day we just were not finding anything open. Mid afternoon, we had gotten lost in Quimper and had gone around the town in circles far too long. We were trying to find either a street name or two that was on our map or the route out of town. Both seemed illusive. We finally found ourselves on a road, with no route number, that took us out of that dreaded city. We drove the two lane country road and everything was closed. We arrived in Concarneau just as it was getting dark and I was really starting to fret. We saw an open gate, it said "campground" with a little symbol on the post and we pulled in, very relieved. The place was deserted.

The groundskeeper, wearing baggy brown corduroy pants and several layers of dark colored, shabby looking sweaters, approached with a giant black dog plodding along at his side. In a friendly manner, he explained to Paul, in French of course, that they were closed for the season. I petted the dog, who looked up at me with big brown, soulful eyes and I asked, in what little French I knew, if this was a Newfoundland dog. Mr. Baggypants was surprised and delighted with my recognition of what was a rare breed in France and the conversation continued, a little more animated.

Paul asked about a campground nearby that might be open and when he explained that I was frightened and refused to sleep in the town square, the man relented. Although the campground was officially closed, he would leave a washroom open for us. He apologized for not being able to turn on the hot water. I was thrilled with a safe place to stay and after the groundskeeper left, we set up camp.

Several hours later, long after we had eaten and settled in for the night, the groundskeeper returned, scaring the hell out of me when he knocked on our window. My heart pounded even after I realized who it was and was sure, just for spite, he was going to tell us to leave. He didn't.   The radio, he advised, had predicted a bad storm and he suggested we move around to the back of the shower block where the building would offer us some protection from the wind and rain.

We secured the dishes in the sink, closed all the cupboards, unplugged the electricity and following him to the spot around the back. Settled in for the second time, Paul removed a bottle of Calvados, apple liquor, and offered a shot glass to our gracious host and guardian. The smile, showing teeth that could use some dental care, was unmistakable. He was an obvious fan of this beverage, as was Paul. Someone drank my share. I found it unpalatable and poured myself another glass of the same red wine that Paul and I had shared at dinner. The evening ended around midnight with all of us well fortified with spirits. We barely heard the van being pelted with rain, hail, strong winds and horse chestnuts all night.

It was in the early stages of our love affair with France that we learned that red wine doesn't travel very well. The same red wine that might produce a wicked migraine headache in North America, did not do the same in the country of origin.....and can there be a better country of origin for the drip of the grape, than France?

We started haunting all the small town wineries. Once

inside, we sampled several vintages that we thought we might like. While slightly inebriated we would make our selection and buy as many bottles as we dared. The wineries were slightly cheaper than the stores and we always loaded up. It was the year that Paul and I did not make it to France that the French government complained about the lack of wine sales. Where else, but in France could we have free wine samples. Well, to be honest.....Spain, Italy, Greece.....any of the wine producing countries gave free samples. They are so civilized.

Also in France, we learned the joys of grocery shopping at the open air markets, where everything fresh, canned, bottled or dried is displayed. We chose what and how much we wanted just by pointing. My investment dealer husband figured out the value of the money instantly. We cooked most of our meals ourselves so we got into the habit of wheeling and dealing and especially loved market day. Every town and village had its own special day and we would pick up fresh produce every day or two. As far as meals were concerned, I still handled the inside work, while Paul did the barbecuing. On rainy days, I steamed up the place cooking indoors. I was becoming a master of the stew pot.

One particular day, early in our French adventure, Paul chose a half pound slab of a very lean red meat. I added diced potatoes, whole button mushrooms, sliced carrots and a couple of leftover green beans. Any vegetable left in the refrigerator including a dabble of spicy vegetable spaghetti sauce went into the pot. Nothing ever went to waste and since the base was always bouillon cubes and watered down wine, the taste was superb. If it had a different flavor, I invented it and possibly would never be duplicated. That didn't matter.

This stew was the best we had ever tasted with meat so tender we cut it with a fork. I was determined to reproduce it at a later time and sat down immediately and made notes as to exactly what the stew contained and in precise proportions. A week later, we tried again, using the same lean meat. Didn't work. A week or so after that, we tried again. Didn't work. As a matter of fact I was never able to reproduce the wonderful stew of that day, no matter what I tried.

All I know is that it was right after that first magnificient stew, that we learned about the two different meat counters in

France, one for beef and one for horse meat. Once we were made aware of the two different counters, we always made sure that we went to the beef counter and we never had that wonderful stew again.....and why do I feel like saluting every time I see a person on horseback.

A mystery.

Chapter 6

One of the many special delights of traveling in a country where the natives did not speak our language, was when we found someone who did speak, in our case English, they looked forward to talking to us as much as we desired to converse with them.

As we headed south, we discovered well traveled, well spoken, street smart people from various and exotic parts of the world, who were as keen for company as we were. Friendships, although some lasting only through coffee, dinner or a few glasses of wine, were made instantly.

After a few days in France, we ran out of the British pounds we had changed at the bank into francs. We needed money before we could spend another night in a campground. Driving along the Loire valley, we entered the first large recognizable bank we came across in Nantes, with passport and Visa card in hand. We left with a fist full of French francs and were so excited knowing that our traveling money was as close as any bank accepting Visa, we promptly got lost driving around the city. We left town.

We stopped at Champtoceux, one of the principle sites in Angers, for a picnic lunch and spent an extra hour talking with Margaret and Dave, a young British couple who were just finishing a fortnight (two weeks to the rest of the English speaking world) camping holiday in the Loire Valley. They were a fountain of valuable information, and although we planned on spending a lot of time in this region, it was interesting to hear their views. Put simply, they loved it.

After spending the night in Angers, we visited the chateau, famous for its fine collection of tapestries. These masterpieces influenced future medieval tapestries and a special gallery was built to house the magnificient one known as the Apocalypse.

The afternoon found us at the Bouvet - Ladubay winery, sampling their wares and once again overstocking our supply. After a short, but intensive tour through Saumur, we ended our day in Chinon. The large treeless campground was situated right by the water, a short walking distance to all the shops, markets, pubs and restaurants.

David and Betty Dyers were our neighbors. They were camping directly across from us, on as open a plot of ground as we had. They were both in their early sixties. Their haircuts were almost identical and both heads were covered with thick, gray, unruly, hair. Both were stoutly built, but while she blended into the smallest of crowds, he was instantly recognizable by his huge salt-and-pepper handlebar mustache. We took to their friendly, outgoing manner immediately. It was easy to wile away the hours exchanging stories with them. When we felt a change in scenery was needed, we moved to a pub in beautiful, downtown Chinon. We occupied one of the outdoor tables and watched as the local folks went about the daily business of life in rural France.

We awoke the next morning to the clanging of a cowbell and the delicious aroma of freshly baked croissants. A double tray full of the tasty goodies had just been delivered to the campground office. It didn't take Paul long to get dressed and stand in line for a couple of them. By the time he returned, the coffee was on the table, along with butter, jam, cheese and pate.

The day was already warm and filled with sunshine. We decided to spend an extra day or two in Chinon, just to unwind from our hard life. We had been on the road about six weeks.

Our last day in Chinon started with a kipper and egg breakfast. The kippers, purchased from a local fishmonger, were a treat for Paul, dating back to his youth. For me, it was a first time shot, which I must confess, I enjoyed, not to the degree that Paul did, but certainly enough to consider preparing the delicacy a second time.

After breakfast, we drove to one of the most beautiful chateaux in the Loire Valley, Azay-Le-Rideau. It was surrounded by trees and reflected majestically in the lake. Just as we were wandering the last of the spectacular sixteenth century rooms, we heard, what we knew unmistakably to be, American English. We came face to face with Jerry and Dee from San Francisco and before leaving the chateau decided to follow them to a lunch spot where we could continue our frantic discussion of favorite spots in the area.

At a little outdoor cafe, we finished our sandwiches, washed them down with the smidgen of beer left in the bottom of our glasses and were on our way to Villandry, famous for its specular gardens. We toured and talked for another hour and at the garden gate, we bade farewell to our new found friends and drove off in different directions. We also waved goodbye as we passed the Chinon campground and stopped at one more castle, Chenonceau, before leaving the Loire Valley. As beautiful as the sixteenth century castle was, it was becoming difficult to remember the various chateaux and castles. They were all starting to look alike. Fortunately we got into the habit of buying postcards of each exterior, with each postcard displaying a room or two of the interior. They helped to jog our memories. We decided to stop visiting castles for awhile and concentrate on other interesting places, such as museums or unique architecture, that we came across.

We visited Loches, a three star town according to the Michelin guide. The beauty of Loches' trim white houses set in the idyllic countryside, contrasted keenly with the sinister reputation of its bastille, where those unwise enough to displease the kings of France were imprisoned in dark, dank dungeons.

We arrived in Poitiers at rush hour and promptly got lost. All the signs for an open-all-year campground ended abruptly. Paul became impatient looking for the next sign. We never found another campground sign even after heading down each of the possible roads. You know why Moses wandered in the desert for forty years. Right, well, my husband would not stop and ask directions either so we left Poitiers and headed south. We stopped at four or five other campgrounds only to discover they were all closed for the season. We arrived at St.

Maixient just as Paul finished threatening me with "we can pull into the woods, you know." My eyes darted from signpost to telephone pole to stop sign before I glimpsed the small campground sign with an arrow pointing straight ahead. We followed the arrows and I prayed silently that they wouldn't end abruptly like they had in Poitiers.

We were so cranky at this point, that we had started snapping at each other. We were hungry and it was getting dark, which increased the tension. We pulled up one last side street and saw the open gates. What a relief. There were very few campers in the place, but it was, indeed, open.

At the far end of the campground a cluster of campers had congregated and one lonely camper was parked near the restrooms. The closer we got to the lone camper, the easier it was to see the insignia on the van. To our delight a "GB" sticker was displayed prominently. We assumed they were English speaking from Great Britain and at this point we welcomed the company of others.

As Paul back into the spot, we noticed a well dressed, distinguished looking man standing beside his camper.

"Do you mind if we park in your back yard?" Paul queried.

"Your day's driving is done," said our neighbor, "how about a brandy?"

As we were getting out of our van to join our new found friend, a woman raced past the van on the way to the restroom, we assumed. We did not give it a second thought and joined Don Jones in his camper. Don handed each of us a drink and we quickly shared our day's events and sights.

Marjorie, returned, smiled and greeted us warmly. We again introduced ourselves and were instantly involved in a lively four way conversation.

We never did get around to cooking dinner. When our stomachs growled loudly enough, we went back to our van and retrieved some wine, a can of sardines, two packages of cheese, turkey slices and several varieties of crackers. In our absence, the Joneses found more wine, some pate, a few cheeses different from ours, stuffed olives and sweet pickles, a tin of Planter's nuts and dried fruit pieces. By the time we returned with our offering, a spread had been placed on all the side tables and our glasses had been refilled.

The hours passed quickly, especially when they started talking about their new life together. Don was American. Marjorie was Welsh. He was sixty-nine years old. She was sixty-seven years old and they had been married a month.

Don told us about meeting Marjorie in Spain where he had been visiting, after the death of his wife. He and his first wife, had left the United States several years before. They had taken to a life of travel because she had inoperable cancer and "did not want to die sitting still." They had been traveling for a couple of years and although she had been hospitalized for brief periods of time, she loved the transient life. They decided that a larger van, with a permanently made up bed, would be more comfortable and ordered a larger motorhome. Don was forced to accepted delivery of it the day his wife died in an Italian hospital.

We all listened quietly, knowing that it was breaking his heart to tell the story. In an emotional turmoil, Don continued to travel and went south to Spain because of the warm weather. "You can't imagine how many dinners I paid for, just so I wouldn't have to eat alone," he said, his voice touched with sadness. "When I met Marjorie, my life changed forever," he continued, reaching over to take her hand.

Marjorie's story was different. Her first love had died at the beginning of World War II. Marjorie had been totally devastated at the time, but did go on to marry twice and have two children. Neither marriage had been very happy, nor had they lasted very long. She preferred telling us about her war effort which included being a rat catcher in England. This part of her life she described in infinite detail. She regaled us with stories of how they caught the rats, some the size of cats. Most were killed humanely but she and her coworkers played games with others. Some of the rats were tossed like frisbees after being twirled by their tails, some were kicked like footballs, others were used in target practice. It's hard to imagine, so elegant a lady, grossing us out that way; however, what an entertaining evening we spent.

It wasn't until the next morning that we found out what really happened the night before and why we had been given such a pleasant greeting by Don. The newly weds had just had their first disagreement. Marjorie had rushed past us, not to use the facilities, but to call her son, Neil, tell him about the fight and advise him that "she was leaving the son of a gun and coming home." Neil was not at home. When she returned to their camper to continue the argument, there we were. Being too well brought up, she would never continue the argument in front of us, so she acted like nothing was wrong. That she accomplished admirably. We never, for one instance, suspected. We all had such a good time we parted on a high note. Of course, they resolved their problems.

We had coffee and breakfast together the next morning. They gave us their address in Albir, Spain. It was the start of a friendship that would last many years.

Chapter 7

Leaving our friends to go their way, which was directly to their home in Spain, we headed for the coast and found a colorful haven in La Rochelle. We discovered a charming seaport lined with elegant boutiques going miles in all directions. The sidewalks were all under cover with simple but elegant archways going out to the streets. We spent the afternoon wandering in and out of the shops and checking all the side streets for interesting architecture. When the rain started, we went back into the stores to stay dry. At the first sign of the rain letting up, we sprinted back to the camper. Although camping close by, we did not go back into town that evening. The drizzle abated around midnight.

The next morning, on our way south, we stopped at a giant flea market in Rochefort and bought ourselves a luncheon delicacy like none other.....two dozen oysters, a shucker and a couple of lemons. I don't know where or when I acquired the talent, but I shuck oysters like a pro. While Paul walked around the dock, I prepared the feast.

He returned to find the oysters scrubbed clean, opened and set on the only large platter we owned. The lemons were cut into wedges, heaped onto a small side plate and the hot sauce stood open and at attention. A glass of white wine sat on the table to the right of my plate and a bottle of beer, open and ready to quench his thirst, was in front of Paul's place. A large pot, lined with a plastic bag, yawning at our feet, waited to catch the debris. The only thing missing was a bed of crushed ice to keep the oysters at a perfect temperature. The twelve tiny cubes our freezer produced would have been lost on the platter.

His eyes beamed with pure pleasure when I invited him into the van. Without saying a word, he scanned the table, smiling. Before sitting down, we toasted each other and I asked my usual question, "I wonder what the peasants will be eating today?" To which Paul responded, "probably caviar." We used the expression over and over and it always brought a smile. We always kissed afterwards.

The region we entered after our fabulous lunch was the most unique we had ever experienced. Art and modern man have their roots in the Cro-Magnon past and in the Dordogne, there are traces of history dating back tens of thousands of years. The history of the earth, where slow drops of water carved out the famous rock shelters, stretched out before us. We were in the world famous limestone caves and grottoes, where the paintings left by prehistoric man floated eerily among stalactites and stalagmites.

The Font de Gaume has the most beautiful collection of cave paintings, open to the public, in France. I was stunned to realize that a needlepoint I had completed less than a year before and totally different from anything I had ever done, was taken directly from these walls. The Combarelles contains France's most important collection of rock engravings, while Laugerier Cliffs is famous for its coral-like mineral deposits. The first drawings of a mammoth along with the first skeleton, thirty thousand years old, of Cro-Magnon was discovered in this area and the only thing that marred our visit to the area was the poorly constructed, giant replica that stood outside the museum. It spoiled the image completely.

Just driving in this region was captivating. We always found a new winery with wares to sample, or a picnic spot by a fast moving brook, or a cave carved out of the rock half way up a cliff, that we had no way of reaching. When we drove into the town of Sarlat, it was time for another in depth tour. The Renaissance and the Middle Ages still live in this town. The houses were old, many blackened with age and you could imagine the "burnings" that went on in the oast houses. After a day of wandering the narrow, winding streets investigating every shop, house and museum, we camped on a horse farm nearby. We returned to town the next morning for freshly baked croissant and coffee.

It was a short drive, after breakfast, to Rocamadour. The village is built into the cliff beneath a road that leads to a spectacular view over the town. The seven sanctuaries of Rocamadour have a number of treasures, particularly two twelfth century frescoes. From a little cafe at the top of the hill we enjoyed lunch and the view.

Once back in our van, we headed towards the coast and ran out of spectacular viewing, so we just drove. The night in the campground was cold and uncomfortable. We were shivering when we woke up and Paul discovered he had accidentally left his window open. By the time we reached Agen, he had a scratchy throat and could not control his sneezing. On the way to Labenne, Paul had to stop and rest. I hated the challenge, but I drove while Paul stretched out in the back. We stopped for the night in Labenne.

A sick husband in a tiny motorhome was no fun. Every move or sound I made, disturbed him. We drove to Bairritz, checked into a guest house with a private bathroom and stayed. Paul slept the first day away, waking only for homemade soup prepared in the van and hot tea prepared in the room. It didn't take him long to feel better but we stayed warm and cozy for a few days while a storm raged outside.

The calm weather of the interior had turned cold, rainy and windy on the coast and we had never seen such an angry sea. On the third day, from the safety of a seaside restaurant, we watched huge waves crash onto the dock, spewing water hundreds of feet into the air, before returning to our room.

We awoke the next morning to the final insult..... snow on the ground. We had our motorhome serviced that morning in St. Jean du Luz and crossed the border into Spain a little after lunch.

We turned the page in our book of maps and realized that there must be some mistake. In the enormous section of maps on Spain, there were only a few roads shown. We started out, sure that we would come across interesting little side trips. We found ourselves climbing and climbing and stopped at the Chapel of Our Lady of Guadalupe just for the view of the beach, the town and quay side, and from the end of the headland, the French coast and the town of Hendaye. We continued our climb. We thought the winding, twisting ribbon of road into the Pyrenees, with a view of nothing but pine trees and gorse, would never end.

After several hours of the slow assent, we found ourselves on, as the song says, the plains of Spain. We stopped in Pamplona for some essential banking. For years Paul fantasized about running with the bulls in this fair city so we drove Ernest Hemingway Boulevard to the end and took a picture in front of the famous bullring. The bulls run in July. We decided not to wait.

Once back on the two lane road heading across country, it again stretched out endlessly. There were no turnoffs, no side roads, no campgrounds and no hotels that came close to suiting us. The land was flat and devoid of anything green or alive and each town passed seemed poorer and as colorless as the last. It was still light, but as the hours of driving passed, with nowhere to stop or stay, I was again beginning to worry.

In the middle of the emptiness, stood a lone sign post with a symbol of a little house. "Great," said Paul, who had obviously done his homework, "a Paradour."

"What the hell is a Paradour?" I asked.

"It's a government run hotel." "It could be an old fort or a castle that has been converted into luxury rooms." "I've had enough driving," he said, "I need some luxury."

We had failed to see the dramatic change in the landscape as we followed the signs to Alcaniz and drove into the center of town. We turned left and drove up a long, winding street. The road was narrow and although our van was small, we had trouble maneuvering around the curves. At one point we had to stop, back up and turn sharply up one of the roads, but we made it. We entered the large empty lot surrounded by fencing and parked directly in front of two giant wooden doors. We walked into the grandeur of what had once been an eighteenth century castle.

Our bedroom was the size of a small house. It had twin beds, my only immediate objection, a large oak dresser, a huge writing desk and a set of stairs, running the entire length of the room, leading up to a wall of windows for looking out at the countryside. We were, indeed, up on a hill and the scenery surrounding the castle was most impressive. The town, for as far as we could see, sat amidst orchards and fertile olive groves. This was a total change of scenery from the hours of nothingness on the road.

What totally impressed us about our room, however, was the floor. It was covered in a stiff, brown-red leather. We went down on all fours to feel the unique rough texture or perhaps to kiss the ground that we found a place to stay that was off the road and safe for the night. With all we had heard about wild camping in Spain, we dared not stay anywhere outside a campground. The room was our sanctuary.

The bathroom was only slightly larger than our motorhome. A large bathtub, just waiting to be filled, sat to one side. I would forego that pleasure until after dinner. We were famished. We were advised when we checked in that the kitchen was closed for the evening and most of the staff had gone home. Paul and I were the only guests in the hotel.

We went back to the van and raided the refrigerator. Eggs, onions, fresh mushrooms, a canned ham from our bulging cupboards, kept on hand for emergencies, was made into a feast. Since we were both starving and my hands were shaking a bit, I managed to slice into my finger while cutting up some tomatoes. The omelet was delicious and once we had a bit of food in us, we felt human.

I rushed back to the room. I could wait no longer to luxuriated in the tub. While I enjoyed my personal bit of heaven, Paul roamed the confines of the castle. He returned long before I was out of the tub having read all about the history of the Paradour.

With the unfamiliar beds, no one to snuggle up to, a strange room and sheets starched so stiff, my elbows were rubbed raw from my tossing and turning, sleep eluded me. Paul did not suffer from the same problem .

At first light, I decided to treat myself to another bath while Paul went to get us coffee, a ritual he performed faithfully. He was back within ten minutes.

"You have to come downstairs," he said.

"Ok, I'll be down shortly," I hollered from the tub.

"No, now," he said, sounding totally flustered. "Come

now," he insisted.

I stood, dried off in the huge anteroom that was attached to the bathroom and got dressed. Bewildered by his insistence, I followed Paul to the dining room.

"I ordered coffee for two," Paul explained. When the waiter said "completo" I said "si, completo" and I assumed they would bring cream and sugar.

At that moment we entered the dining room to find a table set for two with flowers. To one side on the table, there was a tray with an assortment of cheeses, another tray with an assortment of meats and a third with fruit and breads and a steaming pot of coffee sat in the middle. We would have had leftovers had we fed the Spanish Armada. We decided to stay cool for another hour or so and thoroughly enjoyed whatever had been placed before us, since the waiters had no intention of cancelling or removing our order.

When we paid the bill, we discovered that the breakfast, fit for a king and his court (and their families, neighbors, friends and enemies) added sixteen dollars to our sixty-five dollar room charge, a major extravagance for the Spanish people. We left the Paradour just before noon, thrilled with what had been our first day in Spain and delighted to have learned our first word in Spanish, "completo" meaning "screw the tourist."

Chapter 8

The drive down the mountainside from Alcaniz to the coast was a painstakingly slow procedure with all its twists and turns. This was El Cid country, Spain's national hero. Rodrigo Diaz de Vivar, better known as El Cid, was banished in 1089 and unjustly accused of disloyalty. Our only stop in this region was Morella to visit the fantastic fortress. The fourteenth century ramparts, punctuated by towers formed a mile long girdle around a hill on which the town had been built in tiers. Crowning the rock summit are the ruins of a medieval castle.

That night we camped near the coast in Vinaroz. The place was a large, flat, sprawling, fenced area, not terribly interesting and for the most part, vacant. We wandered the campground after dinner and met a few campers who were staying only a day or two before moving farther south.

Our favorite permanent resident, however, was a little black and white mongrel that seemed overly friendly. We stopped to talk to the little guy, whose tail wagged constantly at any sign of recognition, so I bent down to pet him. Since he followed us around and sat and stared every time we stopped and talked, I felt I owed him. At dark, he vanished. We had no idea where the short haired, floppy eared little guy went that night, but the following morning he stood wagging his tail in anticipation right outside our van's side door. When I treated him to a dabble of the oatmeal that I scraped out of the bottom of the pot, it was devoured with one swat of the tongue and a gulp. The poor thing was starving.

Being a sucker for dogs in general and starving dogs in particular, I could not resist the temptation and threw a couple of spoonfuls of uncooked oatmeal back in the pot with some milk. In my world the gooey concoction should not be for human consumption anyway; but, since my husband loved it, I always kept an open bag and one to spare in the van. I certainly did not mind giving the dog my share. I made another small pot of the stuff while Paul's bowl cooled. When it was ready, I topped both with some milk but sprinkled brown sugar only on Paul's portion. I don't think the dog missed it. When the little beggar was through eating, he did not stick around for the thanks that I felt I richly deserved. He gobbled and fled.

Later that day, while Paul and I relaxed in the sunshine, we had a return visit from the dog. This time he was followed by a camper who came over to say hello. While I petted the dog, the fellow asked if we had fed him.

"Yes," I answered, "I made him some porridge".

"No wonder he would not eat my paltry offering of bread soaked with milk," he volunteered. "Today you ate like a king, you little beggar," he laughed and bent down to stroke his head, who responded immediately by licking his face.

This would be the first of many stories we heard about the dogs that needed a passport to get home. They also needed transportation. Paul and I listened, in fascination to the heartbreaking story of this little mutt.

People usually like to travel with dogs. They are not only good company but provide a bit of protection. When leaving a motorhome unattended, a barking dog is a real asset since a vehicle with a ferocious occupant of any size will not usually be broken into or vandalized.

The British are usually responsible for the problem. If they bring their pet out of the country, they cannot bring the animal back into England, so they leave their own pampered pooch at home. All animals brought into Britain must spend six months in quarantine due to the fear of importing a rabid animal. Most family pets do not survive the ordeal.

Once the offender crosses the border into France, they have been known to pick up a stray that is hanging around the docks. The dog is taken to a vet to ensure reasonably good health, bathed, probably deflea-d and then taken traveling. The animal is treated to be best of everything for a month or more, possibly the winter, and before returning to England, the dog is dropped off at any campground or sometimes by the side of the road, to fend for themselves. During the high season, these little beggars have no problem finding food; however, during the lean months, they often go hungry. If it were a problem with just one or two dogs, the campground could cope for the season; however, some of the dogs, when food is in very short supply, resort to running in packs. Then it becomes a problem for everyone concerned. The locals have no choice.....the once beloved family pets are poisoned or shot.

This scenario is true, more often than not, of the Britishers wintering in Morocco, since the locals are terrified of rabies. They will not go anywhere near a vehicle that has a dog of any size or description in it.

Listening to the tragic story of this one little cur, I suddenly thought what a remarkable story this would be from the dog's point of view. If only they could talk.

Little mutt Pierre, who is bored with being a spoon fed, sniveling little moocher decides to   check out the action at the dock. After scoffing down a bowl full of pate sans croissant, he jumped off the balcony, rolled in a bit of dirt to disguise the overpowering scent of Eau du Chien and headed off to meet his destiny.

Little Pierre definitely has the advantage. He is small, by no means intimidating, but big hearted and eager for adventure. He quakes a little to show he is cold and easily approachable. Who could resist? He is picked up almost immediately by a family heading south. He blows kisses to his pals left on the dock from the back window of the camper.   His winter is one of luxury. He flourishes in the warm climate and has to exercise his vocal muscles only a few times before strangers know to stay clear. By the end of his trip to Morocco, he is a fearless protector.

Our dog nappers are back on safe ground when they arrive in France and Little Pierre is returned to the same dock, well fed and tanned. It doesn't take long for our pampered pouch to start regaling his pals with travel and adventure stories of warding off those terrible Moroccans, with their dark swarthy complexions and penetrating black eyes.

Of course when Pierre tells the tale, he is the hero of the trip. Even the French poodle, Fife, cannot resist the charm of this little vagabond. Our daredevil returns to his French family, who has not stopped mourning their little Pierre. All is happy.

Seen in the eyes of Pierre, it is a funny story; however, the sad situation is very real. The dogs are usually picked up in France because the French pamper their pets. Unfortunately the dog is rarely dropped off where he is picked up. The poor little animal in dropped off anywhere the people feel like dropping them off. Winter months often spell disaster.

As sad as the story is, it is only one of hundreds, possibly thousands.

*   *   *   *   *

We stayed in the campground in Vinaroz one more day and shopped at an enormous outdoor flea market. We purchased enough groceries to restock our refrigerator and cupboards. Our van got a thorough cleaning and when we needed a break, we relaxed and read our guidebooks. The following morning, refreshed and rested, we were on our way.

The weather was clear and sunny one minute, raining the next and pouring a minute after that. We drove in and out of sunny spots, so we continued straight through Valencia and camped that night at El Saler. There were only a few people in the campground. The following morning we pushed on to Albir. It didn't take us long to find our newlywed friends Don and Marjorie Jones. We were given a warm welcome and a bottle of Chinon wine came out of the larder in celebration. They had purchased several bottles of our favorite wine just in case we took them up on their offer to visit.

Their new apartment needed some cleaning, painting and some decorating. We stayed to help.

Chapter 9

We stayed in the area long enough to help get all the work done, meet their friends, play a little golf and accept an invitation to a traditional Christmas dinner. Although our home was in a nearby campground and all our new friends had apartments, we enjoyed being part of the close knit, English speaking, community. When anything of interest cropped up, like a card game or a group going to a movie or if they were meeting for lunch or dinner, Marjorie and Don came to the campground to fetch us. We kept in touch daily.

Albir was a quiet but affluent town, thanks to the tourists who wintered there. They had paved streets, a few sidewalks, lots of little shops and restaurants and a drug store selling newspapers from around the world.

The town also had an interesting myth connected to it. One of the many hills that surrounded the town had a singular tooth-like bite out of the top. It is said that when the giant awoke, still groggy from sleep, he accidentally stubbed his toe on the mountain. It not only produced the gaping hole, but the mound of earth that was kicked out became Calpi Rock. On our trip through Calpi we had stopped to see the colossal mound that sat about a mile off shore. The myth made perfect sense since we had seen both parts of the puzzle.

Every few days, we lunched with Marjorie and Don at Penny Lanes, a British pub, and listed Adrian and Morris, the pub owners, amongst our friends. All was right with our world.

It was the third week of November. We had been on the road about two and a half months and were still in the habit of counting off the weeks. We were, once again, itching to explore new worlds. We promised to be back in time to celebrate Christmas.

The twenty second of November found us in a beautiful campground, overlooking the deep blue water of the Costa Blanca, just south of Cartagena. We moved a little slower since we heard there were both rain and snow storms in the area and we had no intention of getting caught in either. We stayed in Puerto de Nazarrone and since it was warm and sunny, Paul took out some fishing equipment and we lounged on the dock for a couple of hours. While Paul concentrated on catching nothing, I read.

When the sun came out the following day, we knew it was time to move. The fifteen mile trip from Mojacar to Carboneras was spectacular. The road skirted the shore before turning inland to climb the pyramid-shaped mountain by way of serpentine bends. The terrain appeared to be made of coal with the color in spots ranging from purple to mauve rock. The trip down to Carboneras Beach was intimidating, since our van was British and the passenger wheels inched close to the cliff's edge. I held my breathe until the bottom, trying to enjoy the spectacular view. Paul was so intent on keeping his eyes of the road, he missed almost everything. We stopped in a rest area part way down for an unobstructed view.

The road through an area, distinctively desert-like in appearance, led us to a campground just outside Almeria, where we spent the night. Back on the road the following morning, we stopped to do some sightseeing in Guadix, home of troglodyte dwellers. The snow covered Sierra Nevada were on our left as we headed towards Granada. The distant mountain view was striking, but we had no reason to stop except for lunch and the odd tea break.

In Granada we reverted to typical tourists. We spent the entire day at the Alhambra, one of the most remarkable fortresses ever built and Generalife, the summer palace of the Kings of Granada, all part of the same magnificent complex. We stopped only long enough to have a conversation with a mother and daughter from California who had come into the

Alhambra via the exit and had no idea where they were or where to start their tour.

We spent the next day walking around Old Granada, visiting churches and schools, studying statues and carvings. While lunching in a small restaurant, we listened to the news in English. The area we had been in the day before, Almeria, had been hit with a violent rainstorm and had sustained major flooding. We didn't have long to wait the next day, we left Granada in a downpour and headed for Cordoba.

From our campground, on the outskirts of town, it was an easy bus ride into Cordoba's center. Again we played the typical tourist. We spent at least two hours in the Mezquita cathedral (Mosque). The forest of pillars are unique, but the red and white Moorish arches, extending in all directions, was a traditional Muslim one. We could not believe the vastness, but we walked it all.

The same afternoon we toured the Old Jewish Quarter and visited a fourteenth century synagogue, one of only two synagogues left. Queen Isabella was responsible for ousting the Jews from Spain in the late fourteen hundreds so most synagogues had long been destroyed. Before catching our bus back to the campground, we toured the gardens of the Alcazar. The Arabic style gardens are terraced and refreshed with pools and fountains and surrounded by cypress trees. The vegetable garden, still being cultivated, dates back to the caliphs. By the time we returned to the campground, we were exhausted, starved but very well educated. While I prepared the salad, Paul lit the barbecue.

Strolling the grounds after dinner, we met Jack and Bev from England. Their long haired German Shepherd sat chained to the van. When Paul said "hello" the demon eyed monster sprang to his feet, barking madly and straining at the chain. Before introducing himself, Jack locked the dog in the van, who barked threateningly at us from the window long after it was necessary. The dog unnerved me, but we stayed for a glass of wine and some conversation.

By the next morning, we were on our way. Portugal was calling.

Chapter 10

The Spanish don't seem to like it when you leave their country. We left anyway, waving goodbye to the border and suddenly ran out of road. We were in no man's land, driving across a well-worn cow path, patties and all. We maintained our direction, staying on the path, hoping we wouldn't run into the herd that had left the deposit on our escape route. We soon hit a gravel road for a few hundred feet, then a paved road for another few hundred feet and were suddenly welcomed by the Portuguese border patrol. We stopped, showed our passports and were waved through. Paul asked if they would mind stamping them, which was a mistake because they took forever putting our names into their computer. With everything in order, we went on our way.

One of the first signs we saw, when we entered Portugal was the now familiar symbol of a house. This time we both knew exactly what we were looking at and decided we would again treat ourselves to another fabulous evening. The Pousada is the Portuguese version of the fort or castle style luxury.

We arrived in Evora late morning and drove directly to the Pousada. Only a few rooms remained vacant and we booked one of them, never asking the price. While our room was being readied, we wandered around the town. Evora harbors both a Roman temple and a Renaissance palace and everything medieval in between. We played tourist until hunger pangs set our stomachs to growling. When we could not find an open bank to withdraw money on our Visa cards, we went back to the

48

van for lunch.

We had arrived without an escudo to our name, but since we were seasoned travelers, we no longer worried about such incidentals. All banks were closed. It was the first of December, Independence Day in Portugal so we would have to rely on the Pousada to exchange some of our Spanish money and wait until Monday to find an open bank.

Our stay at the Pousada was enchanting. Within an hour after our arrival, every room was occupied and before going back outside to continue our wandering, we made dinner reservations. We were advised there would be two sittings for dinner and we chose the latter. When we returned a little after mid-afternoon, our room was ready and we relaxed awhile. The room did not have the unusual charm of our Spanish room, but it was more than adequate. Besides, it had a bathtub. I needed nothing more.

That evening we enjoyed our three course dinner consisting of consume soup, salad, baked fish and flan for dessert. Every table was occupied with two or four guests and from the various languages we heard, they represented at least a dozen or more countries. We ended the evening having drinks in the lounge with a couple from San Francisco who had arrived that day. The date was December of 1989 and this was the first we had heard about the devastating earthquake in California that had wrecked havoc a week or so before. We listened, totally fascinated, to a blow by blow account of the man who survived for days buried under the rubble. It was a lively conversation and we enjoyed catching up on the news about America.

We had been on the road for close to three months and it was at this point, that we started losing track of time. We stopped talking about "the weeks" that we had been on the road. Since we had no problem borrowing money on our Visa cards, we knew our friend Pat Thomas had been depositing our mortgage money and paying our bills on time. Paul no longer felt guilty about not getting up early every morning and going to work. I was getting used to and enjoying my gypsy life. We were free.

Before leaving Evora that Monday, we found a bank, lined our pockets with escudos and headed towards the coast. Much to our delight, on our journey inland, we discovered that

English was a second language for the people of Portugal. Most of the natives spoke it to some degree, or tried. That helped me since Portuguese was unlike any other language I had ever heard and Paul, as usual, had already mastered hello, thank you, good morning and good evening and took every opportunity to add a word or two to his vocabulary. I had just started to learn a few words of Spanish when we found ourselves at Portugal's back door.

We enjoyed the driving since the price of gas was a little cheaper than Spain and the roads seemed to be in a little better shape, until Paul suddenly had to swerve around something large and deadly looking on the road. We stopped and walked back to the object. In what would have been a reasonably jarring hole in the pavement, someone had placed an enormous concrete block, with one corner jutting, pyramid-style, up in the air. Hitting the hole would have jolted us out of our seats, no doubt. Hitting the concrete block, on the other hand, would have broken our axle then jolted us out of our seat. Paul removed the offending object and together we dragged it to the side of the road away from, we hoped, anything with wheels. We ended our drive day in a lovely seaside resort of Cascais, just north of Lisbon.

Cascais was a little tourist village where we could do some grocery shopping. We found a second hand bookstore with some English books available and spent an hour or so pouring through them before choosing several. Book buying was serious business for us, but such a treat. The day we arrived was also market day and we wandered up one side of the street and down the other seeing the goodies of the region. We purchased a variety of fresh fruit and vegetables.

We checked into a campground and were thrilled to discover that they had a television room, something we had not seen often. Knowing that Portugal did not have a movie industry and that movies were shown in language of origin, we hoped that the television might be the same. (Even we found it amazing the different bits and pieces of information that we gleaned along the way about the places we visited. We were becoming a store house of useless information.) Perhaps we could see a bit of television and understand something (or anything) for a change. After dinner, while Paul took care of the dirty dishes, I checked on the state of the television room. The room was occupied by a man in his mid fifties, who was lounging on one of the overstuffed chairs. His legs stretched out on a coffee table as he watch television. Since I understood none of what was said, I presumed it was Portuguese.

I was immediately drawn to the man, who did not even look up when I entered the room. He was wearing a black track suit with the word "Canada" printed in bold white letters down one pant leg. I couldn't resist and asked, after he acknowledged my presence, if he was from Canada.

"No" he said, very excitedly upon hearing my Canadian/American accent, "are you?"

He was thrilled when I responded "yes" and wanted to know exactly where we were from, how long we were staying and where we were traveling to next. He was dumbfounded to learn how long we had been wandering aimlessly around Europe. Just then Paul walked in. It didn't take him long to introduce himself to Dieter Haueisen.

Dieter was originally from Germany but had lived in Portugal over half his life. He had returned to Germany only long enough to see that his two daughters had German University schooling before returning to Portugal.

While we talked and exchanged all kinds of information, Dieter translated the news that had just come on television. It was all local events and nothing that was of any real importance to us, but it was interesting anyway. By the end of the evening, we had become fast friends and the next morning Dieter and his wife, Helga, stopped by our camper to invite us to share in some of their dinner. They were in the process of preparing their national dish, bacalhau. Bacalhau, we learned from Helga, is reconstituted salted cod served with garlic soaked olive oil. It took several days to prepare and much of the preparation, she explained in relatively good English, was in removing the salt from the cod. This was done by frequently changing the salted water to fresh after the fish had been soaking, then allowed to drain completely.

Since it was only mid-morning, we brought out the coffee and shared some of the many cereals we always kept on hand. The coffee started a wonderful, long eventful day, that continued through a mouth watering barbecued bacalhau and steak (our contribution) dinner and an evening of non stop talking and exchanging stories and ending close to midnight.

The next day the Haueisens gave us a guided tour of the sights of the Cascais area. We drove to the most westerly point in all of Europe, Cabo St. Roca and our hosts insisted that we each get a certificate to say that we were there. By the time we returned to the campground it was too late for a hot dinner. I heated up the soup pot and Helga made sandwiches. Again we picnicked and again we ended the evening close to midnight.

Dieter came to retrieve us early the next day. The morning news predicted severe storms and Dieter felt uncomfortable with us being so close to the coastline. He suggested that we pack and leave with them. By late Sunday morning, we were following Dieter and Helga into Lisbon and to one of the local campgrounds. We would be safe there, he told us. We said our goodbyes late afternoon and before parting, decided we would all get together the next evening for dinner. The Haueisens were not out the gate, when the rain started.

With the torrential downpour, it did not take long for the campground to flood. We were happy to be inland but Paul decided that instead of sitting around the campground, after dinner, we would wend our way into Lisbon and perhaps go to a movie. Since movies were shown in the language of origin, we hoped we could find an English one. All the movies had Portuguese subtitles. We figured, if we couldn't find a movie, we would enjoy walking around the mall. It had been too long since we were in a big, modern city and from what we saw on our way into Lisbon, it certainly was a big, modern city.

The trip into town beat sitting around the camper in a deluge. We tried not to notice that the streets were really flooded. We drove slowly since the water was half way up our wheels in spots. We took our time driving around the city and found a shopping center that had theaters. It seemed everyone in Lisbon had the same idea and the mall was overflowing with shoppers, diners, lookers and much to our dismay, moviegoers. Although there were several English movies, the only one with available seats was Return to the Bridge Over the River Kwai. No, I had never heard of the movie either and there wasn't a recognizable name in the list of credits. After seeing it, I knew why. The only interesting thing about the movie was that it was in English with Portuguese subtitles and when they were speaking Japanese, the subtitles were also in Portuguese. It did not take a rocket scientist to figure out the plot, not that there was much of one.

As we were leaving the theater, the mother and daughter from the United States whom we had met two weeks earlier, at the Alhambra in Granada, Spain came over to say hello. We went out for coffee together and shared some of our experiences. While they were frantically running around Lisbon in the last days of their vacation, we confessed that we had just started relaxing and had no idea how long we would be traveling.

Paul found the way back to the campground. We located our spot and settled in for the night. The rain had abated sometime during the movie so we had no problem getting back to the campground. I always admired Paul's sense of direction for places revisited. Even if he got lost, he always managed to find his way via an alternative route, even in a foreign country. In this instance; however, being on the main road, he did not get lost.

The following evening, when we arrived at the Haueisen's, Dieter was most upset and demanded to know where we had been the night before.

"We went to the movie," Paul responded, "why, what's wrong?"

It seems, as Dieter explained it, right after we left the campground to go into Lisbon, they closed off some of the major roads due to severe flooding. The roads must have reopened before the movie let out because we knew nothing about it. Dieter had spent many hours trudging through the muddy campground looking for us, wanting to invite us back to their apartment, where we would be really safe. When he returned home without us, Helga had been most annoyed with him and told him so, in no uncertain terms. While he had soaked himself to the bone looking for us, we were snug as a bug in a rug, stuffing our faces with popcorn. His anger was very short lived and we went on the have a wonderful evening and even have an "it's a small world" story to relate.

Dieter and Helga spend one month every year in Ontario because Helga has a brother living in Ontario, north of Toronto. They showed us home videos of the Elmvale Flea Market. The same flea market, where for years I was a vendor and much of the footage was taken from my empty booth. I had a ninety mile drive and would stop and call on customers along the way so I arrived later than most of the vendors. The Elmvale Flea Market was where Dieter had purchased his track suit with the word "Canada" written down the side and he had purchased it from the vendor right next to my booth.

Our days in Lisbon were filled with wonder. We toured the old part of town and watched as the sidewalks were repaired with five or six men sitting cross legged the entire width of the repair zone. One man would shovel the sand into the hole and the rest would tap in the stones with tiny hammers to keep them in place. A more tedious job we could not imagine.

We visited Sao Jorge Castle, the Tower of Belem, the Coach Museum and we sauntered around the harbor area, looking at the sights and reveling in the sunshine. We toured the Jeronimo Abbey, the Maritime Museum and, of course, the crowning glory of Lisbon, the Monument of the Discoveries, which is the front end of Christopher Columbus' ship and all crew members looking out to sea.

We had one more dinner with our friends in Lisbon. The restaurant was a fifteenth century home that had been converted to a gourmet restaurant. The following day was overcast and by the time we left Lisbon to take the ferry from Setubal to the South Coast, it was raining again. What a fitting end to a wonderful city. We actually felt like crying ourselves. We had left a beautiful city, some new friends and were once again out in the great unknown.

We drove all that day in the rain and ended up in Mirafront. The sun was up early the next morning and we did three loads of laundry. We spent the next three days putting out the laundry and taking it in when it rained, which was often. We finally started heading south in the hope of finding drier weather.

There were very few times that I missed America, but this was definitely one of them. I longed for one of my big, fluffy sweatshirts still warm from a dryer.

Chapter 11

We camped that evening in Sines on the coast. The weather had finally cleared up. Paul prepared our marinated barbecued chicken wing dinner. The nastier the weather became, the more we looked forward to our infrequent outdoor dinners. I set up the picnic table with utensils to take full advantage of the serenity of our surrroundings and the warmth in the air.

After cleaning up, we headed to the dining room to see who might be available for some conversation. It was still early winter and most of the campground was vacant but a small intimate group sat around a huge wooden table, sampling wine. A blazing fire, hissing and spitting from a brick fireplace that took up one wall in the lounge, lit up half the room and warmed it to an inviting temperature.

The couple turned to greet us and with very little urging, we joined the conversation. The dark haired young man in his early twenties was surrounded by wine bottles, some empty, some full, and was regaling the couple with stories of the goings on in the campground. Even without knowing who he was talking about, the stories were amusing. Some friends, he told us, would be arriving that evening and he had not seen them in more than a year. His English was excellent.

For our benefit, he volunteered a little of his life story. While his parents owned the campground, he owned a small but productive vineyard in the next county. He had loved growing grapes and blending wines since he was a teenager and his parents had purchased the vineyard for him to indulge his hobby. The wine that was offered around the table was a sampling of his own product. We could not have been more impressed. The full bodied red wine was rich and flavorful with just a touch of sweetness. Three months on the road, having tasted the best of France and Spain, had changed me into a connoisseur of wines and I dubbed the vintage set before us, a very good year. I should however advise that before leaving America, I drank sparingly and had more headaches on one glass of wine, than I cared to admit. I was now not only a connoisseur but rapidly on my way to becoming a lush.

We exchanged stories, we sampled wine down to the dregs, we laughed and we talked some more. When several hours had gone by and a platoon of empty bottles lay like soldiers on a battlefield, with droplets of their blood splattered on the table, the young man decided he could wait no longer. He introduced us to another Portuguese delicacy, Frango Piri Piri. Chicken pieces marinated for several hours in Portuguese hot sauce, called Piri Piri, was barbecued over an open fire. We were all starving and this magnificent offering was considered an elixir of the Gods by the ravenous troops.

By the time his friends arrived, the wine was gone, the food was gone and we were close to being out of conversation. It was after midnight and the new arrivals were exhausted from their long flight from London and an even longer drive from Lisbon. After a warm greeting and some small talk, Paul and I headed for the aspirin bottle and bed.

We slept in the next day and did our best to rid ourselves of the hangover before the festivities resumed the next night. And resume they did.

By the time we left the campground on our trek south, we knew that Portugal would be another one on our list of favorite countries. Although the weather did not lend itself to what we would call ideal, the people would stay in our memory as being warm, friendly and most hospitable.

It was overcast when we left and raining by the time we arrived in the Algarve. Our campground was just on the outskirts of the town of Lagos and we used it as our headquarters. We toured the area extensively. We walked into the heart of town and had no trouble finding a spot for an afternoon libation. How could we resist a place called Club Canadian, a small community bar run by three young Canadian men, two from Winnipeg and one from Toronto. Lagos was one of the few places where we ran into many English speaking North Americans.

That evening Steve, from our now favorite watering hole, directed us to an off the beaten track restaurant that we never would have found on our own. It was at the end of a street that had run out of street lights, a sharp turn to the left and there it was, lit up like a Christmas tree. Steve's only request was that we return his flashlight at the end of the evening. We, once again, enjoyed Frango Piri Piri with all the delicious side dishes, like french fries and coleslaw. Not typically Portugese, but certainly to our liking.

Lagos was built like the spokes of a wagon wheel and we never knew which spoke we were headed up, because from the town's open air center they all looked similar. We enjoyed them all so much, we just kept walking. Each spoke had its share of restaurants, gift shops, cafes and bars.

From Lagos we took a day trip to Sagres and enjoyed a bit of isolation in the small community. We visited a local resort, loving the massive rock formations seen from the beach in Albufeira and Portimao. We stopped in Faro for some grocery shopping. We stayed by the water long enough to enjoy the scenery, write a few postcards and letters before continuing on towards the Spanish border. It was a short ferry ride from Portugal to Spain and not too long, nor too interesting, a drive to Seville.

On our first day of walking Seville, again in the rain, Paul fell in love. "This is the real Spain I wanted to see," he repeated over and over.

It was true. Seville was filled with wrought iron and beautiful red flowers in white hanging baskets and tiny doorways leading into courtyards filled with simple beauty. The buildings were complete with second and third stories, unlike much of Spain that waited to be renovated. (In Spain, taxes are not payable on unfinished buildings so many remained incomplete and in desperate need of attention that was never received.) We both loved Seville.

We left our camper at the Dos Hermanez campground and took the bus into the heart of town. From the bus terminal we walked to and through the University, which had been an eighteenth century tobacco plantation. We toured San Telmo Palace, once a naval school and residence of the Dukes of Montpensier and now a seminary. We admired the Gold Tower from a park bench and discovered the bull ring. We toured the immense Gothic style cathedral and walked up the thirty five flights of the Giralda for the splendid view of the capital of Andalusia. Before heading back to the campground we visited the magnificent gardens of the Alcazar.

By the time we return to the campground, we were soaked to the skin, very cold, very thirsty, very hungry and utterly exhausted. The following morning we didn't let a little car trouble, due the dampness, keep us from leaving and heading south, again in the hopes of finding drier weather.

We drove to Tarifa. Travel agencies stood on several corners advertising trips to Morocco. Until that very moment, we had not ever thought of going there.

Chapter 12

From Tarifa it was a short drive along the coast to Algeciras, where we had a breathtaking view of The Rock, as it is called by Prudential Insurance. We knew we would be heading in that direction and since they did not have any campgrounds, we knew we would not be spending the night there. We also learned from our guidebook that it was a tax free haven and we could purchase a few things that would make our lives more pleasant, if that were possible. We followed the route signs, according to our Spanish map.

"Christ," I complained to Paul, "where the hell is Gibraltar?" There was not one indication that we were getting close or even on the right road. We passed a welcoming sign that said "La Linea" and were lost, until we rounded a bend in the road.

La Linea, it turned out, was the last stop in Spain. Again, as in Portugal, we passed through no man's land and there was the sign in big, bold lettering.....Gibraltar and an arrow pointing straight ahead.

You'd think we would get used to the bizarre Spanish way of thinking. Their fondest desire, as far as Gibraltar is concern, is to own the country. Since Britain is not willing to relinquish its hold, the Spanish prefer having nothing whatsoever to do with the country, including putting up the tiniest of signs, pointing the way.

We parked our van in a lot just over the border, on the

Gibraltar side, and went shopping. The whole town was one giant strip mall. Electronics were being sold in every store. "Cheap, cheap, cheap" the signs screamed in fluorescent lettering, over the store windows, with most windows protected with wrought iron bars. Luggage was available cheaper than anywhere we had seen. Fortunately we didn't need any. Gift shops were everywhere, including extravagantly decorated little carts set up at street corners. We were dodging street hawkers selling watches and radios and trying anyway they could to entice us into the store that offered them the highest commission.

The sun was shining. The weather was warm. We walked in and out of nearly every store and priced anything we might be interested in buying, hoping we would remember where we could get the best deal.

We purchased a short wave radio, with a built in cassette player, in one of the shops that seemed to be doing a hefty business and where the prices were marked in both British pounds and Spanish pesetas. The radio was equipped with a Spanish plug and the salesman showed Paul how to convert it. Paul was now well acquainted with all kinds of strange plugs, since British plugs were different from French plugs which were different from Spanish plugs. A now seasoned traveler Paul knew that correcting the problem would be a snap.

We purchased some English novels in a second hand book shop, had a fish and chip lunch wrapped in newspaper, as good as any we had eaten in England and walked from one end of the town to the other visiting all the shops, the narrow alleys and stopped to rest awhile at Alameda Gardens. We filled our van with cheap gasoline and toured the Island. We stopped on one of the back roads long enough to watch a few Barbary apes that inhabit Gibraltar.

It was said that the British, who captured Gibraltar in 1704 with a naval force under Admiral Rooke, will remain as long as the apes survive. When there was a danger of the apes becoming extinct in 1944 Churchill sent a signal ordering reinforcements. The colony has flourished ever since and they are everywhere.

We refilled our gas tank and returned to Spain long before nightfall. We left relatively early because we had been advised there was often problems at the border. The Spanish are very unhappy when you visit Gibraltar and often keep the lineup long just to be a nuisance, we were told. Perhaps because we had Canadian stickers all over the van and flashed our Canadian and U.S. passports at the border crossing, we were motioned through without stopping.

We had enjoyed our day in the British haven. We drove back to Algeciras, found a suitable campground and spent the night. The following morning after hearing that we could leave our camper unattended and free of charge for a couple of days, we walked to the port in the downtown area and went directly into a travel agency.

Chapter 13

"There's no God damned way I'm going to Morocco without a tour," I argued with Paul. "Every time you hear people talking about the place, all you hear about is the stealing and the pick pocketing and the garlic breath and I'm not going without a big group of people and a guide," I made my point as quietly as I could.

"Oh, come on," said Paul, "they said the same about Spain." "Every country we've been in, someone has told us not to go somewhere." "I'll take care of you," he insisted. "I won't let the bogeyman get you," he said, furrowing his eyebrows and giving me that funny little grin I found irresistible and that always made me laugh.

"I know you're right. They did say that, didn't they?" I continued. "I'm still nervous though. Those people are really weird," I insisted. "How about we book a two day trip and if we like it we'll go back on our own," I continued hoping to convince him.

"OK," said Paul, "that sounds fair."

The entire conversation took place at the travel agency, whispering as best we could. The agent had left the room and let Paul and I hash it out in peace. I'm sure it was a discussion they heard over and over again.

We booked a two day tour from Algeciras, Spain via Tour Africa. The name itself, Tour Africa, conjured up mysterious images, dark and forbidding, but since I had a tremendous amount of confidence with what I thought would be lots of other people around, it was starting to sound exciting.

The following morning, with only one small overnight bag between us, we were picked up at the campground gate by taxi and delivered to the dock. We boarded a ferry that would take us to Ceuta in Spanish, Morocco. The weather was gorgeous which did wonders to lift our already soaring spirits. On board, we basked in the sunshine. Sitting on hard wooden benches that lined the upper deck of the ferry and leaning against the railing, we watched as Gibraltar faded away and we sailed the open seas.

Standing in the doorway of a full sized tour bus, was a dark haired young man, holding a white cardboard sign with a name that looked only slightly like ours. There was one couple on board. They were occupying the two front seats, catty corner behind the driver. The young man, about twenty five seemed really thrilled to be there, but the older woman, possibly his mother, sat stiffly, staring straight ahead. She seemed very agitated, almost frightened. With one glance, she gave us a quick skimpy smile and shot us a "please get me out of here and I'll give you my first born child" look. The doors closed and we were off, roaring down a partially paved road, swerving to the wrong side if that piece was paved and ours was not. The drive to the border took about fifteen hair raising minutes.

The bus, standing in a long line of traffic, seemed to take forever at the border between Spanish Morocco and French Morocco. When the young runner, who had greeted us at the bus with our name sign got off the bus with all our passports in his possession, I was not too thrilled either. I had a sudden image of being stranded in no man's land, without passports, anyone speaking our language or access to our money. My vision was short lived. In a matter of minutes he came running back, hopped on the bus, but insisted on holding onto our passports.

As soon as the runner returned, the bus pulled out of line and drove over the border. We were on our way again for a short distance. When we arrived in Tetuan, we were welcomed by our official guide, dressed in a long white robe and the traditional multicolored skullcap and hordes of ragged looking children all with their hands out, hoping we would give them money. With this unkempt group gathered noisily around the bus, the lady refused to get off. We all, including the guide, promised to protect her. She was absolutely miserable and I could only sympathized with her. Eventually, after some prodding, pleading, promising and threatening to leave her on board with the doors open, we did persuade her to join us and we all huddled together. I must confess, it was wonderful being with someone more intimidated than I was.

Our first stop was the medina (marketplace) in Tetuan. There were a thousand tiny streets and doorways that all looked alike. Some streets had only four or five doorways. There were streets that went nowhere and ended abruptly at a crumbling wall of mud and stones. There were streets that went on and on and seemed to end except for the ten step alleyway that took you onto another street or into another alleyway. The guide took us through the area like he had lived there all his life. No doubt, he had.

Although I was not quite as frightened as Pat, I was thrilled to be with a group, as small as it was, and with a guide, who seemed to do a fairly good job keeping the beggars at bay. Halfway through the tour, Mohammed, our illustrious leader, opened one of the thousands of doors. The five of us stood stark still in a magnificent, open air, courtyard. This was where we were to have lunch. We were flabbergasted. I could not take my eyes off the colorful and unique decor. Even Pat became verbal for the first time looking around the room oohing and aahing.

The room was brimming with beautiful and decorative rugs, overlapping in spots, piled high in other spots and individually displayed in others. The handwoven pillows were gigantic. Some were heaped in a corner while others were placed strategically around the room. It was a feast of color after seeing so many ordinary streets that lacked even a hint of individuality. The wooden tables were inlaid with mother of pearl and built low to the ground so we could admire the intricacies on the tops of the table.   The servers, all men, walked around in gauzy, brightly colored belly dancer costumes. This was major overload for our poor starved senses.

Our group was ushered to one of the low slung tables. We were each seated on an individual small pile of rugs and served mint tea immediately. Only after we sat down, did we all realize how ravenous we were. Stewed lamb in a sweet sauce made with raisins and orange pieces and served over couscous, their traditional fine grain pasta, was our only luncheon choice. It didn't matter, Paul and I loved it all and were totally caught up in the delights of the moment. The food, although totally foreign to us, with a sweetness we were unaccustomed to in a main course, was delicious.

Once lunch was over, however, we were accosted at our table by a large framed man in a dark business suit, whom unbeknownst to us was obviously part of our tour. He tried to sell us pictures that he had taken of us along the way.

"No, I don't want them," I said and shook my head at him.

He showed the pictures to me, then to Paul and around the table. "No," I repeated waving him away with my hand, even though everyone complimented the quality of the photo. I have an aversion to my picture being taken and did not want them.

He reduced the price from fifteen American dollars to ten dollars. I still refused. "Everyone buys the pictures," he yelled. "It is for your memories," he shouted.

"No," I argued, "if I wanted pictures, I would have brought my own camera." "No, I don't want them," I continued, trying not to raise my voice to the level of his. The louder he yelled, the more adamant I became.

In the end, he threw the pictures at me. "For free," he said and stormed out.

Our guide was not with us during the episode, so with this bit of unpleasantness over, he returned and had, no doubt, heard about the fiasco. We left our fabulous luncheon spot and went back into the medina. Again we wandered the streets, all looking alike and when we arrived in an open air piazza we were immediately circled by more street urchins, most of whom were once again kept at bay by the guide.

When a man approached out of the crowd, we did not take any notice until a snake was draped around Paul's shoulders and another slithered around his arm. My breath caught. I suddenly couldn't get enough air. The head of one of the snakes started fanning out in front of Paul's face. His face registered the terror in his heart. A cobra.....my God it's a cobra, my mind screamed. I don't think I said anything out loud. No one moved. I dared not yell. Where the hell was the guy with the camera now, I wondered for a brief instant. I stood glued and staring, gasping for air. The guide said and did nothing. God, how I wished we were back on the bus.

Willing his body the slightest movement, Paul inched his way. Painstakingly slow, he put two fingers into his pocket and extracted a ten durum note (seven durums to the American dollar). With his fingertips, he held it out to the charmer. The snakes, as smoothly as they had been applied to my unsuspecting husband, were removed instantly and whisked back into a basket. Grateful that it had not been them, everyone in the small crowd that had gathered threw money at the man who came very close to causing my death due to heart failure. We slunk away, horrified, our eyes darting in all directions. A bit of color was just starting to return to Paul's face. He was as frightened as the rest of us, but was the first to start joking about it.

Mercifully, the show was over. Our guide took us to a shop with trinkets, knickknacks, toys and various and sundry dust collectors, which was the part of any organized tour that we hated. When he saw we were not buying anything and seemed immune to the proprietors rapid price reductions, we did not stay long. Out of the medina and on our way back to the bus, we were surrounded by another group of kids. It was definitely not pleasant.

Mother and son got back onto the bus and we were ushered into a taxi, our passports given to the taxi driver. They were on a one day tour, which thankfully for Pat, was coming to an end. We said our farewells and waved goodbye as the bus door closed and tires squealed as they raced away from the stop.

The drive to Tangier was restful and we enjoyed the comfort of the back seat of taxi. The driver spoke but a few words of English and said almost nothing on the way. Paul and I were a little on the weary side from our frantic escapade and just relaxed, admiring the scenery, not saying much ourselves.

The landscape on most of the two hour drive was desert like with people tending their camels and working the fields. We were not surprised to see that the needs of the animals or the plowing of the soil was done by the women while the men sat on blankets, usually under an umbrella, sipping something and directing the work that had to be done.

In Tangier, we were deposited by our noncommunicative chauffeur into the Chellah hotel. We showered and changed for dinner. The room, although considered a four star, was sparsely equipped. The bed was comfortable enough and we did have a writing desk, but one lamp with a fifteen watt bulb was expected to light up our lives. We could hang our clothes in the closet on the two hangers provided but the room lacked a dresser. We solved the problem by leaving our clothes packed in our overnight bag. Fortunately the bathroom had familiar toilet facilities for which we were very grateful. The water in the shower was certainly hot enough, but it dribbled out so while I lathered, Paul showered and we reversed the process, afraid that even the dribble would quit at the whim of some unforeseen water bearer. What the heck, we were veterans. We could handle anything.

During dinner, we were seated at the same table with a British couple and thanks to Rae and Jack, we learned a little about a custom not usually known by the tourists. We were being accosted everywhere we went because we were on a tour and suspected of being "rich" tourists. The four of us went sightseeing on our own that evening and much to our delight, were totally ignored. We toured the area around the hotel, walking down all the little side streets, checking out the tiny, hole-in-the-wall stores before walking down to the beach to feel the sand under our bare feet. We were incognito for the first time since arriving in this unique country and loved it. To celebrate our newly acquired knowledge we ended the evening sipping a couple of brandies in the bar.

We slept well and started the next day with a typical tourist breakfast of scrambled eggs, orange juice, toast, grape jelly and strong coffee. Our new guide, Hassan, again dressed in the traditional long white robe, met us at the hotel desk at precisely ten o'clock in the morning, ready for a tour of the countryside. Our taxi, complete with another non verbal driver, awaited.

Again we observed the rolling hills in the distance and didn't comment too much when we saw the men sitting on blankets under umbrellas while the women toiled in the fields under an unrelenting sun. Our guide, fully prepared to explain the history of the country in any one of four languages, was fascinating. Since we had studied the country's history in our guidebooks, we were more interested in his personal history. He had been a guide for over twenty years and all official guides must speak a minimum of four languages. He was from Casablanca and although loved living in Tangier, he missed his family. He did not see them often because it was an expensive bus ride and money was scarce.

We were appalled seeing elderly women stooped from carrying heavy loads of firewood or young girls carrying baskets filled to overflowing with vegetables or fruits, carrying a child or two slung on their back while the men sat in the shade doing nothing. Hassan explained that it has been this way in his country for thousands of years and would likely go on for thousands more.

Paul was sure he saw a woman carrying a donkey, but I assured him he must be mistaken. Women performed back breaking labor and even I wasn't absolutely positive that he was joking.

After the tour of the countryside, we returned to walk the city of Tangier, with the guide pointing out all the places of interest. What had us mystified were all the chickens that sat perfectly still in a ring. Paul asked if they had been drugged.

"No," replied Hassan, "all their legs are tied together." "If they cannot move," he continued, "they make no sound and do not struggle."

Once again we found ourselves wandering the medina, and once again, all the doors looked alike. Hassan assured us, that while some lived modestly, many lived in absolute luxury behind these doors. "In Morocco," he said, "you must not flaunt your wealth."

The actress Rita Hayward, we learned, kept a home in the medina in Tangier and was reported to have been fabulous. Paul was also intrigued with the Parisian Cafe, where all the spies of World War II traded their secrets. We occupied one of the outside tables and treated Hassan to Nescafe coffee, one of his favorites. Paul and I each had a sweetened Turkish coffee, which surprisingly, I found tasty considering the bottom half of

68

the tiny cup was the texture of mud. By the time our guide returned us to the hotel, we were totally enthralled. Hassan had painstakingly explained that it took many years to become an official guide and if we wanted more of a tour we should contact our hotel manager and a guide would be hired. Guides, he explained again, must speak at least four languages well and be knowledgeable in all areas of history, geography and the culture of his people. That he was. We tipped him the equivalent of return train fare to Casablanca, thanked him and returned to our room at the hotel.

Our two days in Morocco had just whetted our appetite. Besides enjoying the gorgeous sunshine, unusual scenery and delicious food, we were not too upset about being awakened at five in the morning for the first call to prayer, even if we did pray for more sleep. Also fascinating were the posters at the Tourist Information Center and the travel agencies that indicated we could get on a ship in Agadir, Morocco and sail to the Canary Islands. We were definitely coming back.

The trip on the ferry back to Spain was a long tiresome one and the drizzling had started. By the time we landed in Algeciras, it was raining heavily and there was not one available taxi. We walked the three miles back to the campground. Someone, probably me, had left one of the windows open in our camper and our bedding was soaked. That night we slept on the bare cushions with one dry blanket between us and dreamt of snakes crawling all over our bodies.

Chapter 14

It was after the middle of December and since we had received a wonderful invitation from Don and Marjorie Jones for a traditional Christmas turkey dinner feast, complete with family and friends in attendance, we lingered in the Algeciras area only long enough to watch giant goldfish swimming around in the campground swimming pool, being fattened for the traditional Spanish Christmas dinner.

Just before we were ready to leave that morning, the owner and manager of the campground hearing of our problem, offered to wash our bedding and then treat the once soggy mess to the pure luxury of having it put into a real life, proper dryer. How could we refuse. It was returned to us before noon, clean and warm and fluffy. We said goodbye to the friends we had made and were once again back on the road to adventure.

By this time in our travels, we had witnessed and coped with enough rain to cause flooding the likes of which we had never previously experienced. We saw chimneys sticking up in the middle of what we had thought was a lake and wondered where the people had gone. We saw field watering equipment protruding from newly formed ponds. We saw barns floating on their side in the fields. We saw animals standing on a bare patch of grass just big enough to accommodate their body and bawling mercifully. It was heartbreaking. We knew the people of this region were in a disaster area and most had lost all they had. We saw few people. We drove through in silence.

The problem this awful weather created for me was that my knee never stopped aching. I limped noticeably in damp weather. I still wore the brace and Paul spent many hours gently massaging my sore thigh muscle.

In our drive up the coast, we visited Torremolinos, but didn't stay long. The name itself has become a by-word for two week tourist holidays. We stopped in the resort town of Malaga for some banking and to browse in an English second hand bookstore.

We drove on to Nerja. The sun came out briefly but we missed much of the fireball in the sky while exploring the Nerja Caves. The caves are so large and beautiful and filled with so many colored stalagmites and stalactites that ballets are held inside. Since we were not permitted to wander alone, we took the guided tour which lasted over an hour. We left the caverns and basked in the glorious sunshine for only a few minutes. It was a treat to be driving in pleasant weather. It didn't last.

It was late afternoon when we left Nerja, driving the coast road. We headed north, towards Almeria We hadn't gone far when we started looking for a place to stay. The recent flooding had closed many of the campgrounds and although we had wild camped frequently in France, Spain was not the place for it. We were to stay in campgrounds and if we chose to leave the camper for a night's stay in a hotel, we were warned, we could be assured that the camper would be broken into while we slept, if the hotel was not surrounded by walls or had a guard on duty. We drove on. Fact or myth, we were not taking any chances. Everything we owned was in the camper.

All the campgrounds at Almunecar were closed. Before leaving the area and returning to the main road, we saw lightning in the distance. We checked our camping book. There were no campgrounds, open or otherwise, along this coast road but we had no alternative. There was nothing open in the area we had just left. We had to keep going. We stayed on the coast road.

During sunshine this would have been spectacular scenery but the wind had picked up and was producing formidable gusts. Paul used all his muscle and concentration to keep our van on the road. It became treacherous so quickly. There was nowhere we could turn off. There was a mountain wall on our left and a sheer drop into the sea on our right.

Debris started flying at us. The van was being pelted with what sounded like chunks of wood. A broken table umbrella slammed onto the road in front of us. Paul ran over it. The passenger side of our van was hit with a chair that suddenly sprang to life. We dodged large tree branches that planted themselves wherever they wanted.

We stayed on the cliff road. Even if we wanted to wild camp at this point, there was nowhere to stop. By the time we reached Motril, a driving rain complete with tiny ice pellets, battered and bruised us. Within minutes the water in the middle of the street became a raging torrent, smacking the rubber half way up our wheel, threatening to defeat us. We stopped only long enough for the light to change to green and we moved on with the rest of the traffic. We were terrified. We needed higher ground. We continued driving slowly, afraid our van would stall, but we drove.

Weeks earlier, we had spent one night in a campground in Almeria. If nothing was open before that, surely Almeria would not have been swept away. It seemed a long way off in the downpour but at least we had a possible destination.

We drove through Adra. Nothing was open but we felt a little safer because we were now inland a bit. The rain let up a smidgen. Our windshield wipers were doing the best they could, but we couldn't see much. As we drove, the rain lessened even more. We were close to Almeria and prayed that the rain would not have wiped out the campground situated so close to the water. The gates were open. We drove through them.

It was around seven thirty in the evening. We got out of the camper to put our shaky legs on solid ground. It was sprinkling only slightly and, for the most part, the ground was dry. The keepers of the campground shop at our port in the storm knew nothing about the deluge. The drizzle had just started a minute or so before we drove through the gates.

Muttering to ourselves and shaking our heads, we walked around the campground like zombies trying to rid ourselves of the dread we felt. We had just spent four hour driving through the most ungodly storm and no one even knew what we were talking about.

We set up camp. We made ourselves coffee and threw

enough brandy into the cup to settle our stomachs and give us a hangover at the same time. Before the evening was over, we calmed down enough to make some dinner. Our insides were so scrambled, we decided to eat lightly. I prepared scrambled eggs and ham and.....what the hell.....more brandy.

The sun came out early the following morning. Glorious, life sustaining sunshine. We could not remember when we had seen it last. There was not a cloud in the sky. We packed up right after breakfast and were back on the road. Our bodies needed a treat and we were going to get it. We were off to Fortuna to "take the waters."

Needing the healing waters desperately, we did not do any sightseeing. It didn't take us long to get to Fortuna. We stopped only for groceries. We wanted to stock up for several days because this would be a perfect spot, we thought, to rest and unwind. Paul hated to admit it, but even he was tense, not only from the hazardous driving conditions of the day before, but from the fact that he did all the driving. He tried pleading with me to help in taking the wheel from time to time, but his pleas fell on deaf ears.

There was no way I would drive on the left side of the road, while sitting on the right and shifting with the wrong hand. "No way," I told him, "I'm never driving." "I have my chores, you have your chores and one of your chores is doing ALL the driving." "Get used to it, Buddy," I added. Then I kissed him on the chin, his lips and the tip of his nose just to let me know that I was taking full advantage of the situation and knew it.

We left the shopping area of downtown Fortuna, fully stocked and ready to relax for as long as it took. About three miles out of town is the little community that boasts of "the healing waters." We found a campground, pulled into a spot, made sure we were on level ground and turned off the motor. We were fascinated to discover that in this tiny, out of the way, village there were at least three large campgrounds, all open and ready for business. We chose the campground closest to the mineral pool. We were home.

We walked the campground and met several people doing exactly what we were planning. We stopped and chatted, comfortable in the fact that we didn't have to go anywhere for a

73

few days. We walked the main street in town, which contained one small shop to purchase milk and the barest of necessities. There were no other stores. It was totally unimpressive. People visited Fortuna only for the waters. When we returned to the campground it was close to dinner time. Paul marinated the chicken pieces that we had just purchased at the butcher in town and started the barbecue. I put the rice up to boil and prepared the salad. When my homemade soup was hot, we had a bowl of it.

The following day, we took "the waters" for the first time. If I had to describe it in one word, that word would be "heavenly." I could feel the warm water seeping into my tense and weary bones. I flexed and exercised my aching knee and taut thigh muscle. I stayed in the water for four hours. I think the book recommended twenty minutes to start, but what do they know. Four hours seemed just about perfect to me. By the time I got out of the water, I knew exactly what I would look like at a hundred years old.

We talked to everyone pool side. There were people staying a week or so. There were people who had come for the day from Murcia or Alicante or farther. One particularly fascinating couple we met, Jay and Andy Stewart, came from England and stayed six months, rarely leaving the area.

Jay and Andy were both in their seventies and lived full and hectic lives in England. Jay, although crippled with arthritis, worked her law practice in England for the six months they lived there. When she became so disabled that she could no longer get out of the wheelchair, they would pack up and return to Fortuna. Their schedule for the first twenty-one days was as follows. They both took the waters every day. Jay's body slowly healed itself, moving from wheelchair to canes to nothing at all and then they spend the next five months, just feeling great, taking the waters perhaps two or three times a week.

Since both were avid fixer-uppers and loved the joys and triumphs of physical labor, they persuaded the post office in Fortuna to rent them a broken down house for one hundred pesatas per month (approximately one dollar). They promised they would, at their own expense, fix up the house and make it livable and comfortable. They would totally renovate the house and return it, after many years of use and tender loving care, to the post office. They seemed to be enjoying this immensely and took great pride in showing us their progress. They would have fun doing it and take care of their bodies all at the same time. What a joy it was spending an afternoon with them. Since there was not much to do but read and relax and not much to see in the area, Paul lasted three days and was anxious to be on his way. That was fine with me. It was just a few days before Christmas and we were looking forward to the celebration with our friends.

We drove back to Albir via Elche, the city of one hundred thousand palm trees. The Phoenicians planted the groves on the east side of the town hundreds of years ago and driving amongst the stately Queens, that swayed regally in the breeze, was spectacular.

We received a warm and wonderful welcome from Don and Marjorie. Although the people at the campground in Almeria had not heard about the storms in Malaga, our friends had and they had been worried about us. They didn't know the exact date we would be returning, but intuition told Marjorie that we were in that area around the time of the storm. It all sounded very exciting to them. They were glad it had been us and not them.

We decided to stay put and recuperate awhile. The apartment adjacent to Marjorie and Don's was vacant and our friends were acquainted with the owners. With one telephone call, we rented it for two weeks at about the same price it would have cost us to stay in the campground. We enjoyed a real bed that we could leave disheveled if we chose, a full sized kitchen complete with an oven, a bathroom inside the house and glory be.....a bathtub. Does it get any better than this?

We had a wonderful traditional Christmas feast with the Joneses and our newly made friends. We spent New Year's Eve at a posh restaurant for a fish dinner (I don't remember what kind of fish we ordered, but it certainly wasn't goldfish) and dancing. We were fascinated by a group of Dutch people enjoying their meal at the next table. One tall, pretty, young woman wore a black, tight fitting dress and when she danced, exposing the front of the garment, there was a piece cut out and her nipple without benefit of bra showed through. When I pointed it out to Paul, he said simply "no, you can't have one."

We enjoyed entertaining friends in our home. The group gathered at our apartment for drinks since we had more than two chairs to sit on and a balcony that overlooked a garden. We went for long walks in the Benidorm hills. Paul played golf a time or two at the Altea Hills Golf Course. We haunted the flea markets and other places of interest. We picked up English books to read wherever they were available.

Early one morning we drove into Alicante to check the bus schedule for our trek back to Morocco. On the fifth of January 1990 we hopped on a bus and had an all night, uncomfortable ride back to Algeciras.

Chapter 15

We arrived at the bus depot/ ferry dock absolutely exhausted, looking like a pair of unmade beds, rumpled and out of place. It was only five forty five in the morning and the sun had not even begun to think about what it wanted to do this day. While Paul stood in line for our ferry tickets, I waited on a bench with our two pieces of luggage. A medium sized blue canvas bag lay at my feet while our bright pink and black knapsack sat snuggled next to me on the bench at my left side.

A dark skinned man approached. He had a large denomination Spanish bill in his hand and leaned towards my right side, saying "change, change." Bleary eyed and close to sleep, I just shook my head. In a flash he was gone. So was my knapsack. I blinked. It took a second or two to realize what had happened. For an instant I forgot I even had the bag and thought perhaps it was with Paul. I shook the cobwebs from my brain. I awoke immediately, feeling like someone had whacked me in the back of the head with a two-by-four and sprang into action. I scooped up the remaining bag and gave chase. When the corridor ahead was empty, I stopped and heard some noise behind me. I turned and discovered a bar crowded with people. Holding onto my bag for dear life, I entered. Standing in the doorway, hoping my eyes would adjust to the darkness quickly, I could feel my nostrils starting to flare. I was furious.

My mind was in a dense fog as I looked over the mass of humanity and realized that all the men looked alike. They were short, thin, dark, swarthy complexioned and too many to count had an identical pencil thin mustache. I really had not paid attention to the guy who had stolen my knapsack. In a frenzy I ran around the bar looking for my bag and spotted it, left unattended, under some seats at the counter. I grabbed it, scooping up the precious cargo into my arms. Without releasing the death grip on either bag, the knapsack bobbing up and down as I shook my fist at the guy standing closest, calling him a thief and a bastard. He didn't bat an eye. He glanced my way, giving me that "have you lost your mind" stare and continued talking to his friend or accomplice.

When Paul returned, tickets in hand, I was fully awake and animated. I relayed the story in infinite detail. When he asked me to point out the offender, I couldn't. Even though I had by this time, had a good look at him, he still blended into the crowd.

Paul, however, had a story of his own to relate. While he waited in line for the tickets, he had felt nimble fingers poking and probing in his back pockets and had been accidentally bumped a couple of times. Someone had ended up absconding with used tissues that Paul kept stuffed in his back pocket. Not quite the haul the culprit had anticipated.

We vowed to keep our wits about us at all times and guard our possessions, keeping them close to our bodies. We would wait until we got to our room in Tangier before releasing the stranglehold grip we now had on our luggage. If we had to rest on the ship, we would do it relay style. Once on board, the sun came out seeping its energy into our travel weary bodies. It was delightful.

When traveling, I learned, one has to be flexible. I tried not to become unglued when I boldly walked into the ladies bathroom on board the ferry and came face to face with a bearded old man washing his feet in the sink, one foot at a time.

I turned, quietly closed the door and found another bathroom, gingerly opening the door, almost expecting a similar scene. By the time we arrived in Tangier, the warmth from the sun had penetrated right to the marrow of our bones. Our good spirits had returned and we were determined not to let anything spoil the trip, however, not one taxi driver we asked would take us to the Chellah Hotel without giving us a tour of the city. Looking around the dock, Paul found a few familiar landmarks, recognized the way we should be heading and we walked the three miles, totting our luggage. The knapsack was slung over Paul's shoulder and we each took one strap of the canvas bag. Fortunately our shoes were comfortable. Walking on the broken, or in some cases nonexistent, pavement was not the easiest, but being determined and without choice, we managed.

Once settled in our room and we rested for a couple of hours, we felt refreshed. We found a quiet little restaurant close to the hotel and ordered a sweet and sour lamb couscous dinner. We did not linger over our meal. The day had been a very long and tiring one. We returned to the hotel, crawled into bed soon after dinner and slept like the dead.

Since this was a return trip to Tangier, we stayed only a couple of days and enjoyed the beach. We could not remember when we had last experienced continuous sunshine and it was so soothing to our bodies and uplifting to our souls. For the first time on our walk around town, I left my knee brace in the hotel room, since we were not going far.

At the Tourist Information Center we picked up maps, hotel information, sights to see and places to enjoy in the various cities in Morocco. We settled on Rabat, the capital of Morocco, for our next stop. The train trip was surprising comfortable. A great way to get around the country, we thought. We left Tangier at seven in the morning and arrived in Rabat at noon. We deposited one piece of luggage in the hotel lobby, extracting a promise from the clerk that he personally would be taking care of it. Our precious knapsack containing our camera, spare glasses and other important incidentals was slung over my shoulder, to be guarded with my life, if necessary.

We took a long walk to the Royal Palais and then walked back to the hotel. Once rested, we took a walking tour of the Hotel Hassan with its luxury gift shops and the Mausoleum of

Mohammed V, the tomb of the popular king who led the country to independence. On the way back to our hotel, we stopped for an early dinner at a tiny hideaway restaurant and before bed, took a dip in the hotel pool. It was all very civilized.

Jack and Rae were correct. Except for the touters waiting for us at the train station, whom we discouraged immediately, we were not bothered much. When we would stop to look for directions on the map that we picked up at the Tourist Information Center, they approached. Gradually we learned to leave the maps in our bags, removing them only when we were sitting and having coffee.

The following day was medina (old city or marketplace) time. I knew that Paul's sense of direction would come through in the clinches and did not worry too much when we were lost in the Casbah. We walked, totally fascinated by the strange world around us. All through the narrow streets, locals were hawking their wares. We could buy silk threads in hundreds of colors. Spices all smelling wonderfully sweet, pungent or a mixture of both assaulted our senses and were available for a pittance. Animal furs with bits of fetid matter clinging to it, baskets in all shapes and sizes, kitchen utensils, animal innards and outers could all be purchased, reasonably, if we could bargain. Also included in the delicacies of the day were rows and rows of skinned and cleaned goat heads with dead eyes staring at us as we passed.

The fruit and vegetables, piled high on the stands, were the cleanest we had ever seen. It was a relief to leave the animal area and arrive where the air smelled sweet and familiar. We never left the market without buying at least a kilo of oranges from the dealer with the cheapest price. The oranges were huge, thick skinned and juicy sweet inside and it never took more than five to make a kilo. We bought them daily and most were consumed sitting outside on a bench or a flat rock. Few ever made it back to our room.

It took several days to tour the capital city and we enjoyed every one of them, but then it was time to move on. We took another train from Rabat to Meknes and shared our first class compartment with a family of four.....husband, wife, a girl about eight and a boy around five.

As the wife lounged on one of the seats, her hand draped

over the side dripping with diamonds, blinding us. She made no attempt to cover up. In the Islamic world, we were told by the husband who observed our eye-popping reaction, you wear your wealth. She was obviously not part of the group that "did not flaunt your wealth" according to the tour guide of our initial trip. She flaunted. She definitely flaunted.

Paul chatted comfortably, in French, with the husband. I understood some when Paul spoke and he translated the answers from our traveling companion. They were a wealthy (although he did not have to mention that fact) family from Casa (Casablanca to us). Since their children had never been on a train, they had left their car and driver in Casablanca, and were off to visit the grandparents in Fez by public transportation.

The children would spend their holidays learning to ski in the Atlas Mountains. When the vacation was over, their grandparent's car and chauffeur would drive them back to Casa. When Paul assured them that they would love the skiing, the father realized that Paul could probably teach them and invited us to Fez. Since there were many rooms in grandparents' home, we would be made welcome as their guests. It took a while with much stammering and spluttering, but Paul assured them we would meet up in Fez.

As soon as we got off the train in Meknes, Paul realized he had accidentally smudged the napkin containing the telephone number, written in blood red lipstick. We tried to make out the numbers as best we could, but to no avail. It was gone and so was our first and last opportunity to experience luxury, Moroccan style.

We chose a hotel from a pamphlet and map given to us by the Tourist Information Center at the train station, arranged for a room, left our bags in the hotel lobby as we had done before and were off to explore Meknes. The main street was full of stores and little shops and, again, we became fascinated with the colorful and unusual bric-a-brac in the windows. There was nothing we wanted to buy since we would have to carry it on our backs, but we enjoyed the window shopping. While strolling, we realized that we were being followed and not very discretely. We walked, he walked. We stopped, he stopped. The stranger was tall, very slender, had dark hair, dark eyes and the now all too familiar swarthy complexion. He wore jeans, a

81

dark sweater, covered by a brown leather jacket. His head was covered with the traditional, multicolored cap. I was beginning to panic.

After several streets of this, Paul approached. "Why are you following us? What do you want?" my six foot four inch, two hundred thirty pound husband demanded in a voice that meant business.

"I'm sorry if I frightened your wife," he said softly, "but you were speaking English and I thought you might be from America." "My name is Soulimani (Solomon) Mohammed," responded our stalker extending his hand hoping Paul would accept the handshake, "and I'm from New Mexico." "I would love to speak English to someone."

We accepted an invitation to his office and once seated, we were served our first taste of fresh mint tea. The deliciously sweet, flavored tea warmed our insides and soothed us instantly. He again apologized for scaring me. His hospitality and soft spoken manner put us at ease almost immediately. He had been back in his homeland seven years and had returned with a Japanese wife and although he enjoyed being with his family, he missed America. We brought him up to date as best we could and answered his many questions about our life in America. With the niceties out of the way, he jumped at the opportunity to discuss a little business proposition. He was in the import/export business and would love to trade the finest Moroccan leather products, samples of which we fondled and caressed, for a favorite Canadian product....."perhaps maple syrup," he volunteered.

We listened but not too closely. Our working days were temporarily over. We did take several of his business cards and promised that we would think about it. The following day, Solomon met us at our hotel and gave us a complete tour of Meknes, back streets included.

Knowing that we had no chance of meeting up with the friends from the train, we decided to pass up going to Fez. The towns were starting to look alike. On the return trip to Casa, we discovered that the train continued on to Marrakech. We could not resist. Casablanca, we knew, was a large, industrial city with none of the charm depicted in the movie with Bogey and seductress, Lauren Bacall. We changed our plans in a split second and stayed on the train heading for Marrakech. We found the local Tourist Information Center, picked up hotel information and more ferry information for our trip to the Canary Islands from Agadir. Agadir would be our last stop in Morocco before cruising to Lanzarotte.

Marrakech was unique. More than any other city it conjured up images of intrigue and danger. Their marketplace, unlike any other in Morocco, is a large open square and to get the full effect, we were told by some American school teachers, we had to go just before nightfall. We did. The hordes of people, all getting too close, unnerved me. Strangely forbidding looking people, most wearing layer upon layer of dark clothes, squeezed between Paul and myself and I struggled to hold his hand so I could feel protected. We were jostled and bumped, nudged and poked, handled and mishandled.

Large groups gathered around blankets where the snake charmers with baskets of cobras, performed. We stayed away from that blanket. There were belly dancers gyrating in full costume. There were groups of children sitting on tattered blankets learning to pick pockets. After each close encounter, I padded my money belt containing all our valuables. It was against my bare skin with a t-shirt over it that was tucked into my jeans. A belt added another measure of protection. Over the t-shirt, I wore a sweat shirt. I took no chances.

We walked and watched, our eyes darting in all directions, hoping not to miss anything, but when the sun went down, I could feel my mouth going dry and my heart starting to pound. I needed to get out and it was an effort going against the flow. Once out of the square and back on the street where locals were walking and talking and not crowding, we both felt better and slowly wandered back towards our hotel.

The marketplace in the evening was where locals met their friends. During the day, this same square was crowded with tourists and for me, possibly us, it was far more comfortable. That was our last venture in the evening.

The following morning we were at the bus station picking up tickets to Agadir. There was no train service to that part of their world, much to our disappointment. All we saw were old, broken down buses but we knew that we had to take one of them. How else would we get to Agadir and to the ferry that would carry us to Paradise, better known as the Canary Islands.

We boarded the bus. We should have known better. We were the only non-Moroccans on board. Our luggage, along with everyone else's, was thrown up to a young, shirtless lad walking on the roof of the bus. Crates of chickens, large jute bags containing God-knows-what and cardboard boxes held together with string were tied down beside, over and under our luggage. It did not take long to get really sick of this trip. I could not remember the last time I felt so cramped or so uncomfortable on seats with thin, lumpy padding.

The smell, a mixture of unwashed bodies, an unknown lemon fragrance and animals, nauseated me. There would be five hours of this with only one stop to break up this hell. Needless to say, it was long before we got to the rest stop that I decided I needed to use a washroom, and I use that term very loosely.

My diary for that day explains it this way. NOTE: I have gone from not wanting to use the potty in my camper due to the embarrassment of Paul being there, to learning to pee in a cup with two hundred Moroccans on board. I've come a long way baby.

The scenery on route to Agadir was splendid, with a view of the snow-covered Atlas mountains in the distance. When we arrived in Agadir, mercifully there was no crowd of touters to badger us. Agadir was newer and, to us, a little more civilized. We were thrilled with the change.

Agadir was newer indeed. An earthquake in 1960 leveled the old town. It was rebuilt on safer ground thirty miles north of the original site. A little of old Agadir remained, but we never got close to it.   Of all the cities in Morocco, this was where we felt most comfortable. We were a short walk to a sandy beach. We window shopped and walked through all the stores, some to the standard of designer shops.   Most of the local people spoke English, and after almost two weeks in the country, we missed hearing it. Everything was clean and neat and working, including and especially the plumbing and the electricity.   We found a book store where we spent an entire afternoon pouring over novels, biographies and autobiographies and talking to the English-born shop owner. He shared some wonderful tips on where to explore next.

Our second day in Agadir, wanting to get it out of the way, we headed down to the ferry docks to see when the next ship left for the Canary Islands. We could then make our plans accordingly. We could stay a week or two or leave on the next ship, it would be our choice.

"The ship is broken," we were told.

"That's ok," said Paul, "when will it be fixed, we will wait a few days?" "It is lovely here, we do not mind waiting, when will it be ready?" asked my husband innocently.

"Ship broken," the man behind the desk repeated.

Again Paul asked, "When will ship leave for Lanzarotte?"

"Ship broke 1987," we were told.

The date of our request was January 16, 1990. We decided not to wait.

We stayed in the Agadir sunshine a week. In the three weeks of the healing rays of the hot, dry African sun, I discarded my knee brace. For that I will always be grateful.

In the space of the next several days we bussed it back to Marrakech, this time on a tourist bus, which cost us each one dollar and fifty cents more. I would have paid a hundred dollars more had I known that a "tourist bus" existed. We stayed overnight at a hotel close to the train station. We trained it from Marrakech to Rabat, again spending the night close to the station. From Rabat we took another train to Tangier. This was not a sightseeing mission, it was a marathon, and thankfully we were winning. We ferried it back to Algeciras, Spain arriving late in the afternoon. We had few Spanish pesatas and the banks were closed. We decided to sleep on the bus which we paid for by Visa. We bussed it from Algeciras to Alicante. We landed in Alicante before the banks opened and had to wait at a coffee shop for a couple of hours. We had enough money for one cup of coffee that we shared. While Paul went to the bank to withdraw some money, I ordered breakfast. We trained it from Alicante back to Albir.

We showed up on Marjorie and Don's doorstep in record time. We had not slept much. We were unbathed and Paul unshaven. After a fast shower and a tooth brushing we regaled them with stories of our adventures. They hung on every word and once again were thrilled that it had been us and not them. We rested for a full week. We were glad to be back in our camper and cooking our own meals for a change. We did not stay contented for long.....we went into a local travel agency and bought plane tickets.

Chapter 16

For the week we spent in Albir with our friends, we reverted back to our routine. We dined together either at their apartment, our van, or more often than not, at a little hideaway restaurant tucked away in the hills that one of the group found. Paul enjoyed another round of golf at Altea Hills and I walked the course with him. Thanks to the wonderful weeks of sunshine that followed us from Morocco back to Albir, I had not resumed wearing the brace and my knee felt steady and strong. Once we felt settled in and back to being comfortable in our surroundings, we went into a travel agency and purchased a packaged tour to Tenerife, Canary Islands.

Susie Something-or-other was her name. She was the only person I knew who had been to Tenerife before me....but she never saw it. She was my grade one classmate. She went on a vacation with her parents. Tenerife was all I knew. The plane had crashed on landing. Everyone on board died.

I had no idea where Tenerife was and the mere mention of the name, always conjured up visions of that plane crash, however, I always visualized the plane crashing into snow. I was wrong. Here I was, forty some years later, on my way to inspect that ill-fated crash site.

Tenerife, for those choosing not to find it on the map for themselves, is one of the four Canary Islands. They lie, huddled together, in the Atlantic Ocean and are ten times closer to the coast of Africa than they are to Spain, their protectorate. The other islands in the small grouping are Grand Canary, Fuerteventura and Lanzarotte.

Paul and I flew from Spain, only after we had taken a long train ride from Albir to Alicante and an equally long taxi ride from Alicante to the airport. The flight, however, was much cheaper than anything, plane or ferry, we could have purchased from Agadir, Morocco. Assuming, of course, that there had been a plane or ferry going in that direction. Just because they had posters plastered on every wall, in every Tourist Information Center and travel agency, in every city in the country, didn't mean they actually went there.

Although relatively close mile wise, the trip from Alicante to Tenerife was a torturously long and tedious one. The plane stopped in Seville for refueling and we, the unsuspecting passengers, were herded like cattle into a one room lounge to wait for a couple of hours. We stopped, thankfully without deplaning or even long enough to enjoy a good, long stretch, in Los Palmas and once we landed in The Garden of Eden, we had over an hour's bus ride to our fortnight hiatus. We were the last small group off the bus. By the time our bed was within sight, it was one thirty in the morning and we moved with the same exuberance, making similar eye contact, as any zombie. We were just grateful that our "you don't even have to change planes" flight was over.

Bright and early the next morning, with information supplied by the manager of our hotel, we learned where we could rent a relatively reliable car. It was a short walk from our hotel down one of the side streets. One tired looking white Renault, minus a gas cap, awaited our inspection. It had four round wheels with tires that had almost a full day's tread left on them and an engine that started the minute we turned the key. We decided to take a few days to mull over our options and explore the fascinating terrain close to home, on foot. We were also hoping to find another rental agency or two so we could have a choice of vehicles, or possibly find a gas cap for the one car available.

Within a couple of days of hoofing it everywhere, we were ready for a far reaching adventure. We had found several other car rental agencies and by the time we were ready, we knew what the prices were and where we could get the best deal. We went back to the original rental agency, that doubled as a newsstand and coffee shop. The salesman found a gas cap for us and we took the time to go over the many bumps and scratches that were there, before we took off. We drove back to our hotel and had the breakfast, included in our package deal, before setting off into the wilds.

Attached to our room, hidden in a corner, was a small kitchen, stove and refrigerator included. We prepared and packed hard boiled eggs, a couple of bagels, celery and carrot sticks, a chunk of cheese, fresh fruit and a couple of beers in a brown paper bag supplied by the grocery store. It was our plan to explore every nook and cranny on the island for the week that we had transportation and going hungry along the way was out of the question.

From the center of the island loomed a giant, snow-covered, hopefully dormant, volcano, that was visible from almost every inch of every road we drove. Each peek at the splendor provided a unique view with its different hues and shapes and protrusions. While one side of the island appeared flat and desert-like, the other was lush and green and damp. It rained every day, sometimes just a dribble, sometimes a torrent, on one side of the island or the other. Every day the sun shone on one side of the island or the other and being fair weather hunters, we reveled in the balmy, breezy sunshine and magnificent scenery.

On one of our excursions, we drove out to see where the Charleton Heston, Roddy McDowell movie, Planet of the Apes was filmed. Just a small note in our guidebook told us about the filming, but once in the general vicinity it is so easily visualized. Gigantic craters filled with lava rocks were everywhere. We could just as easily have been on another planet in some distant galaxy, so unusual was the landscape.

While most of the beaches sported black volcanic sand, one boasted imported sand from the Sahara Desert in Africa and was sandy white, fine granular and unimpressively familiar. We didn't stay long on the beach once the wind picked up and threatened to blow us, along with the white and granular sand, back from whence it came.

It was on one of the black volcanic beaches that we came

close to tragedy. While I sunbathed, Paul decided he was ready for a swim. The surf looked too dangerous to me and I am not a competent swimmer. I walked down to the edge with him but I refused to go into the water. The waves were frighteningly high and even at the edge, I felt the pull of the surf. Paul went alone. I watched for him from time to time, but there were so many people swimming and playing in the water that I thought nothing of it and went back to the blanket to read. He was not gone long and when he returned, he was breathless. His chest was heaving and his color tinged with purple. He collapsed on the blanket. I rubbed his back and arm while he caught his breath. He had gotten caught in the undertow and was under much longer than was comfortable. In his confusion and struggle, he did not know which way was up and suddenly, just before he thought he was a goner, he popped up to the surface.

"Joei," he said so seriously, it frightened me, "I thought I was going to die and my obit would read "Paul Hossack of no fixed address." "I need a home," he said, his bottom lip curling into a pout.

"Where would you like to live?" I asked. "Should we go back to America or do you want to live in France?" "The world is ours, my love, where should we live?" I asked seriously, never taking my hand off him.

"I don't know," he said creasing his forehead. "I just don't know."

Talking about where to live quickly changed his somber mood, but the incident and the thought of losing him sent shivers through me.

Although we did not have a favorite beach, and as the days went on we had tried them all, we did find a special grazing and watering hole. Since many Britishers inhabit and vacation on the island, we could not resist taking many of our light afternoon snacks at the typically British and exceptionally friendly, Hyde Park Pub. We had been warned by some acquaintances in Spain that food on Tenerife was horrendously expensive so, in our package from Spain, we included breakfast and dinner. The hotel food was dreadful, often cold and tasteless. It was a mistake that we would never repeat, but unfortunately too late for this trip even though we complained often about our meal and even contacted our travel agent.

Not only did we look forward to our midday meal in the pub, we enjoyed many of the unusual characters we met there. Andrew MacDuffy, Mac for short, stands out clearest in my mind. He was short, stocky, with a mop of unruly, gray hair, and just a hint of his Scottish brogue left for all the world to hear. From the minute we met him, he invaded our lives. He was sitting on his favorite barstool, tucked away at one end with the wall supporting his back, talking to everyone. He had been in Tenerife so long they considered him a transplanted local.....colorful and friendly to everyone in his immediate vicinity, whether he knew them or not. The Pub group was one big happy family and Mac took to us immediately. Before we could object, not that we would try, he had volunteered his services to show us his Island.

The following day, three of us met at the Pub. Linda Smith, short time resident of the Island, joined us. Linda, in her mid thirties, had escaped being a hairdresser in downtown London, to this idyllic part of the world. She had been on the Island over a year, and so far, had not been granted immigrant status. All the work she did, hairdressing, a bit of typing and lots of bookkeeping, was hush hush and from the privacy of her home. Hush hush on this Island meant, only people not interested in what you were doing, did not know what you were doing.

Linda hated her home. She was desperate to find other affordable "digs" since the previous tenant, an old gaffer, had died in that apartment and she was sure his ghost watched her every move. We listened with intense interest to her story and in the end I asked, "what's life without a few mysteries?"

"Mystery I can handle," she replied. "This scares the hell out of me. I have to get out before he gets me."

The four of us set off before noon in Mac's car, which was only marginally more comfortable than ours. The first stop was for a bite of the Island's national dish, Canary potatoes. In a million years and with the best maps available I would never be able to find this spot again. We went up so many dirt roads and down enough alleyways to totally confuse even the most veteran of back street travelers. We were on some unpaved back alley street, filled with old shack buildings, when we walked through the door of a dilapidated, unnamed, unmarked

91

establishment and discovered a most charming courtyard.

The open air restaurant was filled with long tables and rickety, wooden chairs and friendly people who welcomed Mac and his visitors immediately. We were seated at a table for four. A red checkered oilcloth covered the simple wooden table and a pitcher of beer was slammed down in the center, spilling some of its contents, before we had even ordered. Small juice glasses were placed in front of each of us and a large, red ceramic bowl filled to overflowing with golf-ball sized potatoes, that were encrusted white, appeared out of nowhere. They were hot, very salty and as tasty a morsel as we had ever consumed. With the beer to wash them down, they were heavenly.

While everyone talked to Mac in Spanish, in voices a little too loud and animated, I took the time to view my surroundings and talk to Linda, who didn't understand but a few words of Spanish. Although she had been out with Mac on several occasions, she had no idea this place existed either. Lush plants and huge red and yellow flowers were growing up the walls. The smell of the flowers, combined with the ice cold beer, was intoxicating. When the beer and potatoes were gone, so were we.

The next spot was for avocados. This restaurant/bar was perched on top of a hill, overlooking a rain forest. The inside of the establishment was sparse but the scenery was enthralling. The moment we sat down on a stool at the counter, a large hand-woven bowl of dark green, thick skinned beauties was placed directly in front of me. Since most people can take or leave avocados alone, I ate most of them, because I cannot leave them alone. They are a major addiction of mine. I don't know how many I ate, nor do I want to know how many I ate, but the calorie count would have sent me right off the chart, and again, it was washed down with beer. Beer I can leave alone, so I sipped at one. Within an hour, we were on our way.

The next stop was for rabbit stew, prepared in a brown, spicy gravy that I would never be able to duplicate even if I had wanted to, and beer. The establishments were now starting to look alike and run together. I usually limit myself to a glass or two of beer. I was now up to about eight or ten glasses.

The stew was tender and delicious, but with that much beer in me, all I could visualize was some little soft white furry creature that had given up his life so that I would have to diet. That was the last place we ate. The next little tavern served just beer and then, with Mac still in charge, we were taken to a very small bar with four seats at the counter and only two tables and where they served only hard stuff. Protests from Linda and myself fell on deaf ears.

I had stopped drinking long before but the three musketeers were keeping up nicely to each other. I was the only one close to being capable of driving and the only one who had no idea where we were. We were all at Mac's mercy and he was taking no prisoners.

Sometime around seven in the evening, Mac drove us, I don't know how, back to our hotel. The wall in the elevator supported Paul and when the doors opened on the fourth floor, he tripped out and staggered back to the room. I had to unlock the door, since he couldn't handle the key nor see where to put it. I undressed him, made him sit up while I fed him a couple of aspirins and put him to bed. He was so drunk, I worried. I did not sleep much that night. I stayed awake listening to him snore.

What a day! What a night! What a hangover! The following morning Paul had no idea how he got home, nor how he got to bed.

At some point during that day, or possibly the day before, or more probably both days, Mac had mentioned something about playing bridge. Paul and I both play, but strictly for fun. For me it was a newly acquired skill and certainly not a game that I would bet the house on. As a matter of fact, I play so infrequently, I would rather not play for money at all and certainly not with relative strangers. Mac mentioned several times that it would be a friendly game. Days went by before Mac recovered from his hangover and, when he did, he returned to his favorite seat, propping up his favorite section of the wall at Hyde Park Pub. Again, we enjoyed a few beers and again he mentioned "a friendly game of bridge." This mention of a friendly game was said several more times before he actually showed up.

When he finally did show up with his partner for a "friendly" game, it was at midnight. Paul and I were tired and just on our way out of the pub. Mac insisted we have one more beer before we called it a night and perhaps he could "persuade" us into a short bridge tournament. My weariness got the better of me and I became really annoyed but did my best to concealed it. Mac was up to something, I knew. After all, who starts a bridge tournament at midnight, friendly or otherwise.

Well, to make a long story short. Mac handed me the deck of cards while he ordered another round of beer for himself, his partner and the two he had planned on fleecing that evening. Paul accepted, I declined.

Put a deck of cards in my hands and, my automatic response is, I shuffle them. I really shuffle them. I shuffle them like I was trained by the head croupier at the International Hotel in Las Vegas.

Slowly at first, the people next to me at the bar started watching intently. The reaction fanned out and their neighbors, who had been poked in the ribs by the person sitting on the next stool, glanced over. They too started watching intently. Pretty soon all eyes diverted in my direction and a hush fell on the crowd. People at the end of the bar ambled closer and a small group gathered around.

My shuffling gradually caught the attention of Mac and his partner who had taken a table outside, along with my husband, in preparation of the card game they had instigated. Mac's eyes widened. His jaw slackened and his mouth opened momentarily as he gawked. A small, panicked tremble escaped his lips as he blurted out in a rather shrill voice, "this is not for money, it's just a friendly game."

"Ok with me," I said, "but are you sure?"

"Yes," said Mac, "this is just for fun, no money."

My shuffling had so unnerved him, we played only one game. Paul and I won.....by sheer luck, or probably, intimidation.

It was years later, after watching my father play gin rummy with his friends, that I learned where I acquired this unique talent.....thanks Mom.

Chapter 17

I returned to Spain a year older and hopefully a year wiser, than I had left. I had celebrated my forty-sixth birthday at a seaside fish restaurant with Paul and a few friends from Hyde Park. After each of our side trips we needed a week or so to get organized. The same was especially true after our trip to the Canary Islands since I was now older and wiser. We again settled quickly into Albir life and enjoyed the company of our friends, card games, golf and another movie or two.

We also needed some time to do our many loads of laundry. Paul helped do a little hand rinsing and we strung it out on a makeshift clothesline that we had tied behind our camper. It was warm and windy so we anticipated our first load drying overnight and the sun finishing the job the next morning. We were wrong. It had sprinkled overnight which normally would not have caused a problem, however, the wind had picked up and deposited a thin layer of a red/brown slime all over our clothes. It had rained African mud. The occurrence was unusual only to us. We bundled up the laundry, threw practically everything we owned into four large black garbage bags and delivered them to the local laundromat. Three days and forty dollars later our laundry was returned clean, folded and only slightly damp. Before wearing anything, we put it out on the line for the sun to do what it did best, finish the drying that the laundromat had neglected.

While our closets were bare, we did some much needed cleaning of our van as well. We treated the carpet to a vacuum that one of the other campers had handy and opened all the windows to expose the interior to the outside world, after spraying it with air freshener. We had the oil changed, tightened all the bolts and screws inside and out and purchased four new tires. One day, around the third week of February, we said goodbye to our friends, like we had done so many times before and headed north. Since we had already driven the coast road on our way south, we decided to make up some time and took the toll road until Valencia. We stayed overnight.

The following day we stopped and toured the old Roman town of Sagunto. We visited the ruins of an ancient citadel and the acropolis before driving onto the peninsula of Peniscola. That night we wild camped beside seven other vans and met Robert and Marianne Bethery. The conversation was a real test of Paul's French skills, since neither Robert, Marianne, nor six year old Boris, spoke a word of English. Paul translated for me while Robert told stories of being a Colonel in the French Foreign Legion. When he lifted his shirt to show deep knife wounds and a chunk out of his side where a bullet had been removed, I needed no translation. Robert explained that only one in ten survive the Legion to collect a pension and most Legionnaires have no family. Pensions of the dead are divided amongst the survivors. He and his family are wealthy and enjoy a good life in retirement. When the conversation turned personal, I learned that Robert was sixty, Marianne forty-one, and Boris was their only child together. Paul translated. By the end of the evening, we were all exhausted from the intense concentration, but a friendship had been established.

The next morning, we would be heading off in different directions, but the Betherys had made us promise we would visit them in Perpignan. Before our departure, however, we had to remove a one foot square police sticker that had been pasted on our front windshield, warning us not to 'wild camp' again. The task required fingernails, a couple of razor blades and finally warm, soapy water to remove the residue. What a pain that turned out to be, but necessary since I wanted Paul to see where he was going.

Heading north we stopped at Vinaroz one more time to

shop at an extensive fish market. Just down the same side street, we purchased some fresh fruit and vegetables at the outdoor stand we had discovered on our first trip. Once our shopping was done, we were off to explore virgin territory. By mid afternoon we were in a campground just outside Tarragona. It was quite crowded so we booked in, paid and picked our spot, leaving our barbecue and chair to stake out our claim before heading back into town and visiting the archaeological museum and the cathedral. We also walked the Old Jewish Quarter of this gorgeous city. The following morning, the parking was so horrendous in Tarragona, we double parked like half the visitors and toured the Roman Amphitheater. Fortunately when the tour was over no one had blocked our way, given us a ticket or plastered no parking stickers over our windshields so we made an easy getaway.

We were off to the monastery at Poblet. The guided tour of the cloister, church, Royal Pantheon and museum were most impressive and we stayed for over an hour.

The Montserrat Massif, where we stopped for lunch, was used by Wagner as the setting for his opera, Parsifal. The piling up of the boulders into steep cliffs, crowned by weird pinnacles, produced a serrated outline. It is nicknamed appropriately, Sawtooth Mountain. We continued our driving and camped that night in a small Pyrenean town, Ripoll. We were the only humans in the campground, other than the woman in the office who collected our money and went home after office hours. We were surrounded by hundreds of sheep. Baaaaaad idea. We awoke early due to the noise of bahing sheep, had breakfast, cleaned up and drove out very slowly, beeping the horn constantly to keep the sheep moving out of our way. The sheep were obviously used to people and vehicles and Paul occasionally had to bump one or two to keep them moving.

Nestled high in the Pyrenees, bordering both Spain and France, is the the tiny country of Andorra. It has a population of fifty two thousand living in an area half the size of New York city. It doesn't matter what time of the year you arrive, you are surrounded by snow covered mountains.

It was a cool, crisp, sunny day at the end of February when we drove from Spain into France and finally into Andorra.

Since we never actually crossed an official border, it was hard to tell exactly when we entered the country. There was a little snow in the fields but not enough to be concerned. The roads were dry. We kept a close watch on the skies, since we did not want, at any time, to be snowed in up in the mountains. We stopped often for a tea break, a snack or just to look at the scenery. Driving the highways, lined with thin, metal rods, topped with red flags to indicate where the road is during a snowstorm, was magnificent and, since they were forecasting warm and sunny weather for several days, we decided to stay. After touring the capital city, Andorra La Vella, and doing a little grocery shopping, we returned to Encamp and settled into a level spot. The campground was in the heart of town, which made sightseeing easy and exercise fun. One item surpassed anything we could ever have hoped to image - the washrooms were heated. This was luxury beyond my wildest dreams, comparable only to, at this point in our travels, a hot tub for two. To add to the luxury of heat, each washroom was a separate unit.

I showered in privacy. I dried and powdered in privacy. I brushed, I flossed, I primped in privacy. I'm sure Paul thought he had lost me permanently to the temptress of the toilet but eventually I changed into some fresh clothes and relinquished my sanctuary to whomever was next in line. We went off to dinner, walking to a nearby bistro.

Dinner out, even though we did it often, was always a treat. We liked to sample the delicacies in each country visited. At this point, we had had so much French and Spanish cooking, that they weren't appealing. We ordered snails in a brown, mushroom sauce as an appetizer, something I would never have prepared myself, and a pizza. Without an oven in our motorhome, Pizza was a unaccustomed delight. Besides, anything prepared in, washed down with, or poured over lots and lots of wine was always tasty. The meal was a success.

The following day was another once in a lifetime treat. In downtown Encamp was a ski equipment rental shack and for a nominal fee Paul was able to outfit himself for the slopes. For seven dollars he rented boots, poles, skis and got directions to the best area for skiing. He left his driver's license as security and we were off to the ski hills at Soldeu.

While I sat in the valley with a view of the hills around, writing letters and postcards in eighty degree slightly overcast weather, Paul was glacier skiing in glorious sunshine.

There were so many highlights on this type of adventure but glacier skiing in the Pyrenees was one of the best for Paul.

We drove slowly down the mountain the next day heading towards Perpignan. We were geared up to celebrate Paul's fiftieth birthday.

The Bethery's had been expecting us and insisted that we use their guest house in Barcares for as long as we chose to stay. There was no use objecting. We followed them to their beach house. They opened the door and handed us the key. We were armed with several bottles of wine, which we finished during the course of the evening in Barcares. We accepted their hospitality long enough to celebrate Paul's birthday and for me to teach Boris how to shuffle cards, Vegas-style.

Chapter 18

Our last lunch together, consisting of my forever experimental but, if I must say so myself, always delicious seafood soup along side Marianne's famous quiche Lorraine, was delicious. Afterwards we hugged and said our goodbyes. It was around two thirty on the first of March that we headed towards Narbonne. The former Archbishop's Palace has been turned into the town hall and museums and it was fascinating to walk through.

On the drive to Carcassone we stopped to enjoy a steaming hot cup of cafe au lait and a fresh croissant while a snow and hail storm blew furiously through the area. Carcassone is the best preserved double walled city in Europe. There were some major renovations in progress so much of the entrance into the city was under scaffolding. We did not have the best view but we enjoyed a walk around all the shops before going to the castle.

Although the sun was shining, it was very cold and windy when we toured the canalled city of Sete. Paul and I kept reminding each other how reminiscent Sete was of Venice, except of course, we had not yet been to Venice.

From Sete we went to Anduze for a mini tour. We stopped at a winery long enough to buy a couple of bottles of "pif" as Robert had called it. In our terms, it was the local cheap stuff that we always kept on hand and used for cooking and drinking. I had become a master of French cooking. Wine, along with water or broth, went into everything I cooked, whether the recipe called for it or not. Paul used the wine as a marinate.

When the wind finally died down we had a picturesque drive directly to the Pont du Gard. It was immediately familiar to me. Calendars in the 1950's displaying this perfect three tier aqueduct hung in every butcher shop, grocery store or garage and here I was, standing and staring at the real thing. We parked with Le Pond in our view for a picnic lunch. Afterwards, while Paul climbed to the third tier and examined it from the top down, I talked with a Swedish girl guarding, or being guarded by, a scraggly looking Irish Wolfhound and a Briart, a dog unfamiliar to me except in pictures. Both animals were friendly yet aloof and stood above my waist. We camped close by that night.

At any given moment, and without warning, we reverted back to the typical tourists. In Avignon we spent hours touring the Palais des Papes (Pope's Palace). It was a beautiful example of a fourteenth century Gothic fortress and palace. It was closed for lunch but I entered via the back door and took the tour backwards. When I got to the front door, claiming I was lost, the guard insisted I turn around and leave through the exit. I had used my guidebook starting at the end and going forward , saw all I wanted and, when told, turned around and retraced my steps. When I tried to redo it with Paul, who was waiting for me at the back door wondering where I had disappeared to, they stopped us and told us to come back later as they were closed for lunch. Paul and I ate in the park, within sight of Avignon Bridge, made famous in the song, Sur le Pond d'Avignon, and laughed at my little prank. Since we would be leaving before the palace reopened, I told him all about the points of interest.

We climbed to the rock cliff town of Les Baux and purchased for the first time, Herbs de Provence in bulk. Herbs de Provence is a mixture of spices.....rosemary, thyme, basil, marjoram, tarragon that was combined with the delicate fragrance of lavender. I used the combo in every sauce I made, occasionally adding other spices for a different flavor.

In Arles we toured the Amphitheater, St. Tropime cloister, the town hall and the museum of Christian Art. That night we camped in Aix en Provence. After a freezing night, complete with frost on our windows, we were delighted to see the sunshine and decided to spend our day exploring this most beautiful town. The squares and avenues were shaded by plane trees and mossy fountains adorned the intersections. We did not go into many buildings because most were simple offices or private dwellings. We were awed by the seventeenth century carvings, statues and doorways and we basked in glorious sunshine, not wanting to miss a minute of it.

We stopped in St. Maximin la Ste Baume for groceries and ending up talking to a Canadian couple from Toronto in the parking lot of the supermarket. We stopped in Barjols. This, however, was not the year they blessed an ox then slaughtered and roasted it, so we didn't linger.

That night we camped close to Draguignan. Jim and Mary Unsworth, acquaintances from Canada, lived in the area. We called. They weren't home. We ended that evening playing bridge with a Dutch couple, after explaining what the card suits were called in English.

The following morning, while Paul showered, I called our friends again. No luck. I left a message on their answering machine. I returned to the camper to find my husband babbling incoherently. "What's wrong?" I asked, over and over again.

"Same showers," he kept repeating.

"Paul," I spoke clearly, enunciating every word, "what is the matter?" "What is wrong?"

"Men and woman shower together," he said, completing his first sentence. "That woman we played cards with last night was walking around the shower room naked." "She wanted to talk." "What the hell was I supposed to do with my eyes?" he said, not expecting an answer. "She was naked and she wasn't embarrassed." "I couldn't wait to get out of there." "She was naked, nothing, no clothes."

Paul was not impressed when I started chuckling. "Let's go say goodbye to them," I said with a smirk.

"Go yourself," he said, "I've seen all I want to."

Before leaving the campground, I tried calling our friends one more time. No answer. We drove to Frejus and after seeing the sights in town decided to camp on the dock. By the time we stopped, it was late afternoon and we pulled up beside a van displaying an Italian insignia and parked. Although the drapes were drawn on our neighbor's van, they pulled them apart just long enough to nod and say "bonjourneau." We smiled and nodded back. It was all very civilized. It was still early and we were not quite prepared to draw our own drapes. We wanted to see who else pulled onto the dock. We hoped for campers that would be a bit more sociable. All the spaces remained empty. We knew we would not lose our place if we left for an hour or two. We decided to find a beach with a picnic area and have our barbecued dinner there. We dared not bring attention to ourselves by cooking on the dock.

The sun was still high in the sky and we were not in a hurry. While Paul fussed with the barbecue, I sliced some potatoes, spiced them with chopped onions and herbs de Provence and drenched them with olive oil. I double foil wrapped my latest cooking sensation so the liquid would not leak out. When the coals started glowing, Paul placed the tin foiled bundle on the grill. I prepared a salad. My part of the meal was done.

Paul retrieved our deck chairs, opened them, blocking the entrance to our side door. We made ourselves comfortable, reading while the potatoes cooked. About thirty minutes later, after checking that the potatoes were well on their way to being edible, Paul dropped my steak on the grill. It sizzled and spit the instant it hit. Since I insisted on my meat being cooked through, Paul nattered at me constantly for having to wait the extra ten minutes before he put his steak on the grill. The coals were losing their glow, but there was enough heat left to cook his food the way he liked it, Pittsburgh style. When he took the time to "ruin" my steak, I savored every mouthful. On this occasion, my steak was perfect.

Well fed and nearer to the time that we would be willing to draw our drapes, we returned to the dock, parked next to the Italian van and, once again, went through the ritual of saying "hello." We closed our drapes and settled in as inconspicuously as possible. We played a couple of hands of cribbage, while our radio, on low, entertained us with background music.

It was around nine in the evening and getting dark when

another van pulled into one of the spots at the far end of the dock. The doors were flung open and music flooded out. With the sudden barrage of noise, we sat straight up and listened. We drew back our drapes and watched the action. Without seeing the license plate, we knew the van had to be French. A visitor to this country would not have dared make such a spectacle.

A table was removed and set down beside the open side door of the old, blue Renault van. The tablecloth was whipped out, shaken and thrown over the black folding table. A candle was produced and lit with a little flourish that only an arrogant Frenchman could muster. A bottle of wine was put on the table along with two glasses, set upright. The wine was opened, glasses poured and, before proceeding, the couple, in their twenties, toasted each other or France or whatever they happen to think about toasting.

I spied on her preparing dinner inside the van, while he set up their barbecue on the dock. Exactly what Paul and I dared not do, this young couple were doing. We watched and admired in total fascination. Nothing was done hurriedly and after each minor chore, they stopped for a taste of wine, a little peck on the lips and a flamboyant toast. Their voices could be heard from inside our van, but we could not make out the words.

With dinner ready and the table set, they took their seats. She wore a bright blue flowered print dress while he relaxed, wearing nothing but his white, brief underwear. He had his feet propped on the floor of the van. They drank, ate, talked, toasted and took no notice at the lateness of the hour. They didn't even think to lower their voices although it was nearing midnight. Paul and I watched all the goings on in the flicker of candlelight. It was all so typically French.....and romantic.

I think what we enjoyed most was the fact that it was in plain sight of everyone and everything, while the rest of us hid as best we could. We also knew that if the police came along, they were the only ones who could explain in the language of choice exactly what was going on, but the police never came along.

The next morning we left the dock about the same time the Italian van left. We had been up for hours, having breakfast, doing the dishes and putting everything in its proper place before getting back on the road. When we drove off, there was not a hint of movement from the French van.

We stopped in Cannes to see the fishing boats, yachts, flower market, alleyways and a gorgeous harbor filled with luxury boats from all over the world, including one marked, Toronto, Canada, that flew a Canadian flag. There was no one on board or we might have stopped to chat. We had coffee at an outdoor cafe on the Croisette, the boulevard dividing the beach from hotels, art galleries and exclusive shops. We returned to the harbor in the hopes of meeting the Canadians but there was no activity on board. We left.

From Cannes we drove to and toured the walled city of Saint Paul de Vence, with its cobblestone streets and tiny but expensive gift shops that lined the walkways. We were told there was camping at the castle in Saint Paul, but it was closed for the season. We spent that night in Cagne sur Mer. It rained all night and into the next morning so we did not rush out. We made our way down to the beach and drove through Nice on the coast road. It was late morning when we arrived in the tiny Principality.

How can any country be so small and so rich. Welcome to Monaco. I must confess that Monaco was a bit of a blur. There were no campgrounds in Monaco. We actually had to camp in France and go into Monaco for day trips only. They even restricted our day parking, not wanting the unsightly motorhome in full view of their residents. Paul, however, could not resist taking our four cylinder motorhome, that went from zero to sixty miles per hour in only four days, on the Grand Prix circuit. The necessary high speed noises were made by his mouth.

We took a tour of the town and walked to the harbor where Prince Rainier's yacht floated majestically in the center. The smaller ones had slips at the dock. All the yachts were magnificent even though they were dwarfed by the Prince's. Our city tour ended at the Palace, a city within a city, and we arrived just in time for the changing of the guards. With hundreds of tourists, who had arrived in tour buses, we watched. We listened as the guides explained each move. We toured the gardens and lunched in view of the harbor. Even in jeans, t-shirts, tennis shoes and jackets we felt like we were the royalty for the day.

The next day we were back in Monaco for more. Being avid fishermen, avid snorkelers, avid anything to do with water, how could we miss the Oceanographic Museum. It is one of the world's oldest, finest, most important and directed by none other than Monsieur Jacques Cousteau. He wasn't in his office. The museum has an extraordinary aquarium, deep sea exhibition and the most incredible collection of nautical wonders and hideous freaks, we had ever seen.

That afternoon we wandered the Princesse Antoinette Park. From the garden we looked over the serene world that is Monaco. We touched olive trees millennia old and sniffed at the strange Exotic Garden with thousands of plants from semidesert countries, clinging to the slopes of the mountain, flourishing in a new environment.

There was so much to see, and we saw much.....but it was a blur.

Chapter 19

What can you say about a country where backup lights on a car are an option. Where swarms of disheveled looking children surround tourists, checking every nook and cranny on their bodies with tiny fingers for money and other valuables, and no one stops to help the unfortunate foreigner. Where entrance fees to museums and archaeological sites are doubled or tripled to accommodate the non tourist season, since locals feel they deserve the same amount of money without having to deal with the volume of visitors. This, and much more, is Italy.

We drove the coast road from France into Italy. We bypassed the border town of Ventimiglia and found a campground a few miles up the road in the center of San Remo. Since there was no one at the gate and no office that we could see, we drove in, found a vacant patch of ground and parked. After taking a cold beer from our tiny refrigerator and putting our chairs outside, we knew we were settled for a few days.

We had been too long without hearing English. When I passed a young woman standing by a wash basin doing some hand laundry and she said "hi" I became rattled. I stopped dead in my tracks and turned away. The word "hi" turned over and over in my mind. What countries use the word "hi" as a greeting? I wondered. Could she be speaking Dutch? I thought. Could she be saying something in German as in "Zig Heil"? After making a total ass of myself with my silence and indecision, I turned back to her, "is that 'hi' as in an English hello?" I asked.

"Yes, yes, yes," she almost shouted. "I'm from Australia." "So good to hear English. Where are you from?" she asked.

It was a question that started three days of nonstop talking. Obviously, Paul and I were not the only ones starved for a little outside conversation.

Andrew and Susan Dove were the first of many Australians we would meet in our travels. They were both in their late twenties, full of energy for sightseeing, hiking and deep sea diving, even though their old VW had been broken into and all their expensive tanks, masks, wet suits and fins had been stolen. The talk of their travels was filled with excitement and they had not lost any of their enthusiasm despite being on the road more than a year. We had heard about the Australian and New Zealand walkabout phenomenon. Once these people start traveling, it is years before they head home. This was our first confirmation.

We left our motorhome in the campground and, as a foursome, walked the entire length and breadth of San Remo.

We spent an evening in the casino. Once inside, after being given the evil eye by the guard at the door for our unpretentious attire, we were dazzled by the bright lights. We all seemed more interested in the crystal chandeliers, the velvet wallpaper, the gaming tables and the clientele than in the gambling, however, Paul did manage to leave a few lira behind at the blackjack tables, before I pulled him away.

We spent one day doing a little clothes shopping. I bought a gorgeous, bright, red sweatshirt with English lettering embossed on it. The words, strung together to form one long sentence, made no sense whatsoever. I loved it for that reason alone and wore it constantly.

One afternoon we walked up and down every street to see the houses, gardens and general landscape before entering the Russian Orthodox church. It didn't matter where we went, we loved having the company. We just walked aimlessly and talked about everything under the sun. We enjoyed dinners together, heating up only one of the barbecues and discussing the day's events. We loved finding out about the different places they had seen and that we had to visit, after leaving San

Remo.

By the end of three days, Paul and I were edgy and ready to move along. We had enjoyed the company of our new friends, but our campground, the only one in the area, was situated beside a railroad track and every conductor took special delight in blowing the whistle. It was an added bonus when they passed in the middle of the night and could blow the shrill and mournful whistle, twice. We never slept through the night.

The following morning, we mortgaged our home (assuming of course, that we had one) and filled our gas tank. There was no place in all of Italy where we paid less than six dollars per gallon of gas.

Goodbyes were said and addresses exchanged and we left the campground after breakfast and a little house cleaning, heading south, along the coast road. With stop signs everywhere, some for no reason at all and many just a few feet past the last one, causing bumper-to-bumper traffic, it took over an hour to drive twenty miles. When our nerves could not stand the pace or the erratic Italian drivers any longer, we hopped on the toll road. We paid ten dollars to drive the next twenty miles. We did that on and off during the entire day's drive. Only when we entered tunnels carved out of mountains, some of them two kilometers in length, did we understand why the autopistas were so horrendously expensive.

That night we discovered, what would become one of our favorite spots in the world, a small town called Lerici. We left our camper parked at the edge of the town, in what looked like camper haven. All shapes and sizes of trailers and motorhomes were parked, but the area was totally void of human life. All evening, we strolled this bit of heaven sitting pretty at water's edge. We climbed to the uninhabited castle perched on top of the hill and sat on one of the benches to survey the countryside. All boats were tied side by side in the harbor, safe for the night. Vendors selling fresh fish, even at that time of the night, lined the streets, while the locals milled around inspecting and gesturing in their bargaining. This was the richness of life that we wanted to experience. This was what the "old country" should be like everywhere, but, of course, it was not.

There were no facilities where we camped that night and

no other people around so one night was all we allowed ourselves. The following morning we purchase a fresh bread at the bakery and haggled with some street vendors for a garlic bulb, onions, a couple of carrots and one green pepper. We followed that with some shopping for black olives in a salty brine and a half pound of sliced Italian cheese in the only large market that was tucked away on some side street that we found while wandering. We left lovely Lerici fully stocked.

The next spot literally took my breath away. From the moment I entered the Piazza del Morcoli and saw the Leaning Tower of Pisa, I stared, completely captivated.

"My God, it's going to fall over," I said to Paul, "and I'm going to be standing right here when it does."

Fortunately just a few months earlier they had closed The Tower for repairs, so I knew that it would not be my weight that brought it tumbling down. Although my mind's eye could always visualize the Tower, it is awesome to be standing within viewing range.

Since the campground in San Remo was free, we were not prepared for the cost of a campground seemingly in the middle of nowhere. For one night, we paid a dollar more than our four star hotel room in Morocco, and breakfast was included in the cost of that room. We had no choice. We needed our laundry done and only a few campgrounds had adequate facilities. We checked in. The washers were terrific, the dryers non existent. Our clean clothes were strung all over our van, a couple of clotheslines that were still available and every bush and tree branch had some piece of our clothing dangling from it. The sun was shining and gentle breezes blew. It worked.

We drove out late the next morning directly to a gas station. It was closed. The second gas station was closed, as was the third. We were becoming desperate. The attendant at the fourth station said they would be open in two hours. We had no choice but to wait. Fortunately we were first in line and several cars lined up behind us. That was where we learned there was a gasoline strike in all of Italy. The few gas stations that had the remains of their supply, were conserving it. We put sixty dollars worth of gas into the tank. Our tank was not full but that was all they would sell us at one time. If we wanted more we had to get to the end of the line.

We changed our plans. Heading farther south was now out of the question. The strike could last one more day. The strike could last one month.....or anything in between. Italy, with its outrageous prices for the necessities in life, was not the place to be stranded.

After a few hours drive inland, we arrived in Florence. The campgrounds were closed for the season. We parked in the town square with a statue of Michelangelo's David watching over us. For three days we did not move our van which was the best way we knew to conserve gas. We were above the city center with a view that could only be described as utterly delicious. We looked over a sea of orange, tiled rooftops, church spires, beautiful domes and small bridges in the distance. At night we watched the twinkling lights.

Each day we walked down the steep hill into town. We hiked every street, saw every magnificent monument and threw coins into every fabulous fountain. We spent part of an afternoon on the Ponte Vecchio, taking pictures from every angle. The picturesque construction, with its lateral shops, were almost all owned by gold merchants and silversmiths.

We toured the Florentine Pitti Palace. We visited the Royal Apartments and briefly reviewed the Museum of Precious Stones. We saw a few of the many parts of the Uffizi Palace. The Uffizi Gallery is world famous and we went through it like a whirlwind, not wanting to miss a thing.

When the gasoline strike was not over three days later, we passed on going to Rome and headed northeast to the Republic of San Marino. We stayed long enough to discover that, although San Marino was a free port, the prices were the same or higher than in the rest of Italy, for camping, gas and food. After touring the town on foot and visiting the fort, our guidebooks indicated there was nothing much left to see.

On our way north we stopped for groceries in Ravenna. Since gas did not seem to be a problem once we were through San Marino, we continued driving and ended up in the Marco Polo campground, one short bus ride from the heart of Venice. We had not even leveled our van when a family of three headed our way. It took a moment to recognize them. Paul actually recognized the long haired German Shepherd dog before we recognized Jack and Bev, whom we had met several months earlier in Cordoba, Spain. Their beast, still extremely unpleasant and vicious was growling and snapping as soon as he smelled us. Before getting too close, Jack returned to their van and locked the door behind their dog. We had lots of reminiscing to do.

The following morning, we were seduced by Venice. On a boat taxi we toured the Grand Canal. Traveling along with us was a British television crew, filming what would be the background scenery for a concert by Pavarotti. Paul and I sat in silence, holding hands, marveling at the misty outline of the buildings along with waterway. It was magic.

Once back on solid ground, it didn't take us long to get lost going up and down small streets, over tiny bridges, ducking in and out of shops. We were in tourist heaven.

Don't ask me how we ended up at Harry's Bar, a favorite haunting ground of Ernest Hemingway. Suddenly, without benefit of a map or directions, we were there. Much to Paul's disappointment, it was closed, as it was every Monday. We made our way to San Marco Square, where we were, once again, the typical tourists. We toured the Doge's Palace.

We found ourselves in a glass blowing factory, fascinated by the most unbelievable artistic pieces that were for sale. A glass blown aquarium, complete with colorful tropical fish, was by far the most intricate. A price tag of six thousand dollars U.S. kept us from reaching too deeply into our pockets. Besides, we thought, where would we put it.

We had three days of wandering, watching, sampling, and loving. Three glorious days and we were on our way.

We stopped in Verona for an afternoon of touring Roman ruins. We spent a couple of days driving the length of Lake Garda, not wanting to go too quickly because of the beautiful weather and the splendor of the mountains surrounding the lake. We stopped long enough to watch a forest fire on the opposite side of the lake. We stopped again farther up the lake to watch hand gliders soaring majestically, catching every air current they could.

That last day we drove farther than anticipated. We camped in Forni di Sopra. It didn't take us long the next day to cross the border into Austria.

Chapter 20

You know that you have crossed the border into a Germanic country when you see the men wearing white jackets pushing sturdy, long handled brooms, sweeping the highways. There will be no dirt, dust or debris on their roads thank you very much. A person would never dream of throwing a candy wrapper or soda pop can out the window for fear of being the only human ever to have violated the landscape that way and, of course, fear of punishment. Swift, severe and permanent punishment.

There were few countries that captured our hearts for its sheer beauty like Austria. Unfortunately we still had to deal with the people and the people, particularly of Vienna, would not be dealt with lightly.

We entered Austria at Arnoldstein. After withdrawing enough schillings to last a couple of days and buying a Michelin guidebook, we were off to find the mineral springs at Villach. If it seems like I am always on a quest to "take the waters" you're right. To me it is one of the great pleasures in life. I do it whenever and wherever possible. Paul humored me by saying it was strictly for my enjoyment that he joined me, hour after hour, soaking in mineral water until our bodies shriveled up like prunes. Personally, I think he might have taken a little pleasure in it himself.

Villach was one of those special places, for no reason at all, except for "taking the waters" and since this type of wild activity had a tendency to wear us out, it was a wonderful place to camp for our first night in Austria.

Fit as a fiddle, after a wonderful night's sleep, we drove through the countryside. We stopped in Klagenfurt, with its lovely flower gardens, then drove to the cathedral in St. Paul. We never passed anything named "Paul" that we didn't stop to visit, just to say we were there. We would have stopped at a St. Joei as well but there was never an opportunity. The year was 1990 and St. Paul, while still in Austria, was spitting distance to the Yugoslavian border.

"Do you want to go into Yugoslavia?" asked Paul.

"Not this time," I responded.

We had been in Austria just one day. After a short discussion, we decided not to go just to get the stamp in our passport. We would go to Yugoslavia when we had intentions of seeing, studying and enjoying the country at length. Of course, in retrospect, we should have gone at length at that time. It was not long after having pressed our noses to the border that they closed it to the casual tourist due to civil strife. Twenty/twenty hindsight is such a wonderful and unique ability.

We went to Piber. The area thrives on horses and has an immense breeding farm for the Lippizaner stallions. We had a close view of the horses and until performing, we agreed, they are not a handsome lot. The breed dates as far back as 1580. They were purchased in 1920 from the Austrian imperial stud at Lipiza, near Trieste, formerly a part of the Austro-Hungarian Empire and now in Yugoslavian territory. Originally of all colors, the Lippazaners are mainly gray with an exceptional bay or brown. They do not get their white coats until they are between four and ten years old. They are short in stature with a long back, a short thick neck and powerful conformation.

We found the breeding farm tour absolutely fascinating and really looked forward to watching them perform at the Spanish Riding School in Vienna.

After touring the countryside the next day, we headed towards Vienna. Our campground was an hour outside the city, but a short walking distance to the streetcar line. One streetcar, we were told, would take us into downtown Vienna. A camper, whatever the size, was a nuisance in any major city and we had already learned that the hard way.

Once in Vienna, we wasted no time in finding the

Spanish Riding School. We purchased our tickets and stood in line for two hours with the rest of the foolish tourists waiting for the doors to open. The school was a giant barn-like structure where the horses practiced. The folding wooden chairs we were given lacked padding of any sort and it was not long before everyone, myself included, started fidgeting. Thrilled when it finally started, we were suddenly witnessing the most boring hour of dressage we have ever seen. They did nothing else. These short, squat, thick necked Lippazaners walked....and walked....and walked. If we were not impressed with their appearance at the breeding farm, we were certainly less impressed watching them walk.

Before lunch, we decided there was still time to tour Mozart's house, located just off the main square, according to our guidebook. We found it easily enough and it was, indeed, a short walk, down one of the side streets. We arrived at eleven fifteen and were greeted by a docent who told us we had forty-five minutes to go through the house. The house was small and we knew forty-five minutes would be more than enough time. We paid the entrance fee, entered the small barren hallway and when the docent followed us into the next room, we thought she would be explaining what each room was about. We were wrong. She immediately informed us that we now had forty-three minutes left to see the rest of the house. She followed us around giving us a time update about every two to three minutes. We did her a favor, we left with twenty minutes to spare. All I remember, other than being royally annoyed with being followed around by our very own town crier, is that the house was small and sparsely furnished. Also the time of day stands out vividly in my mind.

The morning, although not quite to the point of disaster, was very disappointing.

We relaxed on a park bench and shared a picnic lunch of fresh bread, cheese, a smidgen of pate, sliced apples and a small bottle of wine. We never left our camper without our knapsack brimming with tasty goodies. Our permanent knapsack necessities included eating utensils, napkins, the camera, a roll of toilet paper, maps and the name, address and telephone number of the campground where we were staying.

After lunch we visited St. Stephen's Cathedral, which

was undergoing major, necessary renovations. The beautiful spires were under scaffolding and could not be seen from the outside. To our disappointment, much of the inside was cordoned off as well. Before returning to our camper late in the day, we toured the Old Town, hoping not to have to talk to anyone.

Except for brief moments, the day left us with a terrible case of the blahs and we relayed our experiences to the campground owner. He listened patiently.

"Have you been to a Heuriger?" the owner asked and proceeded without listening for our answer. "These are small restaurants, individually owned, and they serve the new wines of the region," he explained. "The food is always delicious." "The wine is sometimes good, sometimes very good, and sometimes not so good and the atmosphere is very friendly." "You walk up and down the streets and when you come to a house with a tree bough hanging over the door, you are there," he continued.

We looked at each other, smiled and were off on a new and hopefully delicious quest. The owner pointed us off in the right direction and suggested a street name or two that would be of interest to us. We thanked him before setting off.

We walked up and down some of the side streets and saw several boughs but one place looked particularly inviting. We could hear the lively polka music from the street and opened the door. The combination of sweet and pungent smells, laughing red-faced people and huge mounds of food on each plate, was heavenly.

We took a seat at a large wooden table, set for as many as could fit. We nodded to others at the same table, who smiled back. It was boisterous, welcoming and extremely warm and cozy.

We didn't order the wine. A big, burly waiter covered in a food splattered white apron thumped down a large carafe of white wine, removed a carafe of red with an inch of dregs on the bottom and replaced it with another full one. Empty juice glasses appeared in front of us and we were expected to partake of our favorite, pouring our own whenever the glass needed refilling.

The menu was on display in a butcher type refrigerator

and it didn't take us long to figure out the ordering process. We went to the window and pointed to what we wanted. Every meal came with dumplings whether we ordered them or not, but this was the dumpling capital of the world, how could we not order them. We pointed to four different types of wursts and each was put on a little plate of its own. We halved and shared the sausages and had dumplings, kraut and wine to go along with them. Extra gravy, apple sauce, mustard and some type of thick sour cream sat in bowls on the table and we helped ourselves to what we wanted. The bread basket was filled to the brim with freshly made, pipping hot biscuits and dark pumpernickel bread and refilled often. The butter, served in small tubs, melted the instant it hit the bread. The food was scrumptious especially when we ended our meal with hot, apple strudel.

They closed the restaurant just after we left, since almost all the patrons left with us. We were totally satisfied with Austria. The rosiness in our cheeks (and our noses) when we left the Hueriger was due to the sunshine during the day, I'm sure. We slept late the next morning. We awoke in such good spirits, we decided to give Vienna another chance. We took the streetcar and went back into town. We walked the town square and visited the Arsenal, one of the best museums we had come across. We toured the park of Schonbrunn. Later that day, I refused to get on the largest, oldest ferris wheel in Europe at the Prater, preferring to stay at ground level. We picnicked by the Danube. Whoever wrote the song about the Blue Danube, never saw it. It was dirty brown with a current so swift, a white water rafting company would have made a fortune doing tours.

Since we did not come in contact with too many natives on our wanderings, over the next several days, we deemed Vienna a success and decided to leave while we were ahead.

We aimed our van in the direction of Melk. It was billed with two stars in our guidebook. If the Abbey of Melk is billed as a two star, I cannot imagine what the Austrians considered a three star. In my life I had never seen so much gold. I needed sunglasses for the glare and Paul kept reminding me to close my mouth. Gold was everywhere. We walked around looking at the gold leaf ceiling and the gold statues and kept bumping into things all made from or covered with gold. Neither of us concentrated on what we were seeing. We just looked, inspecting nothing up close, since most of it was protectively fenced off.

We stayed in Linz long enough to do some indoor shopping. It was raining when we arrived, but when the rain mixed with snow, we headed indoors. We tried to find an electric heater for our van, with no luck. We looked for a movie theater that might be showing an English movie with subtitles, but to no avail. We drove to a campground early and ended up reading, writing, playing scrabble and studying our guidebook. We realized that we were close to an area that had been highly recommended by an America couple we met on the ferry returning from Morocco.

The next day found us in the most beautiful spot in all of Austria, Hallstatt. The town is located on Hallstatt Lake and we drove under a mountain, through a low, narrow tunnel, to get to the town center. Had our van been an inch or two higher we would not have been able to enter.

The town is surrounded on three sides by high mountains, with a waterfall, lit up at night, cascading down into the center of town, and on the fourth side by water. We spent a day touring the town on foot and marveling at the sights. We camped in the town square, overlooking the clear, calm lake, with several other campers. Magnificent is the only word that comes to mind.

The following day we took a driving tour of the area. We visited Lake of Gosau. We had a spectacular view of the Hoher Dachstein and its small plateau glaciers. We toured Abtenau at the foot of the enormous Scheiblingkogel and stopped at the Gothic church with its twin aisles. We stopped at Radstadt to see the winter sports center and my husband could not resist touring the winter resort area of Schladming before going on to Grundlsee just to view the vast Grundlsee basin. At the end of the day, we drove back to Hallstatt. We stayed another couple of days just to enjoy the splendor. We met no one who spoke English.

We left Hallstatt early and drove to St. Wolfgang. We, once again, found ourselves desperate for laundry facilities. We needed a day to clean up our van and, in Salzburg, had the oil changed. We crossed the border into Germany, found a wooded area by a lake and camped for the night.

This part of Germany was a return visit for Paul and Munich had always been a favorite part of the world for him. My background dictates that I am going to have a little trouble enjoying anything German, however, I would have followed Paul to the ends of the earth. We visited the town square at noon and was in time to see the Glockenspeil in action. We actually had quite a pleasant day and ended it in the Hofbrau House, toasting everything with all the other tourists that were there.

We were on the ring road leaving Munich when I saw the sign to Dachau. "I want to go," I said to Paul.

"Why would you want to go there?" he asked, a little annoyed that I would want to ruin our trip to Munich that way.

"Because I cannot NOT go," I said.

Paul and I had very different views of Nazi Germany. Paul always felt that they were sorry for what they did and my view is, and always will be, that "they" would do it again in a heartbeat, if given an opportunity.

Without another word of contradiction, Paul turned off at the proper exit and we went to Dachau. Wordlessly and with tears in our eyes, we went through the compound and pictorial museum. With everything that has been written and everything that is known about what happened and everything that we felt in our hearts, it is different standing on the spot, seeing the pictures, trying to comprehend the horror. It is impossible. We walked the museum. We walked the barracks. We saw the ovens. We did it silently and left. We never talked about it. Words were not necessary.

We stopped at a "restplatz" on the highway. The rain fell in solid sheets. We spent the night there with a dozen other vehicles. No one left their camper. We just settled in for the night.

The following morning, after the rain had abated, we drove down the Romantic Strasse. We stopped for a barbecued lunch in the woods and spent the afternoon in the charming border town of Fussen. In the sunshine we visited the shops and had coffee and strudel in an outdoor cafe. I was relieved, a short while later, when we crossed the border back into Austria.

119

We followed the signs to Innsbruck. Something happened to Paul when he was surrounded by gorgeous mountains. He talked incessantly about skiing and was determined to get me, old cross country ski victim, back on the slopes. We walked the town. At the end of the main street, the snow covered mountain appeared at street level and shot straight up in the air. The view was breathtaking.

"Let's go find a place to ski," said Paul.

We headed for St. Anton. What a wonderful little ski resort it was. I was determined that, just this once, I would join him on the slopes. While he went into a rental shop, I waited in the sunshine. Before he had been gone thirty seconds, a young, dark haired girl, outfitted in a gorgeous royal blue ski suit, left one of the shops. Her leg was in a cast, one arm was in a sling, and she was trying desperately to manage on crutches. The right side of her face was black and blue with giant purple welts. Even from a distance, I could see the welts throbbing. I lost my nerve. When Paul came out of the rental shop and told me he would have to mortgage our van to rent equipment for both of us, I was thrilled.

We walked the main street in St. Anton which was bustling with activity. We watched some of the skiers coming down one of the slopes. We were warm, cozy and comfortable in a bar with a huge picture window. We hoisted our glasses to the health of each skier who didn't fall. There weren't many.

We crossed the Ahrberg Pass, stopped in Bludenz for grocery shopping and to admire the religious portraits, done with colored chalk on the sidewalk. We stopped at Rankwell for a tromp up the mountainside and we camped by the water's edge in Bregenz. We were awakened by tanks and trucks going by our window on a nearby path. Men in uniform carrying rifles were all over the place.

It seems we had spent the night on a military installation and we were now part of morning maneuvers. They waited while we dressed hurriedly and took off. We found a quiet spot, again on the lake, where we thoroughly enjoyed a cooked breakfast, laughing over some of predicaments we found ourselves in since we had left home. Hours later we cleaned up and left.

Chapter 21

I don't think we purposefully went looking for Liechtenstein. We just suddenly found ourselves out of Austria and into the village of Vaduz, the capital of this tiny principality. We did this without benefit of signs indicating we were leaving one or entering another country and without even veering off the road we were traveling.

Liechtenstein has been a sovereign territory since 1806 and since a customs agreement with Switzerland makes the border passage hassle-free, we were just suddenly, there. Once inside the country, however, we went looking for border officials so we could get our passports stamped. We learned from one of the shopkeepers that, for a fee, they stamped passports at the post office. Standing there, we knew where much of the country's income came from, since we were at the end of a long line waiting for that precious stamp.

Since Liechtenstein was described in one of my guidebooks as being somewhat the shape of Idaho and about the size of a potato from that state, we walked the length and breadth of the country's capital. The only items of interest, as far as shopping was concerned, were the attractive postage stamps that Liechtenstein is famous for and their intricate cuckoo clocks. We stopped outside one of the shops to watch a cuckoo clock maker at his craft. He never looked up from his task to see if anyone was watching.

Walking the town and looking in the shop windows was not a long involved project. There were so few of them. It was impossible to get lost since there was only one main street and we were on it. In a couple of hours we saw all we wanted and, included in the price of admission, was a picnic lunch that we enjoyed in the park at the end of town.

We left as soon as our bellies were full and toured the sixteen mile long, four mile wide gently rolling countryside. The ride was pleasant but not overly scenic and before we could comment on any particular sight, we found ourselves on a highway in Switzerland and the border just ahead of us. We were asked if we wanted to purchase a highway pass for twenty-five American dollars. When we refused we were warned to get off the highway at the first exit. We were advised that steep fines were levied to locals and tourists alike. Pleading ignorance or insanity would not work.

Since this was not a race through the country and we wanted to see and enjoy all we could, we heeded the warning and got off the highway at the first exit. Their secondary roads, we were delighted to discover, were as well maintained as their highways. We meandered along until Lucerne. We arrived in the rain and spent the entire afternoon indoors at the Transportation Museum, featuring a three hundred and sixty degree "Swissorama" panorama.

We were prepared to spend the evening in our camper reading, while the rain continued, but a knock on our back door brought us to our feet. Parked next to our camper was a much larger one. The couple, Marty and Susan, were from Australia. Since our van had Canadian stickers on it, they assumed we were English speaking and invited us to join them for a drink. We never needed urging when it came to socializing. Paul scooped up a bottle of French wine from our supplies and when he left the camper, I took an extra few minutes to make up our bed. I learned early in the traveling game, when invited to another's camper for drinks, it was not going to be an early night. Paul always thanked me for my foresight.

The following day we toured the city on foot in the mist. The walk across the covered bridge, that separated the new part of town from the old, was breathtaking. With the outline of both parts of town in the distance, we stopped every few feet to look out over the water and marvel at the scenery. Everyone walking the bridge did the same. The excitement in the voices told the story. The various languages did not. Our visit to the Lion Monument, even though it was overcast, was spectacular. It is a masterpiece of the early nineteenth century, dedicated to the memory of the heroic fight and final defeat of the Swiss Guards in 1792 in the year that marked the beginning of the bloody days of the French revolution with the storming of the royal palace, the Tuileries. The monument, carved out of a rock wall, measures forty-three inches. The animal alone measures thirty inches and the inscription reads "To the fidelity and bravery of the Swiss" and below were the names of twenty-six officers who fell defending the Tuileries. For an instant, the sun kissed the monument.

Lucerne had been enchanting, but we still departed in the rain. The weather started to clear around Interlaken, but not enough to see what was supposed to be the most spectacular of views, the surrounding mountains. Not wanting to wait out the bad weather, we just kept driving.

That night, the tenth of April, 1990, was our fourteenth wedding anniversary. We decided to treat ourselves to a night of luxury. The guest house was just off the highway, outside Saanen. We had crossed the Sannenmoser Pass, high in the mountains and descended upon a fairy tale, two-story, Swiss chalet. This, we thought, would be perfect. There was nothing around but snow covered mountains in the distance and cows, sporting a wide variety of bells around their necks, grazing in the fields. The chalet was modestly and comfortably furnished. Everything we could sit or lie on was overstuffed. This, to us, was total luxury.

I took my first bath, as opposed to the shower, in about six weeks. I relaxed, reading the last chapter of my book, on a ready made bed, for the first time in about six weeks. Before going out, I applied some make up, for the first time since 1975, excuse me, for the first time in about six weeks. Makeup has always been a bit foreign to me. Although Paul always referred to me as "the painted lady" when I put makeup on, he loved it when I took the time and got all dressed up.

We dressed and went downstairs for dinner to their modestly furnished dining room. We were seated immediately and although we were the only guests staying in their rooms, there were local people in for dinner and two other tables were occupied.

"What would you like?" Paul asked rather formally.

"I don't know," I answered, "give me a moment."

"What do you think you might enjoy?" I asked.

"Why don't we make up our minds over a bottle of their finest red," Paul continued.

"Great thinking," I complimented

We poured over the menu after the simple "salut" and a taste of the dry red wine.

"I think I'll have the chicken, with all the fixin's," I said rather decisively. "And for you?" I asked.

Hemming and hawing and checking out each item on the one page menu, he said finally, "Yes, I think I'll join you and have the same."

The fact that the chicken dinner was the only bill of fare did not seem to perturb us. We enjoyed the game.

We reminisced over dinner. How many people could say they celebrated Christmas and New Years in Spain, one birthday in the Canary Islands and the other in France, their wedding anniversary in Switzerland and after fourteen years of marriage, were still very much in love. We had been on the road a few days short of seven months and, for the first time, talked about going home.

After dinner, mellowed by a good meal and a bottle of red wine, we returned to our suite and discovered we had left our toothbrushes in the van. I went down to retrieve them. It didn't take long, after my return, to discover we had left our clothes for the next day in the van. Paul went down to get them. Before going to bed Paul realized that he had forgotten his book in the van and when I went to collect his book, I brought another one for myself.

Although we had not tromped through any city or village, hiked up any mountains, skied down any slopes, or even biked, we certainly had gotten our exercise that evening going up and down those damn stairs. "What a pain," was my only comment after the third or fourth trip. Sleeping in a bed, away from everything we knew to be familiar, we learned, not for the first time, was not always worth the price.

124

The following morning we slept in. I refused to rush, since check out time was not until eleven. I enjoyed my second hot, luxurious bath in two days. We would not be traveling far. The son of a Toronto friend lived in Chateau D'Oex and we followed the signs to the village. We had no address, only a brief description of the house. When we finally became frustrated enough to ask directions, we discovered that we had asked their next door neighbors. Digby and Marika actually heard us ask their neighbors for directions to their house and came to their window to see what the fuss was about. Since they had no idea we were in the area, they were totally mystified as to who belonged to these strange sounding voices asking for them by name. We were welcomed.

We stayed for tea and when the conversation didn't miss a beat, hours later, Marika opened the refrigerator to check on dinner fixings. They had bits and pieces. Our larder was stocked. We combined what they had with our provisions and ended up with a delicious concoction that would be acceptable on any table. We spent the evening and night talking as if we had known them for years and ended up camping in their back yard, beside the small creek that ran through their property. In the morning, after coffee served in a large hand painted bowl that was gripped with two hands, and croissants we bid a fond farewell.

We stopped at the Palace Hotel in Gstaad for some coffee and to admire the view of the snow covered mountains in the distance before heading towards Gruyere.

We visited Gruyere castle, which dates back to the middle ages. The castle was the home of the reigning dynasty from the twelfth century to 1555 when Count Michael gave up his land, the cities of Bern and Fribourg, to his creditors. The castle then became the residence of the bailiffs of Fribourg and later home of the prefect responsible for a part of Gruyere.

We spent a good part of the day walking the grassy knolls of the countryside. We stopped in the village of Gruyere long enough to enjoy a most delicious cheese soup and fresh rolls at an outdoor cafe and to buy a hunk of the stuff to take with us. Grated Gruyere cheese was shredded into or onto everything edible from that moment on, until it was gone. Used to a wide variety of the most wonderful cheeses Europe had to offer, we were thankful when we had used the last of the Gruyere. It had become monotonous.

From Gruyere it was an easy drive to Lausanne. We were once again, back in a large, modern city with lots of concrete and shops and finely dressed urbanites. We were in downtown Lausanne when Paul asked a woman for directions to a spa located on one of the routes heading out of town. This request was accomplished by using his best and most formal French; to which she asked, in English, "Which language would you prefer I use?" "Obviously French is not your first language."

While Paul was polite, but taken aback, I thought, "pompous ass." She did, however, tell us the best route to take to get out of the city and the most scenic route to take to get to Yverdon.

We camped that night by the water's edge in Yverdon, a short distance from Lausanne. Perfectly contented, we would stay a day or so. We ended our holiday in Switzerland with an afternoon of "taking the waters." Surprise! Surprise!

Chapter 22

Our last night in Switzerland was spent four kilometers from the French border. We were rudely awakened by a man playing with his barking mongrel and in that instant, would have preferred strangling them both. Instead of laying there fussing and fuming we chose to get out of bed, fix a hot breakfast and get back on the road. It felt like the middle of the night but it was actually a little after six in the morning.

It was Saturday and all banks in that region of France were closed. We drove to the largest supermarket we could find, overloaded on groceries, added a few French francs to the bill and paid for the lot by Visa. We then filled our gas tank, since the supermarket had a gas station on the premises and again paid for it with our Visa card, before resuming our journey. We were in fine spirits by this time and happy to be back on French soil.

Oblong signs, showing bunches of grapes, indicated we were on the Route du Vin. I'm not sure that any road in France is not on the famous wine route. We visited the three star, completely renovated, town of Colmar, with a section called Petit Venice. This time we could definitely see the resemblance. Tiny wooden bridges were everywhere. Some bridges would accommodate two or three people, others we dared not set foot on for fear they would collapse under our weight.

We drove to Kayserberg, equally as charming, but smaller. We drove slowly through one of the loveliest regions of France, Alsace-Lorraine. We toured each mini town.....Riquewihr, Haut Koenigsbourg, Dambach, Obenai. We sampled the wares at each winery and purchased a bottle or two in each town along the way. This was where we discovered Elzwicker. Each region has its own variety of grapes. At the end of every bottling season the master blender combines the leftover wines into a distinctly new flavor. Elzwicker certainly sounded more exotic than leftovers. Some blends tasted better than others but, to me, Elzwicker from the Alsace-Lorraine region was the nectar of the gods.

We spent a day touring Strassbourg, looking at the sights but mostly looking for a tire factory. Our last set had been fitted just before leaving Spain and we had been sold automobile tires instead of heavy duty truck tires. They did not last long. After seeing a large bald patch on two of our tires, we were in desperate need again.

Without knowing exactly when, and without benefit of being stopped, we found ourselves over another border and back into Germany. We knew that Strassbourg had changed hands between the French and the Germans many times but surely there should have been some kind of warning that we had entered another country. There was nothing.

Again, not being my favorite country, we did not linger. We drove through the Rhine Valley, looking for some good German wines, our never ending quest. We spent part of the day visiting Marksbury Castle and had an in depth tour, complete with an English speaking guide. We got lost in Koblenz as we usually did in large cities but found a perfect spot to be outfitted with four new truck tires. That night we camped on the Mosel River, overlooking the fast moving, sparkling water. The scenery was breathtaking with an outline of the village on the other side of the river.

The morning weather was promising, filled with sunshine and we had used the washing machines in the campground to do three loads of laundry. There were no dryers available so when the rain started, we pulled all the laundry off the line and now had underwear, socks, a t-shirt or two strung all over our van. What could not be strung up, I folded as neatly as I could and stuffed into several large black garbage bags. We left the town of Cochem, Germany because it had begun sprinkling, then raining, then pouring. We hoped to find someplace where it would not be raining and we could get into some clean dry clothes. The ultimate decadence in European travel.....we went looking for sunshine.

By the time we arrived in the Netherlands, we had been on the road more than half a year. Unfortunately one becomes very blase when one has been traveling for that length of time and many things that would normally have thrilled us down to our toes had become a normal everyday occurrence. We were not bored exactly. We just were not easily excited.

Our first couple of hours in the Netherlands were very relaxing. We decided that we needed a break from traveling and stayed on a farm just outside of Maastricht. A few cows grazed in the distance and a small vegetable garden was being tended by one man in overalls. The sun was shining and warm so we put our still very damp clothes out on the line. In the breeze, the clothes dried in an hour and as usual, we took the time to pull everything off the line, refold them neatly and put everything back on our shelves or hung them up in the closet.

We went for a four mile hike on a walking trail. Since this was the only hilly area in all of the Netherlands, we were told, the trail was filled with hikers. Everyone was out. We enjoyed the friendliness of people having a good time and no one passed us that did not give a warm smile or a nod. We got back to the van just as the heavens opened up and it started to hail. Since we had been walking for a couple of hours, we relaxed over a cup of tea before starting dinner.

I was standing at our little two burner propane stove, cooking dinner, with the air vent open at an angle directly above my head. When an ear piercing clap of thunder and the lightening struck simultaneously right above my head, I could feel a shiver going down my back. Paul saw my body vibrate from the shock. I could feel my body shaking when Paul yanked me away from the stove. It was over in seconds. He checked my back for welts or burns or for whatever happens when a person is struck by lightning. There was nothing. Had I been standing outside on that exact spot, however, this book would surely have been written by a ghost writer and that ghost writer would have been me. We stayed indoors the rest of the night.

It's hard to imagine so many people living in such a small country. The country is half the size of South Carolina with half the population of Canada, fourteen million people, living there. And yet, they still manage to be very friendly to tourists. Amazing! The many languages spoken in the country don't seem to be a problem either. We met a grocery clerk who spoke seven languages, "and all about at the same level as I speak English," she said. Her English was very, very good, I might add. "Most people in this country," she continued, "speak at least four and everyone speaks English, of course." She then asked where we were from.

"Canada," I replied.

"Oh, you're not traveling in a camping car, are you?" she asked, not waiting for our reply. "If I meet a man with a camping car," she said, closing her eyes and placing her hand over her heart, "I run away with him."

Everyone in the grocery lines that heard her comment, laughed along with us. She was a charmer.

We spent half a day at the Open Air Museum in Arnhem. We found it interesting and I hate to make comparisons, but Upper Canada Village just outside of Toronto had far more to offer. We expected demonstrations of the various old world crafts like broom making or candle making or spinning and weaving or even of knitting but there were none. It was a collection of dozens of farmhouses, mills, city houses and cottages reconstructed just as they were in bygone days. The buildings were situated under tall trees, beside meandering rivers and tranquil pools or set in the middle of green meadows. The houses and workplaces had been brought there from all over the country and fitted up with antique furniture, plowing implements and toys and games. The only thing missing was demonstrations, but that was a major void.

We spent several days in Amsterdam. On our second night we met a young couple in the campground. We decided on a city tour at night. The evening had started innocently enough. After getting precise directions from the campground manager and had all the information written out for us, we took the train into Amsterdam. Since we were on the outskirts, the journey took about an hour, but the train deposited us right in the

130

center of the city.

We were walking the extremely crowded sidewalks, often having to step onto the street to let a group or two go by, and Paul, the bored pro, had been explaining to this young couple what happens after you've been on the road for so long. They were in their second week of traveling and had planned on spending several months doing exactly as we had done.

"We've seen too much," said Paul. "We are castled out." "We are cathedraled out." "We are museumed out."

We rounded a corner just as Paul said "we are museumed out" and directly in front of us, hanging, if you'll pardon the expression, just above our heads, was a twenty foot long penis, with a sign that read " Museum of Pornography." "Well," said my husband, already starting to blush, "maybe just one more museum."

Laughing almost to the point of tears, it started our city tour on a high note. We now viewed Amsterdam with the eyes of any new and inexperienced traveler never knowing what would be around the next corner. Even for the fun of it, Paul, who was now beet red and stammering, could not be coaxed into going inside.

The sidewalks were overflowing with tourists, street vendors and police. We moved with the flood of pedestrian traffic into the Red Light District. Prostitution is legal in Amsterdam and instead of the ladies of the evening flaunting their wares on street corners, they are sitting on chairs in full length windows, partially clothed, so customers could "inspect" before they "bought." When the prostitute was ready for a new customer, the little red light above the door shone invitingly. When she was entertaining, the light was off and the drape drawn. One street housed all black girls displaying their wares, one street all Orientals, one street all blonds, one street all obese. We walked several streets, losing our way amongst the other gawkers. It was an effort, but I made my husband keep his mouth closed and warned him continuously about the drooling.

The following day, while Paul sat at a table for two, at an outdoor cafe with a beer and the latest issue of the International Herald Tribune, I went to visit Anne Frank's house, for what I was sure would be a quick half hour tour. Paul became concerned when over two hours passed and several beers had been consumed. He stood by the exit to see if he could possibly have missed me. He relaxed a little when he heard people saying, "my God, I've been in there three hours, or two hours or where did the day go."

It was an amazing little house. A bookcase hid the secret entrance to the upstairs chamber, where Anne Frank, her family and friends hid successfully from the Nazis for two years during World War II. Pictures and documents illustrated that terrible time in history and her hand written diary is also on display.

For such a small country, there was so much wonder to see. Just driving through the low, flat countryside was an experience. We spent a day in Edam, famous for its cheese making and, while still in Edam, visited a factory making stained glass.

We drove through areas where all we saw were giant fields of yellow tulips. Several miles later there would be giant fields of all red tulips. We stopped to take pictures of each other rolling around in flower petals. We learned that when the head of the tulip is removed, the bulb grows furiously. Tulips bulbs, of course, are a major export for this country. Everywhere we looked were giant mounds of colorful debris.

Still in this area, while driving down a country road, with flower fields on both sides, a ship suddenly appeared sailing along in the middle of the field, on an invisible river. We stopped and watched in total fascination, and were so engrossed, we forgot to take pictures.

Although there is rarely a time when flowers are not in profusion in the Netherlands, we managed to be there during the six weeks that the Keukenhof Garden was at its prime. We spent half a day walking amongst tulips, all one hundred and twenty five varieties, haughty daffodils with their brilliant yellow trumpet flowers heralding their arrival and nasturtium. A mixture of all the flowers had been made into rivers that wandered in all directions. Each bed of flowers had the names of each type. For as far as you could see and in every direction, a feast for the senses.

The following day was spent at the Delta Project. More than half the land lies below sea level with dunes and dikes protecting the hinterland against floods. Nonetheless every generation has experienced major flooding and in the disaster of

February 1953, one thousand eight hundred and fifty people drowned. The problem occurred when heavy rains coincided with high tide. This was the immediate impetus for the large scale hydraulic engineering project called the Delta Plan. In southwest Holland inlets were closed off, dikes raised and in the estuary of the Oosterschelde, a flood barrage was built. The unique tidal pattern in the Oosterschelde was protected and the hinterland became safe. Objects, models, replicas and audio-visual presentation gave us a fascinating picture of what hydraulic engineering has accomplished through the ages.

Even though we raced through the Netherlands in ten days, we managed to squeeze in three Indonesian rijsttafels, their national dish (rice table). It consisted of fifteen or twenty sample dishes of chicken, curry, chutney, raisins, beef, nuts, shrimp, coconut and a variety of hot and sweet sauces all heaped onto mountains of rice. It was ambrosial.

The Netherlands.....such a tiny country, filled with warm, friendly people, unique places and fascinating natural and manmade objects, so foreign to us. We left a piece of our hearts there.

Chapter 23

Only in Europe and only with an aggressive driver like my husband behind the wheel, can you see three countries in one day and feel that you have done justice to all.

Leaving the Delta Project, we drove to Vlissingen, took the ferry to Breskens and spent the night on a campground. We stopped in Sluis the next morning just long enough to squander the last of our gilders on some canned goods and a large jar of delicious rollmop sardines packed with sliced onions in brine, before flashing our passports at the border guards and entering Belgium.

It was a short drive to Bruges, referred to as Europe's sleeping beauty. Renaissance architecture is better preserved here than anywhere in Europe. Romance is always in the air as horse drawn carriages clickity-clack over the cobblestones, swans glide over tranquil water and remarkable facades reflect in the canals. The picture perfect setting gives the overall impression of a living museum.

Our timing could not have been better, it was market day. We walked up and down the street along the canal to see what all the stalls had on display. In another life we would have wished for some room for the antiques they were practically giving away. The handmade lace tablecloths were a pleasure to look at but did not tempt us. We purchased the usual fresh fruits and vegetables to tide us over for a few more days. We walked across the bridge, found a small table for two at the cafe overlooking the water. We sipped a cafe au lait and watched the world go by.

An hour after leaving Bruges we were walking the old part of Lille, the fifth largest city in France. Vieux Lille has been under restoration for many years but it was fascinating walking amongst the seventeenth and eighteenth century brick-and-stone houses.

Another short drive took us to Vimy Ridge, a key position attacked in 1917 by Canadian troops and the seventy four thousand Canadians who died in France are commemorated there. Much of the area is off limits since unexploded bombs still lie in wait for the unsuspecting. We were escorted to a network of trenches preserved for tourists to wander in and were given an extensive tour by a Canadian student who was studying in France for a year. The war years were of particular interest to Paul, and the young man guiding us had many questions about where we were from in Ontario.

The end of the day found us camping in Arras. La Grand'Palace and Place des Heros, which constituted a perfect example of seventeenth and eighteenth century Flemish architecture, made our tour the next morning most enjoyable. We visited the underground maze. Trap doors leading down to the cellars of the Town Hall and heading toward the Market Square left us with a wonderfully eerie feeling. The dampness and the feeling of doom was soon ignored while we viewed the architectural, archaeological and geological interests presented by the thousand year old site.

We followed the Route of Sacrifice until St. Omer, a quiet village on the edge of Flanders. We toured the seventh century Benedictine monastery. It was the oldest we had ever come across. We continued on to Boulogne.

We purchased tickets on the first ferry leaving the next morning. We parked our van at one of the long term parking spots at the dock and went for a walk on the streets of Boulogne. This was our last day on the continent.

We spent the last of our francs. We had no idea how many bottles of wine we could legally bring into Britain, but we purchased twenty of them. It was all we could carry at one time. The wine, at two and three dollars per bottle, did not deplete our supply of money. We each had a chien chaud (hot dog to you).

We shared a gooey pastry and nibbled on bits and pieces purchased from the sidewalk vendors before sitting on the bench to talk about whatever came into our heads. Mostly we just sat and stared. We were on an incredible journey and had such mixed feelings about leaving.

At five o'clock in the morning we drove onto the ferry and discovered two hundred screaming school children on board. Talk about a rude awakening. Their one day field trip to England had inspired an entire passenger list along with Captain and crew to seriously consider abandoning ship. Years have passed, but that incident still produces a shutter, similar, I suppose, to being struck by lightning.

We tried to ignore them and succeeded only to the point of ignoring a much needed root canal, and went out on deck to watch our approach to England. This was our first view of the white cliffs of Dover. We were most impressed with the beauty of the massive, pure white, bluffs. There had also been an announcement on board that the person who wrote the song, had been on a ferry earlier that week and, although in his nineties, had seen the white cliffs of Dover for the first time.

On our way back to Otford and our friends, the Webbs, we stopped in Canterbury to see the numerous remains from Roman, Norman and medieval times, and for a grand tour of the Cathedral, where Archbishop Thomas Beckett was murdered in 1170 A.D.

We could not linger. Our British license plates had expired several months before and although no one cared while on the continent, we were now back on British soil and a heavy fine would have been issued by the first policeman who saw it. We needed some repairs done to our van before we could get our safety certificate. We needed our safety certificate, before we could get our license renewed. We needed our license renewed before we could get more insurance on the vehicle. It was all one big vicious circle, but it all had to be done and it had to be done before we got caught.

We spent the rest of the day visiting the Webbs. The van went to the shop and while getting our tires balanced and our muffler replaced, the oil changed and the brakes looked over at the same garage that Phil used, we told the Webbs of our adventures. That day the van was certified safe, we received our

MOT sticker, which we took into the license bureau and road taxed (licensed) the van for six more months.

We were on our way again. We headed east towards Ipswich hoping to find a friend we had met in the Canary Islands, Cees. He had wanted us to meet his wife, Hedy and had described his exotic plant nursery in such infinite detail that we wanted to see it. We went looking and, without any effort whatsoever, found Paradise Center. We were given such a warm welcome by both, we stayed. Since Paul enjoyed the occasional stint of manual labor, and loved driving a tractor and lawn mower more than a car, we both worked. When my fingers grew stiff and painful from propagating and repotting plants and Paul could not straighten up from dragging and lifting boxes of plants onto the wagon, we showered, ate a gourmet duck a l'orange dinner prepared by Hedy, and went pubbing at the Red Lion Inn, a local hangout.

We stayed and worked for a couple of days. It was invigorating testing our muscles; however, heavy, back breaking, labor gets old really quickly. They convinced us to leave our van on their enormous property when we returned to Canada, so we knew we would be seeing them again before going home. We left for a short tour of Cambridge, spending most of the time walking the campus of the thirteenth century university. Our short tour turned into a long tour of trying to escape via the Ring Road. We drove in circles awhile trying to find a route that would take us out of town. It was not as easy as it sounds since Cambridge had an inner Ring Road as well as a bit of an outer Ring Road and the route signs hindered rather than helped.

We drove to Scunthorpe and visited with a Canadian friend of mine. Janis had given up on Canadian living, after twenty years, and returned to England. She loved being back in her homeland. She loved being near her parents again. She loved the people. She loved the friendliness of the pubs and the fact that she could walk in alone and not feel self conscious. She made friends easily in England and there was a certain flavor that she had missed in Canada. She hated the English weather; but, she was home.

After a wonderful evening of catching up on all the news on both sides, Paul and I were prepared to sleep in our

137

van. Janis' parents, however, had other plans. They were waiting for us and insisted that we stay in their guest room. We never refused a ready made bed or any of the other creature comforts of a home. Mrs. Ladds made us a special hot toddy before bed.

The following day Janis and Les, a friend of hers, who had also returned to England after many years in Canada, and Paul and I, drove to York. Workmen, digging the foundation for a shopping center, discovered artifacts from a Viking Village. Before resuming the digging for the shopping center, they restored the village on the spot where it was discovered. Jorvik, is complete with sights and sounds and (yuk) smells. The museum is housed on the site as well. We toured the village via an underground mini railroad, ending at the laboratory, watching the archaeologists continuing the work and finally, of course, the gift shop. It was most intriguing. We did not bother going into the shopping center that was built right over top.

As a foursome we visited York Minster Cathedral, the largest Gothic cathedral in Britain. After a wonderful pub lunch we said our farewells and went our separate ways.

That night we camped at Flixton. They had an indoor swimming pool and bar, both of which we used. We toured Filey and walked the mile-long natural breakwater of rocks to Filey Brigg. By the time we returned to our van, it was raining. Late afternoon was spent at Eden Camp in Malton. This living remembrance of WWII was the best and most entertaining museum we had ever experienced. It was constructed in the huts of a genuine prisoner of war camp. Hut number one showed the rise of Hitler and the Nazi party. One of the huts was the inside of a U-Boat. One hut showed the Blitz with all the smoke and fiery blasts. Another hut showed the Women at War. It was absolutely fascinating from one end of the museum to the other and from one hut to the other.

We drove through the moors into Goathland with sheep grazing everywhere and, in a split second of forgetfulness, nearly wiped ourselves out of existence. Paul looked the wrong way before going out into traffic. It had been a long while since we had done that and it unnerved us. Fortunately the driver of the oncoming car was alert and swerved, avoiding an accident.

We walked the seaside resort of Robin Hood's Bay. It reminded us of Clovelly, but not quite as steep. We drove through Whitby, twinned with Whitby, Ontario, a town near our home in Toronto that we knew well. That night we found a campground on the moors and spent the next day at the Beamish Open Air Museum. We again decided that we've seen enough museums, since it didn't come close to the fascination we had experienced at Eden Camp.

The following day we revisited Hadrian's Wall. Paul and I, along with my brother Harry and his girlfriend, had been there in 1978. Unfortunately, by the time we left, late in the afternoon, I had a rip roaring headache. We could not find a campground anywhere in the area and not one was listed in any of our guidebooks. We camped in Redesdale Forest.

Chapter 24

It wasn't like going into Cheers, where everyone knows your name. It was going into Scotland where everyone had your name. Until this trip Paul felt he had an unusual name, but there it was right in front of us, R.D. Hossack, Baker and another sign that read G.B. Hossack, Barrister. The newswoman on television the previous night was Roma Hossack. This all happened after meeting an artist at a London gallery by the name of Rosemary Hossack and on that same day, I picked up a sweat shirt with the London Tower embossed on it and the label read "Hossack." Paul wanted to change his name. It was too common.....at least in this part of the world.

We had been to Scotland in 1978 so this was a return visit for us and Paul loved being there. Although born in Canada, the Inverness and Cromarty area of northern Scotland was where his paternal grandfather fished and owned a cannery before emigrating. We would slowly wend our way back up to God's country.

Paul played his first golf game in months in Leven with my honoring him by performing caddy duties for the first nine holes and just walking the course with him for the back nine. The British golf courses are not groomed as well as America courses. They are lumpy and bumpy and I found the walking, dragging his golf bag a little rough. Paul didn't mind taking over.

140

We shopped in the afternoon and treated ourselves to a barbecued steak dinner in the evening, even though we had decided to cut down on our red meat consumption. We took a little mini tour of Lower Largo, a walk through St. Monans and Pittenween before revisiting Anstruther and finding our Smugglers Inn from twelve years earlier. We passed through Crail before coming to a stop in St. Andrews. Paul arranged another golf game for the next day. There were no open slots but he put his name on the list as standby. That evening we revisited the town and walked in and out of all the shops, buying some golf balls for the next day's play, should he be so fortunate. We walked around the outside of the Royal and Ancient Club House, looking at the simple grandeur through some of the windows. The club house was closed.

What followed was a day Paul would remember and reminisce about for the rest of his life. He showed up at the golf course bright and early. One of a foursome could not make the day of playing and Paul was invited to join the group. They liked the fact that he was a visitor from Canada and an avid golfer. His hosts were three of the organizers of the British open.

After the game, Paul returned to the van where I was lounging with all the windows open, enjoying the sunshine and reading a recently acquired novel. His eyes were aglow. "Would you mind waiting awhile longer?" he asked. "I've been invited for a beer in the club house," he continued. "Sorry, Babe, no women allowed," he said, never taking a breath. "They went to find a tie and jacket for me, do you mind?" he asked again.

"Enjoy," I said, as my lips brushed his. I was thrilled for him. This was a once in a lifetime, dream come true, for him.

He talked of nothing else when he returned to the van and told me about each hole in infinite detail as we made our way northward. Every quiet moment was shattered with some little previously unmentioned tidbit or some unforgettable moment that he repeated over and over.

We stopped at Braemar to visit the castle and we camped in a picnic area near Balmoral. It was late in the evening when we arrived but the sun was still high in the sky and it was light enough to read by, without benefit of additional power.

The following day we started up the Whiskey Trail, stopping at the Tamnavulin Distillery for a tour and a taste of a wee dram. We revisited Cullodin to discover they had redone the visitors center and we watched a fascinating video reenactment of the great battle. That night we camped by Loch Ness. Sorry to say, Nessie did not make an appearance and I did watch for her. Had she been swimming an inch under the surface we would not have seen her. The water was black as pitch even at the shoreline.

We returned to Inverness and found a much more modern town than we had left. Many of the streets had been blocked off and vehicles were no longer permitted in the downtown core. It had become a charming and expensive place to shop.

We drove to Cromarty that evening. We learned from a neighbor that Mrs. Bathie, whom we had visited in 1978 had died in 1980. We walked to the churchyard and had no problem finding her grave since her gravestone was a newer one. We paid our respects.

Mrs. Bathie's brother lived in Canada and was a friend of Paul's parents. To our knowledge that was the only connection, but we remembered and enjoyed how fervently she had discussed what Cromarty had looked like at the turn of the century, when Paul's grandfather operated his cannery. We also remembered how much she wanted Paul to join her in a whiskey. She never drank alone, she insisted, so she always looked forward to guests. At eleven o'clock in the morning Paul thanked her and declined. By the time she finished telling her story, it was close to three in the afternoon and even on an empty stomach, we were all ready for a drink.

The following day was a shocker for Paul. While still in the Cromarty area, we visited Hugh Miller's cottage and although we had been there before, there was a curator on this shift who greeted us pleasantly and asked where we were from.

"Canada," replied Paul, "but my ancestors came from this area."

"And what would your last name be?" asked the curator.

When Paul said "Hossack" she responded with "Ah yes, Scottish." "But," she continued, "you know, that you're only about four hundred years Scottish?" "Before that, you were Welsh".

"Welsh," said Paul dumbfounded, "no, cannot be."

The curator continued telling Paul about the people who had fled Wales around the fifteenth century to escape oppression. We listened without saying a word.

On the drive to Dingwall, I commented that he must be thrilled to find out about his Welsh background.

"Are you nuts," he said, "the Welsh are known for their lying and cheating."

"The Scots are known for being cheap, which would you prefer?" I asked. "The last time I told a friend," I continued, "we were a Jew married to a Scotsman".....she said "great, one knows how to earn it and one knows how to keep it." "Personally," I said, "I think I would rather be a liar, than cheap."

We dropped the subject. Paul did not want to talk about it. His final word on the subject was "Welsh, huh."

We drove slowly across gorse covered Scotland to the west coast. We were on a one lane road and if a vehicle approached, one of us had to pull into a layby to pass. Unlike other parts of the civilized world, a one lane road in northern Scotland, meant one lane for both directions. The traffic was heavy but only with sheep splattered with yellow, red or blue paint. This was certainly a colorful way of showing ownership. It was desolate country with very few towns, houses or other visible signs of inhabitants.

We made our way to Kyle of Lochalsh and waited in line for the ferry going to the Isle of Skye. Skye, we discovered, was equally as desolate except for the capital city of Portree which was a pleasant walking town, with shops and a small, active harbor. That night we camped in a clearing just over a bridge and awoke to a wild and woolly sight. A flock of sheep had surrounded our van. They took no notice of us and we couldn't even get them moving when we started our van and drove slowly towards the bridge. A couple of days touring Skye was enough. Sheep do not have an interesting vocabulary although some bleat a very distinctive and different sound.....besides, they stink.

We ferried back to the Kyle of Lochalsh and had lunch in

the sunshine on the grounds of Eileen Donan's Castle. We stopped in Fort William for some grocery shopping.

On the road to Glencoe we picked up a hitchhiker. A young man in his late twenties, plodded slowly down the main highway. He turned when he heard our van and stuck his thumb out. With the large knapsack on his back, he looked terribly uncomfortable and although he smiled at us, the fatigue was clearly evident in his eyes and creased brow. He thanked us over and over for the ride and explained that he had been dropped off in the middle of nowhere and had spent all night walking by moonlight. "There were few cars that passed and no one stopped," he said. He set his sack down in the corner, sat down on one of the bench seats and promptly fell asleep, his head leaning against our clothes closet. We woke him a mile before Oban, since that was our destination. He apologized for his rudeness and thanked us again for the lift. "I'll be able to find a room here," he volunteered. "I should have removed the American flag from my jacket," he said, "perhaps someone would have picked him up sooner." I had insisted we pick him up because of the American flag.

We stopped at the Oban Glass Factory long enough to pick up some Caithness glass to be given as gifts.

Paul did some fishing in Loch Lomond, catching nothing, and we stopped in Lockerbie to visit the Memorial Garden. Lockerbie, a tiny village in the middle of nowhere with no reason to take any notice of it on the map, except, of course, for Pan Am flight number 103 that was shot down killing everyone on board and thirteen people on the ground. It will remain forever as place of great tragedy. The garden was in full bloom.

Our last stop in Scotland was Gretna Green. Young British couples used to run away to marry in Gretna Green and the chapel still awaits any couple wishing to tie the knot. A preacher, along with a witness or two, is on hand twenty-four hours a day to perform a simple ceremony. It was an interesting place to take our last picture and to end our Scottish adventure. We reentered England.

Chapter 25

We lingered in northern England. We visited Wadsworth's birth home in Cockermouth. We stopped in Buttermere and walked the rolling hills to the falls. A lamb was being born and we waited and watched along with throngs of tourists, speaking only in whispers. We drove too quickly through the beautiful Lakes District. We stayed that night in Meal Bank just because we found the name intriguing.

We stopped in Windermere the next morning and discovered a store that took any currency that you had on hand. Each item was marked in prices of at least five countries, but they quoted prices from most strong currencies, since each salesperson walked around with their own personal calculator. It was interesting to see but we quickly tired of the commercialism since there was nothing we wanted to buy. We stopped in Grange over Sands to check out the garden and the duck pond.

Our traveling became a little erratic. We could feel that we were coming to the end of our journey and Paul really wanted to play just a little more golf. After a couple of hours drive on their super M road, something we never would have done in the old days, we were in Chester. We had loved the place twelve years before and decided that it was worth a more intense visit.

We camped, that night, just outside the wall that

completely encircled the city. We awoke early, threw a load of laundry into several of their tiny washers, then dryers, cleaning up the van during cycles and headed off to spend the day in the medieval town of Chester, England when everything was done. We completed the walk around the wall, looking down at all the activities. We visited some of the shops, built in two tiers. We waited for the town crier, in full regalia, to announce the time so we could take pictures. We toured every side street, every back alley and walked down by the river to sit and watch the ducks floating serenely on the water.

It was late in the afternoon when we drove to Erdigg and since we were too late to visit the castle via the front door, we went to the exit. This time both of us wandered the castle backwards, a little trick I had learned at the Pope's Palace in Avignon, France. That night we camped in a lovely spot, Bala, Wales. The campground was within walking distance to all the shops on the main street. We window shopped that night and enjoyed an ice cream cone, purchased from the only shop that was open.

The following morning we drove to Harlech. We set up camp in view of the Castle on the hill. There were sand dunes in the distance, a beautiful beach and Paul, in a little local shop, booked a golf game for the next day. Arrangements were made with the young man, in his late teens, standing behind the cash register. When he learned we were from America, he spent a good part of his talk trying to convince us that America was discovered by a Welshman.

I looked at Paul and watched as his eyes rolled heavenward. Disgusted, but amused, he shook his head ever so slightly. Liars and cheats he had called them, and here was this young man trying to convince us that a Welshman had discovered America. When we left the shop, Paul gave me a grin and that "I told you so" look and I twittered at him. "Poor Welsh Baby," I soothed.

"Do you see what I mean.....liars and cheats." "I rest my case," he continued.

"Ok," I volunteered, "we won't tell anyone that four hundred years ago, you were Welsh." "I promise I will keep your secret," I assured him.

Forgetting about the non stop chatter from the young

prevaricator behind the desk, Paul really enjoyed the golf game. I walked the course, just for the exercise and the sunshine, and since a husband and wife team completed the foursome, we retreated to the nineteenth hole after the game for a drink and a bit of conversation. They were both Welsh, living in the area and this was their favorite course, so they played it often. The super special of the course, or more specifically the clubhouse, was the food. We stayed and enjoyed a crispy, crunchy fish and chip dinner with them.

Still with a taste for golf, we drove the coast road, stopping at small villages along the way. We stopped again when Paul spotted a golf course up on the hill and he followed the signs. The man had the nose of a bloodhound, when it came to sniffing out golf courses, but this was the United Kingdom and the sniffing was easy. The golf courses and their appropriate signs were everywhere.

We looked over the course, and in doing so, spotted a couple of campers that were parked near the green, off to one side. Since the golf office was closed, Paul approached the campers. According to the two couples, a little older than ourselves, three camping vehicles were allowed to park for a week or less on the local golf course. They assured us that we were welcomed to stay a night or two and invited us into their trailer for a drink. Paul needed no more invitation than that. We were there for the night. When the office opened in the morning, Paul paid for a couple of nights of camping and one afternoon of golf. It didn't take long. Our friendship was established. When the men went off to play golf, the women went shopping and lunching and laughing. The conversation consisted of men and marriage and we laughed so hard our sides ached. If Paul, whether he acknowledged it or not, was part of this friendly group of people, I could live with it, even if he found it unbearable.

When the group of John and Elen Lewis, Nina and Peter Holmes, Paul and myself swelled to three more couples, whose names I cannot remember, we went out to dinner and drinks at a local pub. The following evening they were all back at our campground for barbecues. Sharing our stories, and listening to theirs, was delightful.

To add to the enjoyment, the view was spectacular. We

147

were camped high on a hill overlooking the links and Cardigan Bay. Whether the tide was coming in, and we watched the marshland being covered over with water, or going out and we watched as couples, holding hands strolled on the spongy clay bottom in a trickle of water, the view was sensational.

When our friends had to leave for home and return to work, we left the camping spot as well. It would be no fun without them. We left with addresses and telephone numbers in our little black book. We knew we would see each other again, but it was a tearful goodbye.

We coasted down the hill into the seaside resort town of Newport. We found the second hand bookstore that had been recommended. We did some much needed exchanging of reading material before heading to Pembroke. Since we had been driving in the rain for a good part of the day, we took a break and visited the large and well preserved Pembroke Castle. We continued our driving and ended up camping just behind the grounds of Cardiff Castle.

The following day we toured the castle. The inside was impressive and much of the castle is still in daily use.   Various rooms in the castle are set aside and can be rented for weddings and large parties. It is very well preserved and maintained. The grounds are used as park land. Locals and tourists of all ages were strolling and picnicking. The outside wall of the castle was fascinating. Every few feet, a stone animal in a crouched position, was coming over the wall ready to pounce. Inside and out, it was fascinating.

From Wales, we slowly made our way back to our friends in Otford, stopping to tour Cirencester and the Roman Villa. We drove through the Cotswolds, stopping at Bibury and the trout farm. We stopped at Wayland Smitty to see a five thousand, five hundred year old tomb before walking the cliff to the Chalk Horse hill figure.

We spent a couple of days in Otford with our friends, Phil and Andrea. We took the train into London each day. We saw a play. We lunched. We arranged our airlines tickets. With everything set, we drove back to our friends in Bures-LaMarsh, who had offered to store our van for as long as necessary. A day was spent enjoying our friends, Cees and Hedy, at Paradise Center and making sure everything was in order regarding the insurance for the van. We headed to Gatwick airport by train. We had been traveling for nine months. We needed to go back to America. We wanted to see our friends and family. We had to see for ourselves that all was well. We needed to look for a home.

Chapter 26

I don't know what we expected to find when we got "home" but whatever it was we were expecting, we didn't get. We, of course, had conveniently forgotten that we had no place to live. Everything we owned had either been sold, given away or put in storage. One of our immediate objectives was to find a place that didn't move, except through the violence of nature, that did not have wheels or an apparatus for steering those wheels and where we could be stationary long enough to review our options and hopefully, make a few decisions.

In our nine month absence our friend, Pat Thomas, had lost her husband, Bob, to cancer. She invited us to stay with her and in the days that we lived in Beeton, north of Toronto, we shingled one end of her large country home. Besides enjoying the physical labor, it was fulfilling a promise we had made to Bob. I kept the pool free from leaves, bugs and the occasional frog that jump in to refresh his hide in the chlorine saturated water. Paul kept the refrigerator stocked with food and beer and, in general, we lived life to the fullest with just a bit of work to break up the monotony. We had a fine time. It didn't take us long, however, to want to move on after the shingling was completed.

For reasons beyond our comprehension, our friends and families were anxious for us to get some kind of normalcy back into our lives. Since they seemed satisfied with their status quo, they felt we should be as well.

When each listened to about five or ten minutes of our unique, intriguing and funny travel stories, they wanted to know when we were going to "stop this nonsense and get back to work." After all, they reminded us, I was still only forty-six and Paul had just turned fifty. Most of his well intentioned pals told Paul, in no uncertain terms, that he was giving up the biggest earning years of his life. I was told by the same well intentioned friends, I had closed an extremely lucrative business and if I didn't wait too long, I could reopen without losing many of my customers. We imagined that under all the practical advice, they were grappling with envy.

Our friends went on to tell us about the same problems at work that we heard about before we left. We listened to stories about their children and about the house renovations they were still planning on doing some day soon. We heard references made to the same political problems, financial problems and family problems. We listened patiently. We nodded in agreement. We absorbed every word. A few days later we went out, bought a used tent trailer, hooked it onto the back of our midnight blue Chevy Camaro and left.

We had been back in Canada about three weeks when we pulled off that little caper. Our friends and family were appalled. If, at that moment, any one of them could have committed us, they surely would have.

Without maps, plans, or a time frame, we took off. We were looking for a home, we told everyone who would listen and each other. Since Paul's close call in the Canary Island, he was convinced that he did not want to die "Paul Hossack of no fixed address." The incident had played heavily on his mind, however we needed an area that we wanted to settle in and America was such a big place to start looking. This we felt was also a great excuse for having a good time, seeing America and staying alive, eager and vital. We had a mission.

We headed north from Toronto past Parry Sound, Sudbury and Sault Ste Marie, Ontario. These were all places we had been to many times before and certainly not on our list of places to investigate for our future home. We crossed over into the U.S. at, strange as it may sound, Sault Ste Marie, Michigan. You would think that since we were in a new country, they could come up with a more original name. We spent no time thinking about who had chosen the name first.

We headed west, moving at break neck speed.....snail style. We were looking for a home and were exhilarated by the fact that we were actually doing something about our homelessness.

We knew that we would not be looking for a home in Wisconsin, Minnesota or North Dakota, so we just bee lined through those states. We stopped for meals, always by a river or pond, a picturesque garden, or in a park where we could walk and stretch our legs. If our AAA guidebooks, acquired on route, mentioned an interesting museum, we stopped and investigated. We left the campgrounds late, after a leisure breakfast and we usually stopped early, so "break neck speed" meant good, home cooked and wholesome meals, cleaning a little, setting up and taking down a lot, sightseeing and the odd museum or two, hence the snail style.

We also stopped for the occasional bicycle ride. Bringing our bicycles had been one of those few mistakes we would make along the way. The bikes had to be tied onto the car between the car and the tent trailer. They had to be removed before the trailer could be set up and put back onto the car before reattaching the trailer. We could not cover them during inclement weather because seeing out the back window would have been impossible. To make a long story, short and boring, bringing the bicycles was a major pain in the ass and it was a mistake we would repeat when we returned to Europe. But that's another chapter.....a little farther along in the book.

We continued westward. Never having been to Montana, I was anxious to see Big Sky country. My pulse raced when I visualized the Marlboro Man on his trusty steed riding off into the sunset and I must confess that Big Sky country was wonderful.....for the first fifteen miles. That Marlboro Man could have been five hundred miles ahead of us and we would have seen him plain as day since there was nothing but clean, crisp air to spoil the view. The next five hundred and eighty five miles of Big Sky country with nothing to look at but the Big Sky on a road that was straight as an arrow was pure tedium.

There were few things to see and nothing to stop for on highway 2 on the northernmost road in the state. One small sign in Hill County brought a smile. It said, Welcome to Rudyard, 362 real nice folks and 1 old sourhead. At the opposite end of town it said Leaving Rudyard, goodbye from the old sourhead.

To add to our disappointment, there were few places to eat and, much to our discomfort, even fewer places to camp. At one point, on this ribbon of nothingness, I became extremely anxious. There was no way we were going to pull off by the side of the road and camp in a vacant field. There were no restaurants that we could pull into and ask if we could camp in back after eating in their establishment. There were no motels that we even considered spending an hour in, let alone an entire night. The last place of civilization had been about two hundred miles back and just about the time we decided to change drivers and pull an all nighter, since it was about eight in the evening, there was a slight bump in the road and off to the right was a campground, in the middle of nowhere.

It looked like the Garden of Eden, complete with trees, bushes, outer buildings, lots of other vehicles and people. We pulled in, parked, set up the trailer and while Paul went to register, I started dinner. In a matter of minutes we turned from two snarling, crabby individuals into a lady and gentleman, offering each other a glass of something refreshing. We breathed easier. We ate in silence, enjoying being able to put our feet up and to stand on solid, unmoving, ground for a bit. A tour of the campground, indicated that they had washing machines and dryers. We stayed an extra day so we could have some clean clothes to wear. We lingered in the hot showers. We read, drank an extra beer or wine without hesitation and soothed our aching shoulders. Sore from putting up and taking down the tent trailer, I needed a nightly massage.

Once back on the road, we did not have far to travel, or so we thought. By the time we were close to Shelby, looming directly ahead of us, and jutting straight up from the road, stood the Rocky Mountains, in all its splendor. We headed towards them and could not believe how far we actually had to travel before we got close to them.

Just past Shelby, in Browning, we took a mini jog to the right and headed north on highway 89. We crossed the border into Canada and a whole new camping world opened up to us when we reached Waterton Lakes National Park. We were back in a gorgeous part of our own country, a part I had never seen before.

The park was not quite filled to capacity with campers traveling in motorhomes of every size, shape and configuration. Some campers were in trailers, some were in cars loaded to the hilt with tents, sleeping bags, inflatable mattresses and whatever else one needs to sleep on the ground, cook full meals on a picnic table and eat outdoors. The people were of all ages and descriptions and children were everywhere and a bit too noisy for our liking; but it was energizing.

There were mountains surrounding us so majestic and rugged, we could not believe our eyes. They rivaled anything we had seen in Europe and we, now fully in the know, compared the Rockies to the Alps in France, the Dolomites in Italy, the Pyrenees, nestled between France and Spain and the Atlas Mountains of Morocco. We knew that we were now part of an elite class of folks. We had seen it all and we would flaunt it, assuming of course, anyone would listen.

Deer and mountain sheep wandered the park and the streets like the owned the place. When a dog came too close to one of the deer, it leapt over a fence, effortlessly, into a yard where some children were playing. They ignored each other. It jumped from a standing still position, immediately lowered its head, and resumed grazing like nothing had happened. We watched the deer and looked at each other in total amazement. It was only then that we realized that we had not seen animals in Europe and we had missed them

We set up camp, prepared to stay for a few days. We met a few neighbors, did some scouting of the campground and tried a little hiking. There was something very peaceful about the ambience, until the rains came. The rain started right after dinner on our first night so we regrouped in our tent trailer. It continued, becoming heavier.....and heavier.....and heavier. We went to bed early and listened to the rain drumming out its steady beat on the hard metal top . In the morning, we stepped out of the trailer into an inch of mud. We retrieved our dish washing bucket that had been left outside on the picnic table and it had overflowed so we had no idea how many inches, or possibly feet, it had rained. We went about packing up while the rain abated.

The ground soaking was nothing compared to the inside of our humble abode. The trailer, around the perimeter, had leaked like a sieve. At least six inches on three sides of our mattress was soaked, leaving a dry spot the size of a postage stamp in the middle. We had breakfast, packed and headed for Calgary, where our friend, Hugh Osler was waiting for us. We would dry out there.

As soon as we were on the road, the sun came out, as if to mock us. We had been traveling a couple of weeks at this point and looked forward to seeing our friend. The added bonus of sleeping in a bed, especially since ours was a waterlogged raft, would do wonders to rekindle our now soggy spirits.

Chapter 27

After a quick "hello" and a fast beer, we retreated to the driveway. Hugh moved his car and cleared a level spot. We opened the tent trailer, folding back all the flaps so a cross breeze would waft through, hopefully carrying with it any unpleasant odor. Mildew would be a residual that would plague us for the life of the camper and we dared not risk it. I gathered up all the wet bedding, which Hugh insisted be taken directly to the washer. With the three of us pushing, pulling and dragging, we managed to get the dripping mattress out onto the driveway, laying it down on a tarp. There was nothing more we could do. Over a beer the men caught up on their news, while guess who threw in a load of laundry. A glass of chilled white wine awaited my return.

We stayed in Calgary for a couple of days. We did some shopping, taking full advantage of the fact that Alberta does not have sales tax like the rest of the Canadian provinces. Our car was serviced at Hugh's favorite garage. We were once again road ready. Hugh and his son Geoffrey owned a cottage in Windemere, British Columbia and that was where we would be heading next.

After attaching our still slightly damp but usable tent trailer to our car, we left Calgary early Thursday morning after Hugh had gone to work. We headed for Banff in the Canadian Rockies. Banff, Lake Louise and Jasper are the crowning glory towns in the Rockies and we planned on exploring two of them. After paying for a day pass into the park, it was a short spectacular drive to Banff.

Our vehicle took up two spots in the parking lot, but even with that the parking lot was far from full. We walked onto the main street with all its shops and restaurants and stopped on a bridge to admire the overall view. At one end of town was a garden filled with shrubs, flowering bushes, plants and flowers, all set by a master gardener. There were fish filled ponds and meandering walking trails through the garden designed to be admired by all who visited. From any bench in the garden, the view of the other opposite end of town, where the street ended and a mountain began, shooting straight up in the air, all rugged and craggy and snow covered, was most spectacular. Also from the garden, we caught a glimpse of Banff Springs Hotel, peeking over and through a forest of trees.

We walked the entire length and breadth of Banff before getting back into our car and heading for the hotel to enjoy the scenery and a cup of coffee in the restaurant. That was not to be. They would not let us park our car in the hotel lot and the town had filled with tourists so street parking was impossible. We took a quick tour of the outside of the hotel before getting back on the road and driving to Chateau Lake Louise. Getting there was half the fun since we stopped at every rest area to admire the mountains. Lake Louise is a very, very small town with just a couple of stores, a small museum giving us some background information on the area, i.e. walking tours, campgrounds, and the flowers and fauna of the region. It was worth a stop, but a short one.

We hiked at Moraine Lake. Viewing the seven peaks, crowning a lake of icy turquoise water, pictured on the back of the old Canadian ten dollar bill was spectacular. We walked well worn paths for hours, before going back to the hotel for lunch. It was while touring the hotel grounds that we ran into a friend from Montreal, Jan Northfield. Over a cup of coffee we arranged to meet for dinner. We went looking for, and without much effort, found a campsite, left our trailer all set up for sleeping and returned to Chateau Lake Louise to meet our friend and her new husband.

Only Paul and I could visit Banff, Lake Louise and all

points in between in a day or two and feel that we had seen it, done it, been there and got the t-shirt.

The next morning we drove to Windemere stopping at Golden, Brisco, Edgewater and a few viewpoints in Kootenay National Park. Hugh and Geoffrey were there to greet us on that Friday afternoon. After a couple of beers and wines to remove the road dust from our throats, Hugh set up the barbecue.

The steaks were one inch thick and done to a perfect tenderness. Hugh, unlike my husband, seemed to understand the term "well done" without my having to explain or, more specifically, argue. The mushrooms, sauteed in a buttery garlic sauce, were juicy. The baked potato, smothered in sour cream and chives, was delicious.

"A fine mess of groceries," I said to Hugh, keeping as straight a face as I could. My poker playing expression was short lived. "Do you have any idea how long I have waited to say that to you?" I asked. "Years, Hughie," I continued. "I have waited years."

Hugh had been a good friend of Paul's many years before I came on the scene. After he moved to Calgary, he returned infrequently to Montreal or Toronto to conduct business and usually spent an evening with us. When I prepared a dinner, it was always to the best of my ability and all I ever heard from him, was that "dreaded" expression. Since I didn't know him well at that time, I had to hear from mutual friends, that it was the highest compliment he ever gave. I trembled with anticipation at the joy of being able to pay him back. Even without telling Paul, he knew what was coming. Dinner was an unqualified success.

Windemere was another unqualified success. It was a small, compact community with everything necessary close at hand. While the guys played one more early morning golf game, I slept late, treated myself to an extra cup of percolated coffee and read my book without being disturbed. One afternoon I went shopping, something I rarely do because I hate shopping. The clothes that Paul chose for me were always more flattering than the ones I picked out for myself. I let him buy my clothes.

The restaurant that Hugh chose for dinner that evening

was perfect. We looked out over the water while we talked and ate in subdued lighting. A candle flickered on our table. We caught up on each other's lives.

We stayed a few days to enjoy the hospitality but "we were on a mission" and did not want to wear out our welcome. Besides unlike Paul and myself, Hugh was still a working man and business called.

From Windemere we retraced our steps and drove back through Golden before going on to Revelstoke. We stopped in Salmon Arm because the name intrigued us and drove on to Vernon and Kelowna, our ultimate destination in home shopping.

Paul's parents had lived in Kelowna for a few years and had raved about the place. It took us a few passes and a couple of "I wonder ifs" before he found the house his parents had owned. It was a pleasing looking little bungalow, but nothing out of the ordinary and no way to distinguish it from all the other ordinary bungalows on the block.

We both loved the Kelowna area and Paul assured me that it never got too cold. When a bit of snow fell, he said, it never lasted longer than a day or so. "After all," said Paul, "this is the peach growing area of Canada, you know?" We looked at houses and discovered that the houses in the city of Kelowna, where I would insist upon living, were out of our price range, while the houses in the country, where you could not drag me kicking and screaming, were, in our estimation, affordable.

After a couple of days searching, we put Kelowna on our newly formed list of possibilities and continued our drive through the countryside. We were on our way to Vancouver and Victoria, stopping at every other fruit stand to pick up either plump, juicy peaches or giant, near black, Bing cherries. British Columbia, we knew, had lots to offer as far as comfortable living was concerned, but for the time being, we would be traveling as tourists and just enjoying the sights. We knew we could afford this big city lifestyle if we went back to work. Although we intended going back to work someday, it was not in our immediate plans. This was my first trip to British Columbia and I was loving it.

Vancouver was like any large city that we usually got

lost in, so we drove down to the dock. While waiting for the ferry to take us to the garden spot of Canada.....Victoria, Paul got another one of the many shocks that living on the edge usually produces. Every time we boarded a ferry in Europe and were charged a pittance to cross with our vehicle, Paul always announced, to anyone who would listen, and the only one within spitting distance to hear him was me, that the ferry from Vancouver to Victoria was free of charge, paid for by our taxes. He would then go on to sing the praises of Canada and the Canadian government, the Canadian friendliness and so on. Well, you can imagine his horror when he learned that to go the minuscule distance from Vancouver to Victoria with our vehicle and tent trailer would set us back over a hundred dollars. Needless to say, if he was singing the Canadian praises, it was under his breath with every second or third word not being printable. We had no choice. We paid, boarded, crossed and thoroughly enjoyed.

We walked the harbor. We reveled in the splendor of Butchart Gardens in full bloom. We enjoyed the antics of the Beluga whales on display at the seaquarium and since a craft show was going on in the park, we stopped at each booth and watched the artists at work. We did it all in glorious sunshine.

We spent a couple of days touring the coast road on Vancouver Island. We camped in Nanaimo. We hiked. We bicycled into town. We barbecued freshly caught, one and a half pound, salmon. We watched as the talented native people carved totem poles, using long handled curved knives to shave off the layers of wood. We stopped in Duncan hoping to visit an acquaintance that Paul had worked with many years before. He wasn't home. The area was put on our list of possibilities.

Chapter 28

We were back at the ferry dock in Victoria, when Paul, again, had to hang his head in shame and ante up the big bucks to get to Port Angeles in Washington state. Since we enjoyed one last walk around Victoria, it was late afternoon when we boarded the ferry and by the time we arrived in Washington, we were tired and hungry. We decided to stay in a campground near the port. What a rude awakening that was. Sandwiched side by side, our flimsy door hit our neighbor's door whenever we swung it open a bit too wide. We slept fitfully, hearing noises we would not normally have heard had we been apart another foot or two. We choked down a cold cereal breakfast and were on our way as soon as the sun came up.

We rarely stopped in major cities because it was too much trouble trying to park, turn around or finding interesting out of the way sights while pulling a tent trailer and yes, we still got lost. We became irritable every time it happened. For those reasons we bypassed Seattle and Tacoma and headed for Mount Rainier National Park.

From Mount Rainier, we had a perfect view of Mount Saint Helen. Fortunately it was not in an erupting mood as it had been a couple of times since 1980, so we just looked and admired. The weather was bright and crisp and clear. It was a perfect day for hiking. We could see the snowfields well above us. It was a very gentle slope at first and I had no trouble keeping up to Paul. We held hands and talked as we walked.

161

As the incline became steeper I started to lag behind a bit. The higher we got, the steeper it became until I told Paul to go on without me. My breathing was becoming labored and my knee was acting up.

Paul steamed forever upwards, bursting with energy. I plodded along, making sure that one foot went in front of the other without dragging or tripping. I rested often, but I continued. When Paul reached the snow, he stopped, since his footwear was not waterproof. Like the poor, old tortoise, I trudged on. Gradually, I caught up. We frolicked in the snow awhile, pelting each other with snowballs, laughing, and rubbing our faces with the cold, white stuff that we rarely saw up close anymore.

It didn't take us long, going down hill, to get out of the snowfields and back amongst the tiniest of flowers that grew everywhere.....pure white, delicate pink, lilac and dainty purple. Paul stayed close, holding my arm, since it was more difficult going down than up. I could feel my knee slipping and it would have been an easy tumble that would do a lot of damage. We sat on a park bench, near the bottom, just to eavesdrop on one of the funniest conversations we have ever heard.

An elderly gentleman, talking loud and using animated hand gestures, was asking an Oriental family where their cameras were. He was shocked that these people had come to such a beautiful spot with no camera. "I have never seen a Japanese person with no camera," the old man kept insisting.

The younger Japanese man just shrugged his shoulders.

"I will take picture," he said, putting his camera up to his face and making the familiar clicking noise with his mouth, "and send you copy," he volunteered. "Please, give address," the old man continued, keeping his words simple.

The Japanese man again shrugged his shoulders and the old man repeated himself, more slowly this time and with more gestures.

The Japanese man finally broke his silence. "Great man," he said in perfect English, "we live in Tacoma, Washington and we picnic here almost every Sunday." Everyone laughed, including the old man and us. The last we saw of the group, they were headed toward the restaurant. They had offered to take the old gentleman for coffee.

162

Paul and I continued our way down the mountain. We were almost at the bottom, and I could not resist commenting on the fact that "even with a bum leg, I had made it up the mountain as high as he had."

"No," said Paul, "you didn't."

"Oh yes I did," I argued.

"No," said my husband, "remember when you sat down on the bench out of my sight?"

"Yea, so," I answered, my eyes widening and my nostrils starting to flare.

"Well," said my husband, "I ran up another ten feet and came back down to wait for you."

"You son of a bitch." "You knew I would be so proud of myself for catching up, I would mention it," I laughed. "You really are a son of a bitch, you know?"

"Yes," he said, "I know," as he leaned over, kissed me and took a swipe at my glasses with his tongue.

"Son of a bitch," I repeated one more time for emphasis.

We drove across the state and stopped in Yakama just long enough to visit a motorhome dealership, however, we were fairly certain that we would prefer buying a larger motorhome in Europe. We really loved traveling across the puddle.

We drove through Oregon, stopping in LaGrande for the night. We did not stay long, continuing to head southeast.

The next day's drive took us to Boise, Idaho. We arrived late in the day. The heat had become unbearable, over one hundred degrees, and our air conditioner was not working to capacity. We found a KOA campground with a swimming pool. Paul requested a shady spot but none was available. We scanned the facilities and discovered there was not a tree on the property larger than a sapling.

The swimming pool looked extremely inviting. We found a spot, set up and plugged in quickly. We were in our bathing suits and out the door almost before a blink of the eye. We paddled around in the cool, refreshing water for a couple of hours not bothering nor caring about dinner. That could wait. We lounged at pool side talking to whoever was about and there were many. Something mysterious appeared in the distance. We squinted to try and make it out, but to no avail.

Suddenly others jumped from the pool and scattered in

all directions. We did the same, not really knowing why. We watched as a gigantic wall of darkness loomed in the distance. It was heading our way. We sprinted to our tent trailer, working as fast as we could to get it down and bolted, before it hit. We were suddenly caught in a swirling barrier of dust, engulfing us at lightening speed.

Through their window, our neighbor yelled at us to "get that thing down and get in here." We put little tears in the screen scrambling that way, but we closed it up and by the time we got to the adjacent motorhome we were in the full force of the storm. The wind and the dirt took our breath away. Our neighbor pulled us through the door and while we brushed away the residue, a cold beer was handed to each of us before we sat down.

The dust blew away in minutes. It was followed by an ice cold rain that mixed with hail stones the size of golf balls and that too was gone within five minutes. A fine welcome from Boise. Needless to say, this state did not go on our list of possibilities.

Chapter 29

Thanks to the ferocious, unpredictable storm and the kindness of our neighbors, we enjoyed a lively conversation with our hosts. They were retired school teachers and had traveled extensively, thanks to a system that allowed them to work six years and take the seventh year off for enrichment. Although their travels had not matched ours in intensity, they had been to many parts of the world that had captivated us. We had much to share. When the storm was over and a calmer weather pattern prevailed, Paul pulled the picnic table over and set up the barbecue between our homes. The conversation continued over dinner and drinks.

The following day, friends or no friends, we were happy to leave Boise. It was going to be another scorcher, the weather channel predicted. We wanted some shade, a breeze that did not carry half a farmer's plowed field with it and perhaps a spot where we did not have to watch our neighbors barbecuing next to where a dog had recently pooped and the owner had immediately scooped.

With great speed we traveled through Twin Falls, Idaho, Ogden, Utah and Salt Lake City, Utah. It was all of some interest, but not really what we were looking for, even in an overnight rest spot. We needed a home and were determined to find it, no matter where our search took us.

Once we entered Colorado, my husband started looking

a little more seriously. This was ski country. This was worth considering, even if fishing was not readily available, he thought. We visited Grand Junction, where we stopped for the night in a wooded campground. A relief after the openness of Boise. We drove through Delta and Montrose. Even I had to admit, the San Juan National Forest scenery was green and luscious and embracing.

Between Montrose and Durango, right around Silverton, Colorado lost my vote. The weather was still hot, humid and unbearable when we left Montrose. It started with a sprinkling of rain, which we ignored, as we climbed the Red Mountain Pass. The rain never went beyond a light drizzle that the intermittent windshield wiper cleared away, however, near the summit, rain changed to snow.

"Whoa Nellie," I said to Paul, "this is July." In that instant, Colorado, at least that part of the state, took a nose dive and fell off the bottom of my list. The snow amounted to nothing, of course, and we continued on as before, without a hint of a problem, to Durango.

Our campground for a couple of nights was a pleasant bicycle distance from the heart of town. We parked, set up camp, untied and unlocked our bicycles and were off exploring before we met anyone.

The old fashioned country and western town, complete with dance hall and bawdy-house-turned-saloon and eating establishment, added a point or two in Colorado's favor. Even with all its contradictions, we definitely were enjoying this state.

Back at the ranch, I knew that conversation would turn to "what about Colorado as a home base?" and I wanted to clean up before we got too heavily involved. I grabbed the soap, shampoo, toothbrush and paste, clean clothes and off I went to the showers while Paul started dinner. Alone in the shower room, with fifteen or twenty empty stalls, I hummed to my heart's content. This was as close as we had come to making a decision and I was ecstatic. I continued humming until I turned the water off, wrung out my washcloth and looked around for my towel, which I could now visualize, neatly folded, and sitting on the table in our tent trailer. I must be losing my mind, I thought. I have been camping almost non stop every day for a year. How could I have been so stupid as to have forgotten my towel?

Unlocking the door, one eye peeking out and around the room, I peered into a empty hallway. I sprinted naked to the row of sinks, grabbing as many paper towels as I could in the seconds I allotted myself, and raced back to the warmth of my little cubicle. "Thank God they have paper towels," I mumbled. "The place would have been raided if I had been standing naked under some little hot air hand dryer and someone walked it."

Relating the story to Paul, I blamed the entire incident on the hummingbirds, Colorado's state bird, since we had been watching them in total fascinating before I left for the showers. The campground had three hummingbird feeders accommodating eight birds at each feeder at any one time. The feeders, in constant use, had to be refilled at least half a dozen times a day. While the twenty-four stations were occupied, hundreds milled around, jockeying for position, awaiting a free station. When there was a vacancy, many dive bombed and a squabble broke out. They were not the least bit intimidated by anything or anyone and if you stuck out your finger and stood close to the food, they landed. If a bumble bee was feeding at a station, instant mayhem erupted. These multicolored little birds were fascinating to watch, hovering like little helicopters over their food.

A few people, that we met singing around the huge campfire that evening and whose company we enjoyed, invited us to share their barbecue the next night. Our group of six ended up driving into town after dinner. We enjoyed the show, cancan girls and all, a couple of drinks served by buxom ladies dressed in costumes, and snacks. The entertainment was right out of the gay nineties and we couldn't resist, singing along and getting caught up in the hoopla.

We, of course, told of our mission and when one of the couples mentioned that Santa Fe, New Mexico was not worth a visit because it was so artsy fartsy, I knew that Santa Fe would be our next stop. Snow I can do without, artsy, fartsy, is my passion. The next day we were off to Santa Fe. We loved it.

From our campground we commuted into downtown Santa Fe daily and checked the shops, art galleries, museums, cafes and real estate offices. Although staying several miles out of town with few attractions in our immediate vicinity, they did have a little clubhouse accommodating about thirty people and a different video playing every night. We enjoyed a rerun of Cat Ballou.

Santa Fe was a charming place to wander with beautiful pueblo style homes, but much too expensive for us to consider buying property in town. The shops were mostly designers, displaying wood carvings, paintings, glass works and many souvenir shops. Bunches of red hot chili peppers hung everywhere adding to the color and charm of Santa Fe. The houses for sale, pictured in real estate office windows, were way out of our price range, especially since decent paying jobs would be difficult to come by for an outsider.

Our first major stop northward was Colorado Springs. Almost from the minute we arrived we knew that Colorado Springs, Colorado was going to be our home. We fell in love instantly. It was a perfect sized town with movies, shops and golfing. It was clean, reasonably priced, touristy.....everything we wanted and needed, we found. Also for the first time, found something we had experienced only in Europe.....our campground was within walking distance of the downtown shops.

Colorado Springs was where we stayed the longest. We went shopping. We contacted a real estate agent and went looking at homes. Everything we saw was within our price range or close to it. We traveled every street and looked into every store window. I even thought of going back into business, although I didn't have a clue as to what that business would be. We spent one entire day at Garden of the Gods, a desert-like area with gigantic red rocks standing on a tip or on a side or sticking straight up in the air.....amazing stuff.

We kept repeating Colorado Springs and it played like a perfect melody in our minds. We were a thousand miles from my sister in Los Angeles. We were a thousand miles from our friends in Calgary. We were a three hour flight from family and friends in Toronto and Montreal. We were right in the middle of America. It was perfect. Colorado Springs, Colorado. It had a nice ring to it. We could head back to Canada now. We knew the area that we wanted to live in and it had only taken us eleven weeks to find it. We were gushing with enthusiasm.

We stayed on highway 70, detouring around the larger

cities.....Kansas City, St. Louis, Indianapolis, Columbus. In between major cities, we found nothing of interest to stop for, except our overnight stays. Barren campgrounds were in the middle of open fields and we joked that if a tornado hit, we could not see where it would do any damage. There was nothing there for it to hit, except of course, us.

It took a week of steady driving. The night before we landed in Fonthill, Ontario, where Paul's mother lived, we ran into another one of those tent trailer soaking rainstorms. Like drowned rats we arrived on mother's doorstep, grateful for a warm and cozy bed to sleep in, indoor plumbing, central heating and a few of the other luxuries we tended to forget about until they are gone. Once again we had an opportunity to do some laundry, to empty out the tent trailer and allow it to dry, inside and out, in sunshine and most importantly, to talk about our new home, Colorado Springs, Colorado.

All excited about our find, we shared it with our friends in Toronto. They listened patiently to our entertaining and amusing travel experiences of the past twelve weeks, for about ten minutes and then wanted to know "when we were going to stop this nonsense and get back to work." Paul was still giving up the best earning years of his life and if I reopened my store immediately, I would not lose too many of my customers.

Again we listened to the problems they were having at work and to the same problems they were having with their children. We heard about the same renovations they were planning on doing on their homes as soon as they had time and money. We listened. We nodded in agreement and went out and bought plane tickets.

We returned to Europe.

Chapter 30

Despite the fact that our plane left Toronto International Airport one and a half hours late, and without the entourage of the previous trip, we arrived only half an hour late, thanks to a mighty tail wind. It was early morning on the ninth of October 1990 that we landed at Heathrow Airport, west of London. We were equipped with a return ticket dated April 9, 1991, one piece of soft sided luggage each and one bicycle each. Weighing heavily on our shoulders, we promptly put both bikes into storage at the airport.

We took the "tube" into London's main terminal and found the train heading for Bures-LaMarsh. We ended up at a little pub in downtown Bures, whose entire population could be counted on one full set of appendages, and discovered that our friends, whom we assumed would answer their phone if they were within hearing distance, were not at home. We also learned, much to our dismay, there were no taxies available. Carrying our bags, as light as they were, several miles down country lanes, was out of the question. Finishing up his beer, one of the pub regulars, hearing of our woes, offered us a ride. It wasn't too far out of his way, he said, and although he did not know our friends at Paradise Center, he couldn't leave guests to his country, stranded. We offered to pay, he refused. We offered beer money, he gratefully accepted. We were on our way.

We wandered the well manicured acreage hoping our friends, Cees and Hedy, were out tending the plants. No such luck. No one was around and their large country house was dark and forbidding, with all the drapes drawn. We checked our van. The doors were locked. A side window, although closed yielded to the slight pressure of my fingers. Paul hoisted me up. I crawled through the window and opened the rear door for him. We unpacked, made up the bed, changed into jammies and fell asleep on the way down to the pillow. Jet lag had taken its toll. It was nine thirty and pitch black when we heard our friend's car bump the gate and magically, swing open. We scared the hell out of them by turning the lights on in the van.

It took a day or so to recover from a six hour time difference, loss of sleep and to visit with our friends before getting on our way. We retrieved our bicycles from the airport, that were costing us four pounds sterling a day each and drove to Cardiff to visit John and Elen Lewis. We drove back to Otford to see Phil and Andrea Webb and their growing family and it was on the eighteenth day of the same month that we took the Sealink from Newhaven, England to Dieppe, France. We disembarked around midnight. Included in the cost of the ferry ride was two nights of camping at a local campground which we had difficulty locating in the dark.

We stayed the two nights. It gave us an opportunity to do some much needed shopping, boosting France's lagging wine sales. Paul reassembled our bicycles and we attached our newly acquired bike rack to the front of the van. We cleaned our van, inside and out. The bike rack didn't last long since watching the bikes bobbing and weaving in front of our eyes unnerved both of us. The bikes rode indoors with us and were put outdoors at night. During rainy lunches we cursed and swore at them.

We would travel slower on this trip. What we remembered of our previous nine month trip, even with a daily diary, was where we had met and enjoyed the people, we remembered the places vividly. Most towns and villages, no matter how charming and diverse, which we had toured on our own, were just a blur.

Leaving Dieppe, heading south, the first town we

stopped at was Rouen. There were few places in France that we did not fall in love with, but Rouen was particularly charming. It is the fourth largest port, and is located on the banks of the Seine. Leaving our van parked in the harbor, we toured the town, walking almost every street. We visited the centuries old market square where Joan of Arc was burned at the stake, the exact spot marked by a tall, slender cross near the church entrance. We paid our respects in the church and went to the Rue du Gros Horloge, a lively pedestrian street, which led through a magnificent archway to the clock, a 1390 belfry, a Renaissance pavilion and the Louis XV fountain. The courthouse had been restored and the stained glass in the twelfth century cathedral was brilliant with the sun beaming through from behind.

Two hours of driving southeast and we set up camp in Maisons Laffitte, just one short train ride outside of Paris. It was a huge, sprawling campground that accommodates hundreds so we used our bicycles for the first time wanting to check it all out. We inspected the country of origin stickers on the motorhomes and caravans to see where people were from and discovered few were from English speaking countries. Most were from other districts in France.

Paris is for lovers and walkers and we were both. We strolled the Champs-Elysee and watched the artists painting and selling their wares. We walked up to the second landing of the Eiffel Tower. It was so cloudy, we did not go higher. We would have seen nothing from the third landing since it was above the clouds.

We bought some Brie cheese, a very small slice of blue cheese, a bottle of red wine and a fresh baguette and had lunch on the grass in full view of the Tower. We shared a large apple that I had in my knapsack.

We visited the museum Invalides and walked around the Arc de Triomphe, nearly wiping ourselves out of existence dodging several lanes of traffic to get close. On another day toured the Grand and Petit Palais. Having had enough walking that day, we watched a show on the grounds at the Tokyo Palace. Kids were doing some fabulous stunts on skates and skateboards. There was lots of music and tap dancing and a mime strolling around, saying nothing and everything.

172

We spent one morning walking the Jardin Des Tuileries, stopping to admire each statue and spent an unbelievable afternoon at the Louvre. I have seen the Mona Lisa, Venus de Milo, the Sphinx and the Seated Scribe and all within touching distance. That same day we walked to and through Notre Dame and by the time we headed toward our train, it was night. We watched the lights of Paris from our window and it was magical. Paris is for lovers and walkers and we were both.

We needed a day in the campground to recuperate. We slept late, ate a hardy breakfast and read the latest issue of the International Herald Tribune from cover to cover. We biked the campground and took a long walk into town to pick up freshly baked croissants and a baguette. Day old baguettes were used as baseball bats, weapons or thrown into soup as filler, nothing more. We enjoyed our walk in the tiny community that was overrun with campers.

Once back on the road, it took only a couple of hours to drive to Versailles. We spent part of the day in the house enjoying an official guided tour and walked the gardens on our own, guidebook in hand. We drove on to Chartres where we intended spending the night and visit the three star town in the morning, but the campground was closed for the season. We drove on.

The pity was, we were driving through some beautiful areas that we could not really appreciate in a downpour. It was a perfect time to visit Chateau de Clos-Luce in Amboise. Clos-Luce is where Leonardo Da Vinci, painter, sculptor, architect, engineer, spent the last three years of his life, painting and working on his many inventions. The chateau turned museum was filled with scale models of his machines, based on his sketches and put together by I.B.M.

Leaving Amboise, we were back into some familiar territory and when we arrived at the campground in Chinon, we were surprised to see our mustachioed friend, David Dyers. He recognized us right about the same time that we spotted him. With ready made friends, our need to slow down and the small, intriguing, shop filled side streets waiting for the steady hum of our bicycles tires, several days passed most pleasantly.

From the campground we had an unobstructed view of the chateau ruins up on the hill. On the day that we didn't feeling like riding around on our bikes, we took a walk up to the summit and discovered that our chateau was composed of three fortresses separated by deep moats. It was tough walking but we were pros when it came to rummaging around ruins. We walked the garden area, much of it uninteresting and out of season. We sat on benches looking down at our campground and enjoyed the scenery.

That same day we walked into town so Paul could get a haircut. His French was more than adequate and he had no idea what he had told the barber, but he came out looking very much like the proverbial cue ball.

"How could he do this to me?" he lamented. "Look at me, I look awful," his voice sounding mournful.

"It'll grow back, Baby," I reassured him. "It'll grow back, stop worrying." Oh, what that barber did to him!

On David's recommendation, and since we were headed in that direction anyway, we went to St. Maure en Touraine. To thank the allies for their help during the second world war, camping with electricity, toilet and shower block with hot water, was available free of charge. We had to see for ourselves. It was true. Camping for about twenty vehicles, along with everything else promised, was there. The parking lot/campground was paved and although not aesthetically pleasing, was certainly available and free. Since it was the end of October and not really camping weather in France, there were several vacant spots to choose from. The maximum stay was three days. I don't know if anyone ever enforced the three day maximum or the No Germans Allowed rule, but we stayed overnight. There was not much to see or do in the area. We bicycled all the back streets. We read a lot. We wrote letters and played a couple of hands of cribbage. Since I lost the games that afternoon, I had to wander the town and find an open bakery. I had to 'spring' for dessert. Finding a fattening, cream filled, gooey, finger licking treasure was no problem. I think all bakeries in France stay open twenty four hours a day, seven days a week for just such emergencies.

Late October, 1990 was similar to late October of the previous year. The storms were arriving and doing their best to batter us. It did not make for pleasant traveling or sightseeing. We stopped in Valencay for market day and found the prices for fresh produce very high. We bought a few necessities anyway. We spent that night camping in Bourges and visited the cathedral, famous for its five doorways. We picnicked by the roaring river.

On the ride to Autun, the winds were so strong, driving was very uncomfortable. Our van was bouncing all over the road. We had a pleasant evening in the campground. Patty and Joanne from South Africa were the first English speaking people we ran into since leaving Chinon.

The capital of the Burgundy region, Dijon, was our port in a storm. It was an exceptionally lively, university and business center and considered the heart of Europe. We wandered the pedestrian, historical parts of town. We visited the Fine Arts Museum and, of course, toured the mustard plant. Why else would anyone go to Dijon, but for the mustard. Some of it we toured on foot and much of the outer perimeter by bicycle. Just as we were heading back to the campground, the rain started and continued all night. We left the next morning.

It was a short drive to Beaune, the wine trading center of Burgundy. It was in Beaune, in a little shop just off the much photographed courtyard, that we found a much sought after treasure. We purchased a vrac. My French-English dictionary describes vrac as "in bulk." What we bought was a brown, plastic, barrel shaped, container. We could now buy our wine "in bulk." Our prayers were answered. Our vrac held one gallon of the most flavorful wine we could find. We usually tasted everything the wine maker was putting out that year, before we purchased. By the time we finished sampling, we rarely had any idea what we were buying, but it was French wine, how bad could it be?

That night in Beaune we treated ourselves to a pizza, French style, in a little bistro just off the town square. The crust was delicate and delicious. The pizza, unlike anything we had ever tasted, was cut into four portions. Each quarter was smothered with tomato sauce, cheese, mushrooms and green peppers. Each section also had a generous sprinkling of a different seafood.....mussels, baby shimp, and two kinds of clams. C'est magnifique.

With no open campgrounds in the area, we spent the night in the town square with several other campers and slept little. Tooting horns, cars backfiring or perhaps gunfire, screeching brakes combined with early morning setting up of market day, did a number on us. We got up feeling that we had never slept at all.

The following day we drove through heavy rains, sometimes mixed with snow, to Aix les Bain. We camped alone in a park by a lake taking advantage of the quiet and the smooth-as-glass water. The next day was Sunday and everything was closed, including the laundromat and my beloved thermal baths, two things that would have made our lives more pleasant that day. We were moving quickly towards the Mediterrean because of the weather. We were not equipped for these heavy cold snaps. We had a heater in the van, but I did not feel it was safe to sleep with it on. On those exceptionally cold nights we bundled up in our track suits and snuggled closer than usual.

We left Aix, drove past Chambery and Grenoble and stopped in Gap (very high Alps) to do some laundry. That night was so cold, our barbecue would not work properly. We threw the meat, potatoes, vegetables, bouillon cubes and lots of wine into a large pot and cooked indoors. Dinner heated up our van nicely.

We awoke to frost covering everything, including our van. We drove a ribbon of road, woods on both sides without many places nor many reasons to stop, until we reached the Grand Canyon of Verdon. Not having seen the Grand Canyon in the United States, we had nothing to compare it to, however, the view was splendid, the sun had come out and was warm. We enjoyed the drive. Our day's driving ended in Draguignan. Once again we tried calling our friends, the Unsworths. They were not at home. We did not linger.

The following day we visited Grasse, a small town surrounded by fields of flowers. This little community is the hub of the perfume industry and the smell was intoxicating. Before driving down to the Mediterrean, we stopped in Cannes. Since this too was our second visit, we walked down to the harbor and enjoyed a relaxing lunch sitting on a bench, basking in the sunshine. That night we camped in the National Forest just outside Antibes. It was so peaceful.

Chapter 31

Before walking down the steep embankment to the Mediterrean, we toured the chateau in the old Roman city of Nice. Very little remained of the fortress so we did not stay long.

Unlike the white, sandy beaches in America, this beach was blanketed by pebbles and tiny sharp rocks, that pockmarked the soles of our tennis shoes, even at the water's edge. We took off our socks and shoes and hobbled into the icy water trying desperately to avoid cutting or bruising ourselves. It was a treat just being able to dip our toes in the Med, but toes was as far as we dared venture.

Once back in our van, we drove the stretch of road that snaked along the coastline. It is famous for its spectacular view of the deep azure water that is dotted with small, uninhabited rock islands. It was in the distance, and just for a split second, that we saw a clearing in the woods. Rather enthused about our find, we headed towards it. We could not resist the opportunity to enjoy another one of our relaxing lunches, perhaps spending part of the day hiking and, if it was private enough, stay over, wild camping.

We continued our driving, always looking ahead hoping for another peek at the spot. We marveled at the splendid surrounding view, with mere glimpses of our lunch spot, along the way. Our approach continued. As we neared, we realized to our dismay, that the glade was already occupied. Since the road zigzagged along the coast, we caught only the occasional glance at the couple that was occupying the coveted spot. Each sighting, however, sent a chill through my body.

Their car was parked and fully visible in the clearing. A table had been set for a meal in the woods.....checkered tablecloth and all. The trunk of the car was open. A portly looking, middle-aged man sat at the table wearing what appeared to be a business suit.....tie, bib over his shirt and holding a fork and knife upright, primed and ready to plunge the utensils into a juicy slab of beef the instant it was presented.

She wore a red printed house dress, much of it covered by a white-and-red checkered apron, matching the tablecloth perfectly. Madame was serving his nibs his lunch. We watched as she kept going back to the open trunk of the car. She extracted a bottle of wine, a picnic hamper and finally, when there was nothing left to pull out or accomplish for her companion, a chair for herself.

I watched dumbfounded. "Did people really do this!" I said to Paul, my nose wrinkling up like a bad smell had just invaded our van. This was a clearing in the woods, complete with trees, dead leaves, spiders, creepy crawling and slithery things. My husband then informed me that this was the way he would like his meals served from now on. He would 'spring' for the apron.

I asked him casually if his last wife had served him that way. I also suggested that his next wife might be willing to serve him his meals that way; however, if it was his present wife that he was talking to, there was no way in hell that I would be donning an apron anytime soon and serving him his meals in the woods.....arsenic, maybe.....toadstools, perhaps.....his dinner.....I don't think so.

In the end, we did not stop on this road. That "picnic in the woods" scene did, however, cause many a smile as we continued our travels through our beloved France. During every major, and occasionally minor, shopping spree Paul took the opportunity to ask if I wanted an apron.

It didn't take long driving this route to get to St. Jean Cap Ferrat, home of the rich and reclusive. We parked in a grocery store parking lot, pulled out our bicycles and drove the path running high above the water's edge. We were hobnobbing with the rich and biking in areas where the houses and view was worth millions. We felt secure. The sheer cliff, plummeting to rocks below, was blocked off by heavy chain link fencing. This was the laps of luxury. We lunched in view of the splendor that we had driven and biked.

We drove through Monaco, not stopping. We did not want to insult these people a second time by parking our motorhome on their streets. Their parking lots restricted motorhomes with signs that we had ignored on our previous visit. We continued on to Menton, once again, back in France. Following the international camping signs, we ended up in a campground so far above the city that we instantly thought of nose bleeds, when our ears popped. There was no way we could bicycle or walk down to the town. We toured the surrounding village of Gorbio that must have been rooted in that spot forever. The streets were cobblestone. Burros, carrying baskets laden with firewood, fruits and vegetables or a small child were everywhere, being led by their owners. We had slipped into a previous century without knowing it. The apple-cheeked young ones smiled. The older folks, their faces lined with deep grooves, stared, expressionless as we passed. The campground was nearly vacant.

The following morning we drove slowly down the precipitous streets to Menton, toured the town with its quaint avenues, market place and fairly modern shops. A brace of camping vehicles, similar in size and shape to ours, were parked in the harbor. We approached and were immediately invited by Jean and Bill Higgs from the front van and Thelma and Dick Williams from the second van, to join them as they sat on deck chairs in the sand. Both couples were from Britain and had met that morning. We fit right in, taking up residence at the end of the line. We were home.

We played cards. We played scrabble. We played cribbage. We congregated in Dick and Thelma's van for a pre-dinner cocktail. Jean and I each brought a tray of hoeure d'ouvers and Paul barbecued marinated chicken wings on the beach. Our favorite dinner was new to our English friends.

Since we paid for the use of the facilities at the boat club, no one seemed to mind that we had set up residence right beside the beach. We had steamy hot showers, spotlessly clean change rooms and flush, American-style, toilets available to us. Several days went by before we felt any urgency to move along. We were perfectly comfortable and it was costing us a pittance.

When we were ready to migrate south, and we seemed to get this strange urge as a flock, we planned on heading in the same direction. We made plans to reunite on the dock in the heart of San Remo, Italy. We formed a convoy, moved out together but traveled at different speeds. Since our vehicles were all high tops, we had no trouble spotting each other in San Remo and congregated at one end of the large parking lot. We left our vehicles unattended, walked to the harbor, the shopping streets in town and found our campground up on the hill, just off the main street.

The free campground that we remembered from the previous year was now charging a mini-fortune and offering nothing in the way of decent facilities. Also etched on my brain was that midnight train that screamed its presence as it thundered by our door. We lunched, strolling around the dock. When we returned to our vans the police had covered our windshields with stickers that prohibited us from parking on the dock. It took hours, warm soapy water, fingernails and finally razor blades to scrape away their admonishment completely.

Totally demoralized and with our tails between our legs, we returned, in convoy, to Menton. The boat club manager greeted us with a welcoming smile and an energetic wave when we all pulled into line. "He missed us," he told Paul, the only one of the six who spoke French.

Early the next morning, after exchanging addresses and teary hugs, it was time to be on our way. By late afternoon we were back in Lerici, parked close to the water. It had been a long, slow ride, but we were up and out early the next morning, stopping in Viareggio for breakfast. We drove nonstop through Pisa, Livornia (Leghorn to the English speaking folks) and Grossesto. We spent some time in Porto San Stefano but could not find camping. That night we parked in Lover's Lane in Civitavecchia. It was quiet enough. I know Italians like to think of themselves as lovers, but you could not have proven it by this group. At least no one tried to rent our camper by the hour and by ten o'clock we had Lover's Lane all to ourselves. We slept undisturbed, until the wee hours of the morning, when noisy dock workers arrived.

After a morning of tromping the fascinating remnants of Ostia Antica, a complete Roman town, we picnicked in the restored amphitheater. By early afternoon we were walking the adjacent ancient town, Ostia. The poor of the region still live there, amongst the ruins.

We proceeded towards Rome. We did some grocery shopping before finding our campground in the outskirts of the city. We would stay awhile. We wanted to see Rome properly. Within hours of our arrival we had met half the campground. It was filled almost to capacity.....a Canadian artist and his wife.....a French couple with two small children....a few Brits.....and a couple from America, Amy and Norman Prestup. They had a large cardboard sign posted in their motorhome window that read "English books to trade." We spent that evening swapping books and, as my husband liked to call it, lies.

Amy and Norman had been in Rome, awaiting mail from their home in New Jersey, for over two weeks and they were sick of the place. They did not like Rome and since they looked like the typical hippy couple from the sixties, I assumed that they did not like large cities. I was prepared to love Rome. How could you not, I wondered.

"What do you think of Paris?" I asked Amy.

"I loved it," she confessed.

"How about London?" I asked.

"That's ok," she commented.

I continued the quiz, naming many of the cities we had enjoyed. They loved Madrid. They loved Amsterdam and Berlin and most other cities that I mentioned.

It turned out they loved most of the cities in Europe, large, small and every size in between. They also adored Singapore and Hong Kong but especially loved the smaller places of the world like Bali and Macchu Picchu and had been to every province in China and Japan. Norman had enjoyed one vacation of trekking in Nepal. Their travels, it seems, had been endless.

"Why don't you like Rome?" I asked rather tenuously this time.

181

"Well," said Amy not mincing words, "within five minutes of being in Rome, we were walking through the park and there was some guy with his pants down around his ankles, shitting in the park." "Did I really need that?" she asked, screwing up her face, showing contempt.

The next day, Paul and I were off to Rome. I didn't care what Amy had said, I wanted to love Rome. Within five minutes of being in Rome, Paul and I were walking through the same park and there was, I must presume, the same guy, doing exactly what Amy had described to us the night before." "Did I really need that?" I asked myself.

My diary for that day, Friday, November 23, 1990 read, "Not a charming city. Dirty and unfriendly. We have decided that if you don't have to eat, sleep, buy gasoline or use a bathroom, Rome is the place to be."

The following morning started with a fender-bender right in front of our eyes. One car was stopped in the middle of the roadway for no reason that we could see and another car plowed into the back of him.....backup lights are an option, remember. On the bus going into the city, my foot was mangled in the bus door. With the help of that distraction, Paul's pocket was picked of about twenty dollars by some dark looking fellow that was crowding him. He felt nothing. He knew something had happened only when he looked down and found the instructions back to our campground on the floor of the bus. He checked. His pockets were empty, picked cleaner than bones by a starving scavenger on its prey.

It was Saturday and the banks were closed but we managed to change some Canadian currency at a foreign exchange office. The money had been safely tucked away in a security pouch under my clothes, and it was exchanged at a rate that could only be considered highway robbery. The day was not a total disaster, but it did leave us with a bad taste in our mouths.

Back at the campground, we discussed our day with Amy and Norman. All Norman could advise was, "have absolutely nothing of value in your pockets." "All I have in my pockets," said Norman, "is Kleenex." "Nothing, nothing else." "I have lost so many dirty Kleenex's you can't imagine," he continued. From that minute on, Paul heeded his advice.

182

Had we been Catholic, that Sunday would have been a thrill of a lifetime. Paul and I, standing in St. Peter's Square with throngs of tourists, were blessed by Pope Jean Paul II. We spent the rest of the day visiting the Egyptian exhibit and the Pio-Clementino exhibit at the Vatican Museum and then went through the magnificent Sistine Chapel with a herd of people, most of whom had been in St. Peter's Square with us. There were still parts of the Chapel that were being restored but the 'frescoes were magnifico.' And, for the first time in my life, I stood at Death's Door. No, I wasn't sick. The beautifully hand carved door, one of the entrances to the Vatican, is called Porto della Morte. Each square depicts a different death.....one by hanging, one by stabbing, one by drowning.....charming.

That night I mailed postcards and letters to my Jewish family and friends, telling them about being blessed by the Pope. "It might not help," I said to most of them, "but it can't hurt." To my sister Mona, who followed each step of our journey, I wrote, "I got blessed by the Pope today, what did you do?" Actually, Catholic or not, it was a thrilling experience. After several days of touring the Coliseum, the Forum and the Palatine, visiting the old city and entering every open church, museum and gift shop, we were not unhappy to be on our way.

It did not seem to matter how many accidents we witnessed, and they were too numerous to count on both hands, we did not get used to it. We spent so much time on the road with these maniacs that we worried. On a two lane road, it was not unusual to have two or even three cars passing you, all going around at the same time. When a two lane road became a five lane road, with our van hugging the ditch, it was not fun driving. When it was raining, it added to our misery. The next day was one of those particularly miserable drives. We ended up going through parts of Naples, which my diary describes in many unmentionable words. We did not stop anywhere since we were in an industrial and rundown part of town. We ended up driving directly to Pompeii.

We found our friends, the Prestups, at the campground where we had prearranged to meet. We pulled into the vacant site beside them. We had trouble leveling our camper and I really wanted a fence on one side so I could hide some hand laundry, that I was planning on doing, from the world. We moved our camper to the spot across from them, grabbed a few munchies and a bottle of wine to share and joined them in their camper. The VW LT40 was much roomier and more comfortable than ours. An hour or so later, engrossed in conversation, a thunderous crack startled us. We watched in horror as a huge tree split in two and thudded to the ground in the campsite that we had moved from and that now stood vacant. Maybe getting blessed by the Pope did do some good after all.

Mount Vesuvius erupted in 79 A.D. and successive layers of ash, dust, lava and rock completely buried the city. It was an incredible example of a Roman town from the first century A.D. preserved, intact, cadavers and all. We strolled the ruins of Pompeii the entire day and were fascinated, especially when we came across bodies that were now encased in glass, forever on the spot where they were found. Most victims were in a crouched position, their hands covering their mouths, trying to save their burning lungs from what must have been a tortuously slow death.

By the end of the day, we had seen and walked much and were ready for a quiet, reflective night in the campground. We returned to the ruins of Pompeii the next day, not wanting to miss anything. A cold rain started but we continue touring, trying to steer clear of the slow moving rivulets. At that point, we were, as the expression goes "not happy campers."

Part of our unhappiness in Italy, besides the dirt, crazy drivers, foot mangling, accosted by mangy looking urchins and getting our pockets picked, was being tired of being taken advantage of and spending so much money unnecessarily. We were fleeced "officially" everywhere we went and Pompeii had not been an exception The admission ticket said three thousand liras, over which ten thousand liras had been stamped. We did not want to miss Pompeii, so we paid as we had done so many times before.

The town of Amalfi would have been an interesting place to visit but motorhomes were not permitted to stop, except to fill their gas tanks. The drive along the Amalfi coast was breathtaking. Through a mixture of rain and hail we drove on to Ravello, where we managed to set up camp in the town's municipal parking lot. Part of the lot was covered by a tin roof so we were able to camp in relative security. Not even a dog would be out on a night like that. No one bothered us.

That night we treated ourselves and the Prestups to one of our favorite hot libations.....a Lamumba, the making of which was taught to us by our friends, Don and Marjorie Jones in Spain. It was a mixture of hot milk, rum and chocolate. I have no idea how many we each drank, but we were in bed before eleven o'clock and slept very, very soundly, even though hail stones, the size of peas, machine gunned the tin roof.

From Ravello, we drove the sixty or so kilometers to Paestum and when they tried for ten thousand liras stamped over a ticket marked three thousand, we called it quits. All four of us turned around together and walked away. We had no idea that we would all be fed up at exactly the same time. We ended up taking our own tour, walking the outside perimeter of the ruins. We saw and experienced almost as much as if we had gone inside. We used our guidebooks to point out where the sixth century Basilica was located. We also were able to spot the Temple of Neptune and the exact location of the Amphitheater. We enjoyed our walk and used the money we saved to buy ice cream. It was a delicious treat.

In Paestum, we parted. We promised to meet up around Christmas time in Athens, Greece and made sure that our camping books had the exact same campground available and that the one we chose was open all year round.

The Prestups headed to Sicily while we drove to the east coast of Italy, stopping only long enough to spend an afternoon exploring Castellano Grotto, a cave filled with colorful stalagmites and stalactites. We toured the countryside for a couple of hours to see the Trulli houses. We made up our own fairy tales as we went along because these houses could easily have been occupied by elves and ogres, or nothing that stood over three feet tall.

We drove down to the dock and waited.

Chapter 32

We sailed all night on the Lydia from Brindisi, Italy to Corfu, Greece and although we looked forward to being able to afford the necessities of life, like food, camping and gas, it was a long and uncomfortable voyage.   We were still on board when we learned that all the campgrounds were closed for their winter season and we would have to wild camp. This fact no longer upset me since we were now well seasoned, possibly a little overripe, travelers, and from all we had heard, wild camping in Greece was acceptable.   We did, however, take an extra long, steaming hot shower, just in case it was some time before we found another one.

By the time we disembarked, did some banking, grocery shopping in Corfu City and found a camping spot in a park, just off the dock in Bentsis, I had a rip roaring headache and missed the first bit of warm sunshine. While scouting the immediate area, Paul left me resting in the van with the windows open and all the drapes drawn. I slept fitfully and was awakened by a distant pounding that, for the first time, was not in my head. Before I could sit up, I sighed deeply trying to get my bearings. I lay there listening to the steady rhythm of the beat. When I was finally able to raise myself onto one elbow, I watched as a fisherman, loaded with octopus, pounded his catch. Each small octopus, weighing a couple of pounds, had to be slammed onto the wooden dock, forty or fifty times, "to break up all the cartilage," the fisherman had confided to Paul who eventually relayed the message to me. This was an endless process that I watched with dumbfounded fascination. There was not one unnecessary movement. The arm was raised with the octopus' body held tightly and slammed down on the dock. The catch was rubbed, rotated and picked up to have the process repeated. Over and over, the fisherman performed his duties as the hours evaporated.

When the headache and fatigue from watching the activities overtook me, I lay down again, hopefully to oblivion. I awoke late in the afternoon, and mercifully, the headache had subsided. Weakened and still a bit nauseous, I had some tea to settle my stomach. Paul heated up some homemade soup for us. It was delicious and with some fresh bread, cut into thick slabs, it was all we needed to stave off starvation.

After dinner we went for a walk   Earlier that day, Paul discovered we were camping close to a park with paths and benches and where young people congregated to be mesmerized by the water and the distant mountains, to hold hands and perhaps talk of their future. Most locals, young and old, smiled and nodded at us, but made no attempt at conversation. That night we slept peacefully and undisturbed.

The next day was warm and the sun, once again, graced us with her presence.   Unnoticed the day before, I was now able to survey the snow capped mountains of Albania in the distance.

The Island of Corfu was small enough to tour in a few days and large enough to have some interesting nooks and crannies. The people, particularly the young ones working in the shops, were friendly and took every opportunity to speak English with us.   This was the flavor we had missed in Italy. While Paul always made an effort to learn a word or a phrase in every country we visited, here it was reciprocated.   Even I managed to learn words like parakalo (please) and efkaristo (thank you) while I was still in the country.

We talked with shopkeepers and people on the street, some local and some tourists. The locals wanted us to visit their favorite parts of the Island and took the time to give us instructions in infinite detail. Our maps became their coloring books with circles and arrows and routes marked off in the different colored magic markers that we kept handy.

We went looking for the birth home of Prince Philip of England, but never found it and no one seemed to know where it was located. I don't think we could have gotten close to it anyway. We enjoyed the looking and searching out of the interesting things on the Island, however, this was not the busy season and many of the museums, tourist information offices and shops were closed for the winter.

On two of the nights, the downpour with a bit of hail thrown in for good measure, was so strong we had to batten down the hatches. Leaks around the side windows that were not there previously suddenly reared their ugly heads. Paul sealed them at the first opportunity, but during that first storm we held towels in place and wrung them out regularly through the hours of rain.

On one of those rainy day occasions we drove into Corfu city for an authentic souvlaki dinner and since Presumed Innocent with Harrison Ford and Raul Julia was playing at the theater, we couldn't resist. The movie was shown in English with Greek subtitles and we loved it.

The morning we left via the ferry to Igamenitsu, the sun was shining on Corfu and before landing on mainland Greece, a few hours later, it started to rain.

Although the weather was turning nasty, it did not stop us from heading inland, hopefully to better climes. On the drive through the plains we experienced a steady stream of rain and when we started to climb the one thousand seven hundred and five foot Katara Pass, it worsened. The higher we climbed the worse it became until rain changed to snow. The snow became heavier as we approached the summit. Fortunately the road had just been cleared and we caught up to the plow. It was directly ahead of us for the last several miles or we might not have made it. We stayed a safe distance behind it.

There was approximately two feet of blowing snow and, thankfully, the plow had banked the side so we were not going to fall off the edge of the world, but it was very frightening. Although Paul was an experienced driver on ice and snow, thanks to the many years of enduring Canadian winters, our van was not equipped for this type of torture. (Frankly neither was

188

I.) With the plow still in the lead, we slid over the top. Our van was the only vehicle, other than the plow, on the road that entire trip.

We started our descent and went down the other side of the mountain exactly as we had climbed. Paul must have been unnerved because, as unaccustomed as he was to playing "follow the leader" he drove slowly and stayed behind the plow as long as he could. Gradually, somewhere along the way, the snow lessened, changed to rain and, at the bottom, just sprinkled.

By dark, we had made it to Meteora. The campground was open but it seems we were the only tourists foolish enough to be camping this time of year. Several old men sat around a partially painted wooden table with a half empty retsina bottle in the middle. One of the old men gladly took our money for a night's camping and gave our passports a cursory glance before getting back to conversation and drinking. So far, we were not impressed with the Greek campgrounds, but after a week of wild camping on Corfu, we desperately needed a shower. The night was too cold. We would wait for daylight and, hopefully, sunshine.

The following morning we went looking for a shower. We tried to open the door of what looked like a large, sparkling clean, toilet block. It was locked. Scouring the grounds for someone in charge, we found the owner.

"No," he said, "that toilet block is closed for the season, the open one is around the corner. There is a shower there also."

Again, we found ourselves wandering the empty campground. Frustrated with our efforts, we opened every door that looked like a possibility. We could not find it. I went back to find the person in charge again. Totally annoyed with my lack of understanding of simple instructions the owner/manager/groundskeeper, or whatever the hell he was, stomped in front of us and opened the door to a room we never would have dreamed of opening. We were stunned.

He pointed to the hose, coming directly from a spout on the wall in the laundry room. It was like walking into the freezer section of a refrigerator. One side of the room was bare and the other side contained a large washer, dryer and laundry tub.

"Plenty hot water," he practically spat the words at us.

Wild camping had taken its toll and we desperately needed a shower. We returned to our camper, gathered up towels, soap, shampoo and the rest of the paraphanalia one needs for the task and trudged back to the laundry room. The hot water tank was solar heated and that part of Greece, we surmised, had not seen the sun in about a decade. We stripped, took turns hosing each other down, and washed and rinsed our hair in fifteen seconds flat. We dried ourselves off, rubbing madly in an attempt to get some circulation back into our skin. Unfortunately, a large corner of my favorite pink bath towel ended up being dragged through a small puddle that had formed on the concrete floor, and I just couldn't dry myself fast enough. We worked at a feverish pace before pneumonia set in and put slippers back on damp feet that, in a matter of minutes, had turned blue and achy. We raced back to our camper and I cranked up the heater. It was days before we thawed out completely.

The sights of Meteora were right out of a James Bond movie with monasteries built hundreds of feet in the air and perched atop mountain peaks. Each stone, each piece of wood, each nail had to be hoisted by basket. The cloisters were built in the fifteenth and sixteenth centuries, but steps had been cut into the rock face and there was now a modern road serving the main ones.

When my mind wanders to Meteora, my thoughts are torn between the fascinating monasteries and the shower scene that was right out of a prison movie, with sadistic guards hosing down prisoners in solitary confinement with ice cold water. I couldn't wait to get out of that hellish campground.

The rest of the day was spent driving. We drove through plains and mountains and camped, again in the wilderness, just outside Delphi. Since this was not a winter resort area, the Greeks are used to foreigners camping wherever they can. They were very tolerant and gracious, since the campgrounds were closed, but Paul and I craved a long, luxurious, steaming, hot shower. The uniqueness of the region was worth foregoing many of our creature comforts, but there was a limit and we were tired of sponge bathing in the van.

Everywhere we went, we met up with other tourists,

(most of whom had rented cars and were wise enough to be staying in local hotels or bed and breakfast pansyions) who recommended places that we "must see." The monastery at Ossios Loukas was one of those places. The mosaics were fabulous and a masterpiece of Byzantine art. We camped close by that night. We found a secluded spot under an ancient, gnarled olive tree that cast witch-like shadows on the ground. We were on an old road just outside Ossios Loukas, where we were certainly getting our fill of wild camping.

The following morning, after vacating our under the tree camping spot, the drive from Kiriaki to Elikonas took over two hours. It was a distance of about twenty miles. We had no idea how we had ended up on the path, but it was a road that had been deserted by the goats because it was too steep. Elikonas was a ghost town. It had recently been deserted and all the houses stood vacant for no apparent reason that we could see. Structurally they appeared sound and certainly capable of withstanding whatever the weather threw their way. It was one of the mysteries in our life. We just kept going. Why we kept going was another one of those mysteries of life. We saw so few people, it was a bit unnerving.

From Elikonas to Livadia we were on a switch back road no wider than a cow path and ended up on top of a mountain having to carefully make our way down. We suddenly found ourselves at, what seemed to be, the end of the line. The thought of retracing the steps that had taken us hours to accomplish, was unthinkable. We could neither turn around, nor back up and the road kept getting narrower and narrower. Paul could not get out of the van because he would have fallen down the mountain (it being a British van) and I could not get out because I was pressed up against the mountainside. Inching our way in first gear, we wound our way around and around the mountain. As we descended, the road started to widen and gradually became a two track road.

We could not believe that this had been an actual road but it was. I do not believe, however, that the road was meant to accommodate a motorized vehicle of any size. It was probably meant for a shepherd in a donkey-drawn wagon, herding goats. We were grateful to have made it. That night we found lovely woods to camp in and celebrated by finishing the bottle of ouzo. We would not overtax ourselves on the drive the next day.

We drove to Loutraki, famous for their public mineral baths. Famous, of course, when they're open. They were closed for the season, as was, you guessed it, the campground. We parked with several other campers on the dock. There were so many bathers in the water that we decided to dig out our bathing suits and join them. This was how we learned that the warm mineral springs that made this area famous, emptied into the large body of water surrounding the dock. It wasn't a bathtub or the hot shower that we longed for, but it was cleansing and soothing and for the moment, it would have to do.

Chapter 33

It took several days to tour The Peloponnese. Most of it, unfortunately was done in a cold mist. When the rain was a sprinkle, we donned our bright yellow slickers and walked the confines of the archaeological sites, drove the coast to Gargalia and strolled the fruitful environs of the port town of Pylos. Methoni, our next stop, had an impressive Venetian fort that sprawled beside the beach but we had no sooner started our excursion, when the heavens opened up. We didn't stay. We camped close by and left early the next morning for Kalamata. We needed a bank and a super sized grocery store to restock our larder. One of the side dishes of an extra special Sunday morning treat was the black, sour Kalamata olives, that went along with lox, cream cheese, red Bermuda onions and bagels, so I was also going for a taste from my youth. Everything we needed and wanted, we found. Paul would have to acquire a taste for the black beauties that we purchased by the pound, but I loved the olives.

Just about the time we checked on the available ferries from Gythion, in The Peloponnese, to Crete we heard about an earthquake that leveled parts of Sicily. We hoped that our friends, the Prestups, had escaped it. We were concerned, because we knew that they would be leaving Sicily about this time, or perhaps even a little later.

We headed towards Athens. We did not drive too far off

the beaten path to visit the ancient ruins of Mystra, built on the side of a hill. Even though it was raining, we knew that we could not miss this opportunity. We assumed we would not be back in this regions again. We decided on a self guided tour using our ever handy guidebooks. By the time we climbed to the castle on the top of the hill, above the clouds, the rain had stopped.

The hike, forever upwards, took two and a half hours but each step was one more footprint into ancient history. With each few yards there was another reason to stop, a thirteenth century fresco, a small, intimate museum where only a few people could enter at one time, a collection founded by Gabriel Millet and displayed in the old bishops palace. We stopped at the Brontocheion Monastery, where within its walls are the great churches from the thirteenth and fourteenth centuries.

Just as we arrived at the ruins of the castle on the mount, the clouds dispersed and we could see the lay of the land in three hundred and sixty degrees. It was a most impressive view of the ravine facing Mount Taygetos. We sat on a large, flat rock and emptied our knapsack. While Paul checked the countryside with our binoculars, I spread out the food stuffs, bottled water and some paper napkins. We stretched out our legs and relaxed after the long trek. We enjoyed the view, along with cheese, pate, crackers and a beer that was always nestled in the bottom of my sack in case of an emergency.

Our way down was done as slowly as we had climbed. Taking an alternate route, we stopped at a fifteenth century monastery, now inhabited by a few nuns engaged in delicate embroidery work. We proceeded to the Perivleptos monastery, where we entered through an arched gateway. Inside the church was an exceptional series of fourteenth century murals illustrating the New Testament and the Life of the Virgin.

By the time we reached the bottom of the hill, we were exhausted. My legs felt like jelly and my right knee was just starting to swell. We rested in our van, putting our aching feet up on cushions while a cup of tea brewed. Paul checked our maps and decided we would head back to some familiar territory. We drove slowly to Loutraki.

It was early evening when we arrived and parked in our usual spot on the dock for an overnight stay. There was only

194

one other van and we enjoyed the quiet. The weather the next day was gorgeous. We decided to stay awhile and enjoy the sunshine. After a stint in the mineral water, we used our bikes and cycled over to the Corinth Canal and watched as one boat went through the four mile long stretch. The channel is so narrow that it is not used regularly except by a few coastal traders and cruising ships drawn by tugs. We were fortunate, we had the time to wait for the boat and to watch as it was pulled through.

After an early morning soak and swim, we drove to Athens. We had no sooner entered through the gate of the campground and paid the tariff, that we spotted the Prestup's van waiting patiently for us, the familiar "English books to trade" sign already in the window. It had been three weeks since we had separated and we arrived within an hour of each other.

We had both shopped for groceries before coming to the campground and our combination dinner that night consisted of a kilo of pistachio nuts, five liters of wine, my homemade tziziki, pita bread, three different kinds of cheeses on five varieties of crackers, green olives that the Prestup's had purchased in Sicily along with black olives that we had picked up in Kalamata. We talked and nibbled and drank well into the night, catching up on all the news. They had missed the devastating earthquake in Sicily by one day. They were back on the mainland when it hit but had felt the tremors. This was a joyous reunion. At times, we all talked at once and at other times, we all stopped and sat in silence looking at each other. We were excited, animated and happy to be back together.

After having slept in a little later than usual, we took the bus into Athens. It was one of those busy, busy, busy days. We shopped for a few necessities, like pistachio nuts, sunflower and pumpkin seeds and Halvah, a crushed sesame seed treat with enough calories and oil to clog the cleanest of arteries. We bought our lunch from the sidewalk vendors. We toured all the shop-filled back streets and had we been able to understand the radio or newspapers, we would have known that there was going to be an afternoon strike of all public transportation. By mid afternoon, loaded with packages, we were tired and ready to make our way home. That was when we learned we were temporarily stranded. There was neither a taxi nor a bus to be had. We shopped, ate and wandered until exhausted.

At six o'clock the strike was over and the working people crowded into every breathable square inch on anything that moved. We waited at a coffee shop, too tired to make conversation. It was after seven thirty and dark before we found a relatively empty bus that was going in the direction of the campground. Even with this long, wonderful and frustrating day, and a city filled to the brim with people, cars and pollution, we found Athens charming. We loved it.

We spent one entire day touring the Parthenon, climbing up to the Acropolis. We all recognized the Temple of Athena Nike building, because someone had been kind enough to leave an old tattered Nike running shoe on one of the steps. Another half day, was spent wandering the museum. On yet another day, we roamed the streets, buying up little gifts to exchange with our friends since it was just a few days before Christmas. We lapped up the culture and the food and the colors.

The downtown section of Athens was filled with vendors hawking their edible wares. They sold barbecued lamb on little wooden skewers, spanakopita (spinach and feta cheese inside filo pastry) and chunks of mousaka that dripped when you tried to bite down. These bite sized mouth watering delights were available for a few drachmas. The fact that we were enjoying it with friends, made it all the more special. By the time we had spent our second day in the Athenian campground, we were joined by a British couple, Dee and Dave Hunt, and had became a steadfast sixum.

When we moved on, we moved as a unit and consulted all our guidebooks for places to stay and to meet up, should any of our clan decide that they wanted to see different things along the route. When we left Athens, we headed for an already familiar spot, Loutraki and arranged to convene on the dock, where the camping was plentiful and free and the minerals in the water soothing.

Since Loutraki had become somewhat of a home to us, Paul and I, acting as highly efficient tour guides, escorted the group around the town, pointing out various places of intense interest.....the public bathrooms, the biggest grocery store, a cheap and cheerful restaurant and a store selling second hand books, but none in English. The following day, before heading south, we stopped at the Corinth Canal to watch a ship go by and, again, to be totally awed by the sight.

We couldn't resist stopping for some theatrics at Epidavros, ruins of the Sanctuary of Asclepius. In July and August, classical drama in Greek is still performed in the well preserved theater. Since it was December, we did the performing. With five of us sitting in the top row, one lone performer staged a production of his or her choice. Dee, being English and prone to showing off, performed Shakespeare, starting with Romeo, Romeo, where fore art thou. She did an admirable job, I might add. Amy did a soft shoe while I did some goldy moldy poetry. The men, as usual, did little to nothing. Only Paul tried a chorus from his favorite song, My Way, and although he had a wonderful singing voice, preferred waiting until an orchestra showed up. Everyone listening heard whatever they were supposed to hear, including the delicate shuffling of Amy's sneakers. We discussed, at some length, that with all the advances in acoustics, they still could not build theaters like that anymore.

After Epidavros, we parted so our friends could visit Mystra and we would all meet up again at Gythion where we would celebrate Christmas before sailing to Crete.

Christmas in Gythion, was a joy to our little world. The six of us congregated in the Prestup van for wine, booze and munchies, followed by a barbecued rib dinner and our exchanging of gifts, none costing more than two dollars each. At ten o'clock Christmas Eve, well fortified by alcohol, we went out caroling through the campground. We were the hit of the evening and everyone treated us to an alcoholic beverage when we finished our song. Even the German couple that we disturbed making love, didn't seem too annoyed when we sang our rousing rendition of Oh Tannenbaum without benefit of knowing more than a few words. By midnight, our rowdiness was down to giggling whispers and we returned to the Prestup van to get warm and have a few more drinks.....like we needed them.

We ended our Christmas festivities around three in the morning. Paul opened the door to the Prestup van and immediately fell out and rolled under a tree, too drunk to really

197

hurt himself. He accused me of pushing him and lay there laughing, trying to get to his feet.

The following morning Paul was up and singing long before the rest of us. We needed the entire day to recuperate. Fortunately everything was closed on Christmas Day. While Paul went for a short hike alone, the rest of us did not wander too far from our beds or the aspirin bottles. As a matter of fact, it was very, very late morning, around four in the afternoon, before the rest of us even stirred and even longer before any of us could put a toothbrush in our mouths.

Many of the other campers came over to say "hello" and to tell us how much they enjoyed our singing. Personally, I wished they would have let us die in peace, but Paul greeted all visitors enthusiastically. By the end of that evening, we knew almost everyone in the campground and were ready to socialize quietly. Very quietly. There had been one formal complaint made at the office that day. We had been told about it only in passing. Even the office employees knew that this was not going to be a regular occurrence.

On the first available ship, we sailed to Crete and arrived on December 28, 1990. Although the sailing was smooth and uneventful, we had partied a bit too much even after Christmas and required some rest when we arrived. Side by side, on the dock we pulled down our shades, blocking out as much of the light as we could, and slept for a few hours. By the time we were ready to head into Rethymnon and find a campground, all the banks were closed.   We were limited as to what we could pick up in the way of groceries, since we were short of cash. I purchased a few vegetables and a chicken marked "entero." I was delighted that chickens could be purchased "whole" until I found out what it meant, Greek style. When they said "entero" they meant "entero." All unfolded, the fowl still had its head, complete with beak and face feathers. The yellow feet, sporting talon-like claws, was something I had not seen on a chicken since childhood when my mother bought chickens live. What I pulled out of the chicken's middle caused my stomach to do a little flip flop. I gagged. Not quite so sensitive, Paul took the chicken to the outside sink and fixed it so it was not quite so "entero" while I washed the cooking area, scrubbed my hands and let my innards settle down a little with a cup of tea. He was followed back by a herd of the mangiest and scrawniest looking cats I had ever seen. Paul threw the entrails, and everything else he removed, to the cats and from the snarling and hissing and scratching we heard, we were sure there would be a few less cats, but they persisted. They stayed close in the hopes of another sumptuous meal like the previous, however, living in fear of choking one of these prize possessions, we did not throw them the chicken bones.

New Year Eve, at the Agio Galini campground on the south side of the Island, brought a touch of sadness with it. We had always celebrated and toasted in the New Year with our friends in Toronto, Owen and Elizabeth McCreery and we missed them terribly. We were invited into the clubhouse for a few drinks with the rest of the guests, and after hoisting our wine glasses to our Toronto friends three or four dozen times, we soon got into the swing of Agio Galini living. New Year's dinner consisted of cabbage, meat balls, tziziki and salad. A little out of the norm, but I was becoming addicted to tziziki so I quite enjoyed it. The midnight toast was done with half filled glasses of retsina.

We enjoyed three wonderful weeks on Crete. We did some hiking and lots of bicycle riding. We shopped in Timbaki. We toured Iraklion while picking up our mail. We camped in Elorinda, within swimming distance of Spinalonga, formerly used as a leper colony. When the leper colony disbanded, Spinalonga was deserted. We ate, slept, read, cleaned, lounged and one day, January 17, 1991 we awoke to the news that the Gulf War had started during the night.

The night before had been one of our few arguments in all the months of camping. We had left the campground low on gas. Paul liked to see how low the gas gauge would go before we actually ran out of gas and it always infuriated me.

"I have so little excitement in my life," he complained, "not running out of gas is my only challenge."

At this point in our traveling we had never run out of gas, but Paul felt the need to tempt fate whenever possible. There were so many areas in all these strange countries we visited, where there was nothing but empty space, that I hated the risk. We had visited a couple of small towns and not only had we not found a place to camp, but there were no gas

199

stations. Late in the afternoon, we were heading back to Agio Galini. I was positive we were not going to make it. We were traveling a mountain road and when we came across a large, open clearing, I insisted we stop for the night. A storm was closing in quickly and I wanted to be on level ground, should we run out of gas. When Paul stopped the van in the clearing, he immediately retrieved the barbecue from its hiding place and went outside. I ranted and raved and fumed at him for a long time.

It was too late to barbecue. The wind had picked up and it had turned really cold very suddenly. He opened the back door, poked his head through and apologized, promising not to do that again. Of course, he knew that his life back in the van would have been hell had he not apologized. Before dinner was started, we hugged. Our argument was over.

If we ran out of gas on the way down the mountain, at least it would be daylight and someone would stop to help. Of that, we were certain.

Early the next morning, while I put water up to make coffee, Paul turned on our radio to the BBC. The Gulf War had started in the middle of the night.

Blame the decision about the rest of our lives on the Gulf War. It was after listening to the very abbreviated report that we started discussing our own lives and reviewing our plan to move to Colorado Springs, Colorado. Yes, it was a thousand miles from my sister in California and our friend in Calgary. Yes, it was a three hour flight from our friends and family in Montreal and Toronto. Yes, it was in the middle of America. Yes, it was in the middle of nothing we knew.

"How about Sarasota, Florida?" I asked. "We've always enjoyed it there." "We always said that we would like to live there." "You can play golf all winter," I said.

"Yes, I think I would like that," Paul agreed.

We had breakfast, cleaned up and made our way to the closest gas station which was miles away but all down hill. It was spluttering by the time we arrived and we were sure we were running on fumes, but we made it.

We returned to Agio Galini and talked it over with our friends. Paul and I had seen all we wanted to on Crete. Rhodes was now out of the question. Egypt was closed to tourists and our van would no longer be insured if we went to Turkey, our ultimate destination. We waited several days thinking that the Americans would quickly put an end to the war. We stayed glued to our radio and the BBC broadcasts. Three days later they started issuing gas masks to people in the Hania/Souda area, on the north side of the Island. We prepared to leave while our friends, the Prestups and the Hunts, chose to wait it out.

The day we made our decision to leave, Paul and I wanted one last look at that part of the Island and walked into town to enjoy the scenery and get a bit of exercise. We had just reentered the gates to our campground, when I heard a noise that sounded like whimpering. We stopped for a second and turned, only to see the mother German Shepherd guard dog coming at me like a freight train. I could not get away fast enough and the chain that held her was much too long. She lunged at my stomach. Fortunately the weather was cold and before one fang gouged my stomach, she had to tear through my jacket, sweatshirt, jeans and underpants but one tooth caught me right around the belly button.

Paul threw me out of the way, kicked the dog in the ribs and the demon from hell bit him on the leg. She did not break the skin. The whole incident left us both pale and shaken and fortunately, by this time, out of range. When Paul went to tell the owners of the incident, they no longer understood English. We told our story to Amy and Norman who produced their guidebook "Let's Go Greece." Apparently the guidebook told all to "beware of the guard dog at Camp Agio Galini."

"The dog bites everyone when she is on the chain, supposedly working," said Amy. "You actually have to stand in line to get bitten." "Another lady went to the hospital this week with a torn stomach," Amy continued.

Before we left the campground the next day, my stomach started showing signs of bruising. We were glad to be leaving. I would not have felt safe walking around anymore with that beast roaming loose.

The following day we drove into town in two separate vans. We went for one last mousaka lunch in Iraklion. We hugged our friends and said goodbye and that evening sailed for Pireas on mainland Greece, arriving early the next morning. We would have an all day wait in Pireas.

We decided to check the two main post offices in Athens for mail from anyone who cared to write. Anything was better than waiting on a dock for ten or twelve hours. We purchased our ticket and headed into Athens. Delightfully and unexpectedly there was a letter from my sister Mona and another letter from my brother Nathan. A letter from Nathan could only be bad news, I thought, since he was not a letter writer. All was well after the fact. He just wanted to inform me that our father had had back surgery and was recovering.

We were fortunate on this trip that the Prestups had remained behind on Crete. While we were at the post office picking up our mail, the American Express office, where the Prestups would have been picking up their mail, was bombed. We had walked right by the office an hour or so before the bombing.

With mail in hand, we returned to the dock, to wait for our ship. The dock was jammed with trucks, cars and people all wanting to get away.

Chapter 34

We were the last one to be put on board the ship that was leaving and could have kissed the floorboards to be there. Thinking that there might be a problem getting out of Greece, we had returned early and had been waiting on the dock with hordes of anxious European tourists with their vehicles and agitated British, Italian and Greek truckers, since late afternoon. We were well situated in the queue, but every time we moved closer to boarding the vessel an official came along to motion us out of line and bring others forward. By late night we were tired and frustrated and Paul was ready to argue with anyone who spoke the slightest amount of English. All alone on the dock, close to tears and mayhem respectively, we resigned ourselves to being stranded in a hellish war zone until a dock worker approached and ushered us forward. We were the last one on, sandwiched so close to the other trucks, we had to exit from our rear door. Fortunately we had a rear door from which to exit or we may have resorted to using a can opener on our high top. We were on board and that's all that mattered.

Once our situation was rectified and our blood pressure returned to a low rolling boil, we had time to think more clearly. We worried about the friends we had left on Crete. They seemed perfectly content to wait out the war. Paul, I think, was far more concerned with the threat of all out total boredom than he was of actual war. We had been on Crete for twenty three days and had seen almost every interesting part of the Island. Had the Samaria Gorge been open Paul might have been content one or two more days for hiking, but the Gorge was closed in winter. We were happy to be on our way, since we could not have gone farther than the Greek Island of Rhodes without putting ourselves in serious jeopardy.

Thanks to the friendship of some British truckers, we had a crossing filled with stories about close calls and near misses, funny people, jokes, places not be missed and problems at border crossings. We learned we could have gone into Egypt after all, but would not have been allowed in or near any of their national treasures. Had we gone into Turkey, they told us, our vehicle would not have been insured since all British insurance companies had canceled coverage for people heading into the war zone. Our insurance policy remained in force just long enough to go elsewhere or get out and head back to Britain.

Jim, looking very much like our own Colonel Sanders, recommended the best route traveling through Italy and, at his suggestion, after disembarking and saying goodbye, we stayed on the coast road as long as we could, heading north. There seemed to be very little traffic, for Italy that is, and because it was the coast road, there were lots of places to pull off, have our meals and view the scenery, as desolate as it was.

At dark, when it was time to stop for the night, we pulled onto the autostrada, again as Jim had suggested. We stopped at the first gas station that allowed truckers to rest for the night and set up camp. We enjoyed a safe, cheap night's sleep and didn't allow the noise from the trucks pulling in and out to disturb us too much. The bathrooms had clean showers. We were up early, paid a few Lira for a hot shower, had breakfast and were ready to go.

We filled our gas tank, for the first time not resenting the horrendous price at, what had been our campground for the night, pulled off the autostrada at the first exit and paid one dollar and sixty cents in tolls. We ignored the dirty looks from the toll booth attendant, who knew exactly what we had done and who probably had given us the information, but it was worth the price. We thoroughly appreciated the last bargain left in Italy.

By the end of the second day, traveling on and off the

autostrada, we had journeyed about four hundred miles and it had cost us over one hundred and twenty dollars in gasoline alone and close to that amount in tolls. The scenery to our right was nothing but a fogged in body of water licking the shoreline. The beaches, with white sand and small tufts of grass all along, was not worth a second glance, but we seemed to be making good time. That night we slept on the autostrada just outside Piacenza, approximately one hundred and twenty five kilometers from Genoa.

It was freezing. Sometime during the night, we had awakened bone chilling cold. We had donned our sweat suits and a couple of pairs of socks but in the morning, this had not been enough. We had been huddled together, fully clothed, under several blankets and inside our sleeping bags. We were achy and stiff.

"Someone has to get out of bed and turn the heat on," said Paul holding onto me for dear life, his voice still husky from sleep.

"OK," I answered without hesitation, "how about if that someone is you."

"How about if we both get out at the same time and you turn the heat on and I make the coffee," said Paul.

"How about if you turn the heat on first and then, since you're up anyway, you make the coffee," I said.

The bantering, resting in between the barbs, took about fifteen minutes, while we lay there snuggled as close as we could for precious, life saving warmth. Neither of us got out of bed until we both had to go to the bathroom.

Paul used his shoulder against the back door that had frozen sticky and it creaked loudly in disapproval as it swung open. We raced to the store, gas station, shower block. We stayed long enough to warm up slightly and returned to the van to start our day.

I lit one burner under a pot of water for coffee and then tried to get the propane heater going. Any attempt at warmth took forever. The flame around the gas ring was very low and blue, but it was going.

"I think we're running out of propane," I said to Paul.

It was six o'clock in the morning, still pitch black outside and the temperature was minus six Celsius. We stayed in our track suits and donned another layer of pants, sweatshirts and socks. Paul put his arms around me, holding me close to him, rubbing my back and arms and getting a little circulation back into both of us. It was a little ritual we enjoyed several times a day, warm or cold.

We sipped steaming hot coffee, trying to warm our insides while heating our hands on the mug. We waited for the sun to come up. Our vehicle was covered with frost and the back doors did not close properly after Paul had bulldozed our way out. Our heater, which normally blasted out the warm air, was very inefficient. We just couldn't move quickly in the cold. Trying to warm ourselves by keeping busy, Paul made our bed, while I relit the stove to make us some hot cereal. Again, it took much too long to prepare.

We were ready to get out of there. We didn't do the dishes since we needed to heat the water. We just left them in the sink with sponges all around to keep them from clattering. We were ready to start moving as soon as the sun peaked over the horizon. After several attempts, the van cranked to a start. We let the engine warm up just a little and moved out very slowly, hoping the engine heat would warm us.

We drove through the hills on our way to Genoa. We passed areas with lots of snow on the ground that had been plowed to the side of the road. We were still cold and our feet, particularly our toes, were frozen. Just outside of Genoa, the sun burst through our windshield flooding us with its penetrating heat. The van was suddenly filled with warmth. It was like coming out of a dark, dank, underground cave into brilliant, life saving sunshine. We squinted as the light burned our eyes.

Paul pulled into the first rest area. We couldn't peel off our extra layers of clothing fast enough. The warmth of the sun penetrated layer by layer until even the marrow in our bones ran freely. Our shoulders, so stiff from the tension of the driving in the freezing cold, relaxed allowing our necks to stretch out. Our own fingers rubbed our aches.

I thought if I could get the stove to work, I would heat up some soup. The stove started immediately and the flame, long, narrow and yellow, licked the bottom of the pot as it had always done in the past. It seems we had plenty of propane.

Propane, we learned some time later, freezes in cold weather. That had been our only problem. We stayed at the rest area long enough to heal our bodies and our spirits. Since we are both of hardy stock, it didn't take long.

We were back on familiar ground. We traveled the Mediterrean coastline to Menton, France.

We loved being back on French soil, but it was Sunday and there was not much open. A carnival, complete with rides, games of chance, stuffed animals and cotton candy booths had moved onto the dock at the boat club. We wanted to stay close by so we chose a spot at the far end of the boat club where patrons were parking. There was music and yelling and horns blowing until quite late and the assault started again long before we were ready for it. We awoke early and decided to lounge a bit. It had not been an easy exodus from Greece and our ride through Italy had been cold, uncomfortable and extremely expensive. I prepared a breakfast of scrambled eggs with onions and mushrooms, hash browns, toast and two cups of coffee that we ate leisurely. Had anything but the carnival been open, we might have stayed a day to unwind but in checking the map, we decided on our route for the day. We would stay close to the coast and stop often to stretch, but we cleaned up and left.

It was still too far north for our liking and it was still cold, but nothing came close to that night on the autostrada. On our route south, we had only one mishap. Paul wanted to see if our van could get through a two meter, six inch high tunnel. We couldn't and that smash we heard was the heavy metal, overhead barrier breaking our plastic roof vent to smithereens. Fortunately that was all that broke and we did not get stuck in the tunnel. Our quest for the day was for a soft plastic that would cover the area that had once been a perfectly serviceable opening and closing roof vent. The heavy gauge plastic, that Paul purchased at a hardware store, covered the gaping hole. It kept us dry but did nothing to keep us warm. For the moment, anyway, it did the trick. The night was another cool one just outside of Montpellier.

The next day was an easy drive to Perpignan. Our friends, the Betherys, were thrilled to see us. Instinct had told them that we were in the middle of a problem area and we had been on their minds constantly since the beginning of the fighting. Robert, a retired French Foreign Legion Colonel, had had visions of having to don his uniform and rescue us.

It didn't take Marianne long to set the table in celebration. We had a wonderful mushroom quiche with fresh bread, lots of wine and homemade pate, while Robert explained how he had been out shooting wild mushrooms all night in anticipation of our celebration. Paul told of our adventures in the war zone. I must confess that some of the escapades I did not recognize as having been a participant but they went along well with the wild mushroom hunting stories. We had a heck of a good time, thoroughly enjoying the company of our friends and although we were prepared to sleep in our van, we were given the key to their cottage at Barcares.

We slept in a real bed that night and the following morning, I luxuriated in a bathtub, anointed with fragrant oils. Refreshed and bathed, we picked up fresh croissants and pastries and headed back to Perpignan. We had coffee and breakfast with our friends and they were very disappointed that we were not staying longer. We thanked them, I kissed and hugged them both and said goodbye. By mid afternoon, we were back on the road.

The constant driving, without any real breaks for sightseeing was getting on our nerves and we wanted to get where we were going, so we could unwind properly. We drove slowly through Barcelona, looking at the sights, but did not stop. We camped that night in another familiar setting, Vinaroz.

That was our last day of driving. We arrived at the Jones' house around four in the afternoon. Again, instinct had told our friends that we were in a trouble spot and they were sure they would be seeing us soon. They, too, had worried about us. All fears were put aside. We talked, and regaled them with a little more true-to-life war stories, over a couple of drinks.

The street they were on was completely dug up and much of it was mud, so we walked back to our camper that we had left parked on the main road. We drove to the campground, where we checked in, parked our van and spread out more drinks and munchies.

Our drive was over. We were safe. We were home. For the first time since leaving our Canadian home, we booked into a campground for a month.

Chapter 35

We were in seventh heaven. The weather in this part of Spain was glorious. The humidity free atmosphere brought asthma sufferers from all over the world and we could enjoy its benefits without ever having suffered from the disease. The sun shone every day with only the occasional sprinkle to relieve the boredom of perfection. The beaches of the Costa Blanca were spitting distance from our camping spot. To add to our bliss, we were surrounded by friends, some new, some from the previous trip.

Several weeks before our arrival, Don and Marjorie had moved out of their apartment because of the inconvenience, along with the mud puddles, dirt and noise, of having their street paved. For a few days they trudged up and down the unpaved, gravelly, potholed road. They were not able to park their van anywhere close to their apartment so they moved into their favorite campground. They returned to their apartment every day to see that the note they had left for us tacked to the door, was undisturbed. So sure were they of seeing us. Their trailer was parked right next door to ours.

It didn't take the English speaking campers long to find us. We were fresh faces, had CDN stickers plastered in several spots on our van and that was a novelty to most Europeans and Britishers. The oval CDN is the designated insignia for Canada, however, when traveling through France Paul told the natives it stood for Cote Du Nord. It made us a favorite everywhere we went and, of course, hurt no one. We spent the first few days just unwinding after our long, tedious drive. We read a lot. We walked the beaches located directly across the street from our camping spot. We bicycled up and down the coast road and occasionally biked into Benidorm. Plunked down into the center of Benidorm, you would never have guessed you were in Spain. Everything was either in English only or small Spanish signs translated into large English ones. Fish and chip shops were on every other corner trying to outdo each other in size, packaging (always served in their traditional newspaper) or price. The movie theater showed its pictures in English with Spanish subtitles. Mini shopping malls, extending back from the sidewalks, were on every block. This was not our favorite part of the world, but for the moment, a welcomed necessary one.

Every market day, in every little town around, became our haunting grounds. In Albir it was on Thursday. In Altea we shopped on Wednesday. In Alfaz del Pi it was on Saturday that we scoured the place. We purchased English books at the market or at any one of a dozen or more second hand book stores. We bought our fresh fruits, vegetables, spices, kitchen knickknacks and towels at the market. Whatever we didn't buy was picked up, studied, inspected from every angle and put back. This was our way of slowing down.

We met a special group of English speaking folks. Paul played golf with George Richbell on several occasions at the golf club in the Altea Hills. We bicycled with Keith and Barbara Robinson. The Nix's van accommodated the entire bunch and Brian drove us into Benidorm for a swim at the indoor pool of the Helios Hotel on a couple of occasions. We would have a lively conversation at lunch in one of the local restaurants and we all, except Brian of course, the driver of the van accompanied by his wife Ellen, bicycled back to Albir. We spent our afternoons playing the French game of boules in the several pits dug especially for the game. We played cribbage and UNO and scrabble and talked and laughed.

On one fateful day, we were invited to a barbecue and then for a card game in Keith and Barbara's van. Every other motorhome was larger than our Renault Trafic, but the van we were going to that evening would actually accommodate the entire horde of card sharks around the table. Paul and I were fascinated by what we had heard about the van and were delighted that we were going to get a good look at the inside. The van was a German Hymermobile. This was the first pneumatic bed we had ever seen. When not in use, the queen sized bed, complete with bedding, was power driven into the ceiling above the driver and passengers seats. All other space in the vehicle was livable. It was large and spacious and we wanted one.

The day and early evening had been very pleasant. The weather, as usual, had been perfect for boules. Paul and I left early to set up the barbecue, which was one of our contributions to the festivities. The hot dogs, hamburgers and all the fixings prepared to everyone's specifications, were delicious. We helped in the clean up from the outdoor party before we retired for indoor games and the cook's tour. We talked over a couple of drinks, before getting down to the serious stuff, a card game called UNO. Paul and I had to be taught, but we were game playing people anyway and learned quickly.

We enjoyed the company of our friends and the wine, which poured freely, had loosened our tongues, mine more than others. During the evening the odd joke would be told, but Brit's are not known for their sense of humor and the jokes were simple. It was all in good fun anyway, and when my husband poked me and suggested I tell a joke that he found tremendously humorous, I declined. In his usual manner, he kept goading me. I finally relented.

The joke concerned the man who goes to the doctor's office in a panic. " My wife is really sick," he complains. "She either has AIDS or Alzheimers. I don't know which, but I know she has one of them." "How can I find out which one?" he begs the doctor. "Well," says the Doctor, "put your wife in the car, drop her off in downtown London, if she finds her way home, don't f--- her."

Dead silence befell the room. No one laughed. One person made a slight puffing noise as if a laugh might be in the works and then nothing. You could cut the air with a knife. No one moved. The silence was deafening, lasting an eternity.

About thirty endless seconds later, conversation resumed with a word here and a word there. Eventually even I started talking and glared at my husband every time he opened his mouth or suggested anything. By the end of an hour or so all was pretty much back to normal and things progressed. Much later in the evening, there was several seconds, where people were contemplating their cards or simply lost in their own thoughts, and no one spoke, as happens from time to time in any room filled with card playing people.

"What happened," piped up my husband, "did Joei tell another joke?"

Everyone laughed. Even I had to chuckle. His timing, as usual, was perfect.

At the end of February we had a couple of celebrations to attend. Don Jones' seventieth birthday, fell on the exact same day as Paul's fifty-first birthday. We observed Paul's birthday on the twenty sixth with all our friends in attendance. We enjoyed dinner out, complete with several bottles of good wine and showered him with small presents.

The following day was a big blowout birthday luncheon with fifty people in attendance at the Los Grillos restaurant, overlooking the entire lush, green valley. The music was very lively, very Spanish and danceable. The full course meal, starting with mini bites called tapas and ending with a huge, frosted white cake, was delicious. The gathering of friends, some we had met previously, thanks to the Joneses, and many we had met for the first time at the party, were delightful. We ate, drank and danced well into the evening.

We recuperated for a couple of days. We spent our days enjoying the company of Don and Marjorie, who had, by this time, moved back into their apartment. At the beginning of March, a little itchy from our hiatus, we started touring again. We joined Keith and Barbara, Brian and Ellen and George and Margaret for a few days of free camping and hiking in Finistrat, a tiny community nestled in the hills overlooking our former home. We stayed three days and walked into the town one day to do some banking. Much to our horror, neither one of our Visa cards was accepted by the machines at the only bank in town. We walked to the church overlooking the entire countryside to check out the scenery and for a moment forgot our money problems.

The following day we drove back into Albir and checked with the bank that we had frequented over the previous month. Our Visa was accepted without a hint of a problem and our jeans now crackled with the sound of folded money. We felt better. As long as we were in Albir, we spent another day with the friends we loved, Don and Marjorie. We went to dinner at one of our favorite restaurants and bar, Penny Lane, and talked the night away.

We left the next day and had a long, long, long drive in the rain.

Chapter 36

We were back on the plains of Spain and our only stop, except for gas, lunch and the occasional coffee, was in Almansa. We toured the Casa Grande, a seignorial mansion with a magnificent sixteenth century doorway and twin giants supporting armorial bearings. The exercise continued as we walked the restored fifteenth century ramparts.

By late afternoon we were settled in our spot in Toledo. After dinner we went for a walk in the old part of town, getting lost on the narrow, meandering streets. It wasn't often that I felt the need to purchase something personal but, this time, I could not resist. I bought a pair of damascene (black steel inlaid with gold) earrings.....long, dangling and very elegant.

We visited the hole-in-the-wall shops and kiosks for hours, going in and out of each one until they were ready to close. We wandered around long after some of the shops had packed it in for the night, sure that no more business would be coming their way. It was extremely late by the time we returned to the campground, but we took out our guidebooks and planned the next day's touring. We were so fascinated by this region of Spain.

Toledo, by van and by foot, was on the agenda for the next day. The town, billed as a three star in our Michelin guide, is surrounded by the Tagus river. We drove the outer reaches of the town, using the road adjacent to the river. The surrounding heights were blanketed by olive groves. White houses were half concealed by a truly memorable view of the city. We drove to the third century Alcazar, perched atop the highest of the seven hills in the city. We surveyed most of the rooms, including the steel weapons room and the twentieth century Africa Room. Once parked in the town center, we continued on foot. We saw a collection of paintings by El Greco at the Museum of Santa Cruz. We studied the Spanish Gothic architecture of the cathedral. We walked the Old Jewish Quarter and found the house and museum of El Greco. By the time we got back to our van, we could walk no more.

The following morning, we left in the rain. One and a half hours later, we arrived in Madrid. Our initial impression was that of a large, modern, dirty city. We found a campground on the outskirts of town, but it was dreadful. We drove on to another, which turned out to be worse, with many of the camping vehicles surrounded by mountains of trash and others deserted entirely. Simultaneously we made our decision. We left.

When we drove through the heart of downtown Madrid, we were pleased with our decision. Every fourth or fifth car parked had flat tires, broken windows or ripped up interiors. We were delighted when, without much difficulty, we found the road to El Escorial.

From the road, we could see the Royal Monastery and decided to find a camping spot before taking a tour. After an hour of wandering the countryside looking for the campground listed in the guidebook, we asked a policeman for directions. He was kind enough to lead us right to the entrance or we never would have found it. I'm sure we were not the first he escorted to the gate. By the time we checked in, had a late lunch, early dinner combination and went back to the monastery, it was closed. We walked the town, before relaxing at an outdoor cafe to enjoy a coffee and something sweet. We were surrounded by gorgeous snow covered hills.

After breakfast and before leaving El Escorial, we toured the Royal Monastery. While Philip II and the Spanish Hapsburgs remained on the throne, the Escorial was a place of regal splendor. The king resided in the apartments encircling the church apse. Visiting the New Museum, the church, the kings courtyard, the library and the chapterhouses took almost all day, but we didn't have too long a drive, so we didn't mind. After a snowy drive over the Altos de los Leones de Castille (one thousand five hundred eleven feet) pass, we spent that night just outside Segovia.

It was a pity to have to visit two magnificent cities on the same day, but that was what we did. The morning was spent in Segovia. The Romanesque churches are among its greatest treasures. The Roman aqueduct, with its two tiers of arches throughout, is one of the finest in existence. We walked the old town just to see the decorated facades. It was truly magnificent.

By early afternoon we were driving through the hillside town of Sepulveda to reach our second glorious city, Burgos. We were fascinated with all the Plana trees that lined the streets because the naked overhead branches were all intertwined like lover's fingers. We strolled under the living archway. The rest of the day was spent walking around the most magnificent Flamboyant Gothic style cathedral we had ever seen. It is the third largest in Spain, after Seville and Toledo. We camped that night just a few miles outside Burgos.

The words in my diary on March 11, 1991 were "any day that begins with a gun being waved in the air, is not going to be a good day."

Although the campground had all the amenities, our morning showers had been cold and my husband went to the office to complain. Paul was mid sentence, when wild shouts started behind him. A dark haired young man, waving the gun around was shoving a picture of his (we assumed) wife, under the nose of the owner. The proprietor and the picture-toting, gun-slinging fellow ranted and raved at each other awhile and when they went up the stairs to the second floor, Paul took the opportunity to throw a fist full of pesetas on the counter, grab his passport and run. We took off, safe for another adventure, discussing who, what, when, where and what that might have been about. Heading for the French border and our ultimate goal, Lourdes, we talked excitedly about the incident.

The turnoff, according to the map, was just before reaching Pamplona and traffic had heavied up considerably. Except for the car directly ahead of us, we were behind a long string of slow moving, diesel spewing trucks and my husband was becoming impatient with the drivers. Finally, the car ahead saw a clearing and went for it. My husband did the same, passing a couple of trucks and again pulling in behind the little car.

The driver of the little car stuck his left arm out of the window, attached a small, blue whirling dome light onto the roof of his vehicle and motioned for us to pull over. They were the Guardia Civil and although we had no idea what we had done wrong, we knew instantly that we were screwed. With hand signals and gestures he indicated that what we had done was illegal. We were not supposed to follow him around the trucks although nothing on the road indicated that we should not or could not. With paper and pen the Guardia put down the figure he wanted from us for our offense. That figure was fifty thousand pesetas. I was horrified and pulled out my last five thousand peseta note. He wanted my last fifty dollars.

"No, No, No," he said shaking his head in disgust and rewrote fifty thousand. Double horror. I had fifty dollars. He wanted five hundred dollars.

It was late Friday afternoon. If we wanted the American Embassy, located in Madrid, we would have to wait until Monday and Paul would be waiting in a Spanish prison. God knows where I would go and I don't think the Guardia could have cared less about any of it. They wanted money.

Both kept gesturing for us to make a decision. They indicated that the van would be impounded if we were not prepared to pay on the spot. The longer we talked about our options, the more aggressive the police became and started fingering their weapons, still in their holsters.

"Andalay (hurry up) andalay," the big, fat one kept repeating.

While we were becoming visibly upset, the police held our keys, Paul's license and insurance papers. We had no choice. We followed them to a bank in Pamplona and paid them by withdrawing money on our Visa cards. The Visa transaction left us a little shaken as well since we were withdrawing more than our maximum daily allowance and had to split up the withdrawal on both Visa cards. We were robbed, and by the police, no less.

We drove the many miles in silence and were delighted

to cross the border back into one of our favorite countries. We followed the signs to Lourdes.

The next day, while drinking the sacred water that sprang from the well where Bernadette saw the Virgin Mary, I prayed the Guardia Civil would choke on our five hundred bucks. The sign which read "think pure thoughts while drinking this holy water" was lost on me.

Chapter 37

Every moviegoer has a favorite. For as long as I can remember, my favorite has been The Song of Bernadette with Jennifer Jones. I don't know if it's the message I love, or the foreign nature of the film, or because Bernadette saw the Virgin Mary on my birthday, February 11, the year 1858, being a little before my time, of course. For whatever the reason, I watch The Song of Bernadette every time it's on television and have no trouble staying awake through its entirety at whatever the hour. I don't want to belabor the point, but, I wanted to love Lourdes. I wanted it to be the pilgrimage, along with the four million other tourists that flock there every year, that it was supposed to be. I expected to be awed by the experience. What I got, however, was considerably less than inspirational. In a word.....tacky. The church was magnificent but the village, with its myriad of souvenir shops, selling everything from Bernadette dolls to key rings bearing holy symbols to mugs, mirrors, bottle openers and anything else that would turn a profit, truly saddened me.

Paul and I sat quietly for a long time watching the people praying and touching the walls of the church. We drank the holy water. We examined the turn of the century crutches that hung from the rafters. We walked the beautifully manicured gardens. I said nothing of my disappointment. In secret, my heart wept and withered. I still love the movie, but there is absolutely no connection to the village I saw that day.

The way north took us into Tarbes and with all our driving around the town we could not find Massey Gardens for which, according to our guidebooks, it is famous. They must have taken special pains to hide the place because we found neither signs nor anyone who could tell us where it was. We continued north.

We toured Auch on foot. The interesting part of the old town is on a hill overlooking the countryside. The seventeenth century cathedral, displayed exceptionally beautiful stained glass and carved stalls in the choir.

In Agen we went looking for the eight French franc campground that we had stayed in the year before. We couldn't find it. We camped that night on a farm just outside Fumel, the beginning of the Dordogne region. My diary for that day, March 13, 1991 ends with "now we'll slow down" but we never did.

We revisited some spots. We stopped in Gourdon for groceries and gas. We walked through some of the round medieval buildings in Sarlat, but they were repaving the sidewalks and roads. It was extremely busy with pedestrian traffic, very dusty and unnecessarily noisy with honking horns and drilling equipment trying to outdo each other. We stayed only a few hours.

Les Ezie, from one end of the town to the other, was closed. We had already been to the museum and not one of the stores was open. We drove to Bergerac via Tremolet and visited the horseshoe water basin. We camped in the same spot as we had the year before. We walked and biked in the wonderful sunshine in Bergerac. We lunched that day on two dozen oysters on the half shell, my shucking skills as sharp as ever.

The following day was full of fascinating sights. We walked the medieval town of Perigoux with its long narrow streets. We drove around and around Limoges. With all our travel experience, we still had a tendency to get lost in big cities and this was no exception. We left before frustration set in and headed for Oradore sur Glane.

On June 10, 1944 the Nazis, through misinformation, thought Oradore sur Glane was headquarters of the French Resistance and systematically massacred over six hundred people.....men, women and children.....then burned the town.

The men were shot at their places of business. The woman and children were herded into the church where they were executed en masse. The town remains as a monument. We walked in silence. Each burned building has a little plaque giving the names of the people who resided there and/or what business operated on that spot. Another horror was going through the cemetery at the back of the town. The tombstones had different names, different dates of birth but the date of death on most of the tombstones was June 10, 1944.

We left the monument after several hours and were delighted to meet up with our friends George and Margaret Richbell, whom we had left in Finistrat ten days before. We talked and laughed awhile, catching up on some of the news, before resuming our travels. The Richbells toured Oradore sur Glane while we drove on to Chauvigny for a fast look and ended up camping that night at our favorite free camp, St. Maure de Touraine.

Still heading north, our first stop was Amboise. We had been to Leonardo da Vinci house but the rain had prevented us, the time before, from walking around the town. It was a lovely village with a pedestrian area filled with shops selling local crafts, goat cheese and cream filled pastries. There was a wonderful view of the terraced chateau up on the hill, high above the river. We visited both churches before going on to the chateau at Chambord. We took a guided tour since this chateau was a little different. It had been an old hunting lodge that was converted. We left the lodge just in time to run into George and Margaret who had just arrived. Since we felt our reunion was destiny, we had an early dinner together.

In the rain we toured the old and magnificently shaped cathedral at St. Benoit. The chateau at Sully, surrounded by water, was small and ordinary. Fontainebleau, on our way into Paris, was closed on Tuesday. We walked the outside perimeter, looking through a few windows. Catching glimpses of the interior was just enough to whet our appetite.

The exit we wanted off the expressway around Paris was closed and we ended up lost. With Paul's sense of direction for places revisited, we managed to find our way back to Maisons Laffitte, our favorite old campground, one train ride outside Paris. We were in familiar territory and our bicycles were ready

221

for use before we became too comfortable. The showers had controllable hot water, a rare treat, and the toilets were sheer luxury. They had actual seats, made of a material other than porcelain, which was not the case in most of the campgrounds. (Oh, did I forget to mention that before!)

The Chateau of Anne de Montmorency, one of the most important buildings of the sixteenth century was converted to the National Renaissance Museum. They restored twenty rooms that were displaying collections formerly housed in the Cluny Museum in Paris. The mantels were in the style of Fontainebleau, the tapestry depicted David and Bathsheba, the park and panorama were magnificent.

We took a fast tour of Chantilly but the horse museum and stables, our purpose for being there, were closed. A little farther up the road, we walked the old town of Senlis and wanted to visit the cathedral but a funeral was in progress and we didn't want to intrude. We arrived in Amiens just in time to watch them close the cathedral. At the end of the long, frustrating day we had trouble finding a campground. When we did find one, the gates were open, but no one was there. We stayed anyway. The next morning when we went looking for someone in the office, the door was locked and the lights were turned off. We had a leisurely breakfast and left.

It was a short drive along the beach to Boulogne. The ferry was leaving in forty-five minutes. We were on it.

Chapter 38

Without much fanfare and following a pleasant but uneventful crossing, we landed in Dover. We drove directly to Sevenoaks and closed out what little remained in our Barclay's bank account. The afternoon and evening was spent with Andrea and the children. Phil returned from work about nine thirty that evening and while the men talked, Andrea went to bed and I treated myself to my second bath in five months. It was around midnight that Paul and I returned to our camping spot in Dutton Green, a ten minute drive from the Webb home.

The next day we did laundry in Sevenoaks and were excited about going back into town that evening to see the movie Russia House with Sean Connery. Some time during the day that movie had changed and due to a timing problem we ended up watching Cyrano de Bergerac in French with English subtitles. Although it was an excellent film, I longed to watch the big screen in a language that I could understand without thinking about it. The next evening we went back into Sevenoaks to see Godfather III.

A few daytime visits, was enough lazing around for us. We bid farewell to our friends and drove into Abbeywood, calling in on a motorhome dealership and lusting over some of the new camping vehicles available before checking into the campground. With our camper safely leveled and anchored on a spot, we walked through Abbeywood Park to see the archaeological ruins and the meticulously manicured grounds of

Lesnes Abbey.

The next day was cold and windy and definitely not the day to be outside, but being of hardy stock, the weather didn't bother us too much. We had taken an early train into London and started the day with the changing of the guards at the park before walking to Buckingham Palace. We asked to see the queen, but those uniformed guys in the big, black, furry hats patrolling the place wouldn't even give us a smile let alone the time of day.

After an hour at Westminster Abbey, we waited in line at Leicester Square for last minute theater tickets. We returned to the campground for an afternoon rest and an early dinner. We were back at the Royal Adelphi Theater by seven thirty with front row center tickets to Me and My Gal. I was in my glory when the cast came into the audience and shook hands with all they could reach, commencing with the front row.

We spent one day at Greenwich visiting the shops on the pier and touring the Cutty Sark. We walked the grounds of the Old Royal Observatory and spent much of the afternoon at the National Maritime Museum learning about Greenwich Mean Time. Paul enjoyed anything nautical. We were back in our camper well after dark, soaking our feet from our nonstop plodding.

The next day was on again, off again frustration. By the time we found the Spanish Embassy, it had just closed for the day. The hours at Madam Tussaud's Wax Works were exciting, educational, amusing and mind boggling. Seeing a gray haired, middle aged woman passed out on a couch, a Herrod's shopping bag dangling from a limp, outstretched arm, caught the attention of everyone around. She looked so exhausted.....and so real. She wasn't. The craft booths at Covent Gardens were disappointing, as was our quick ploughman's luncheon special in a pub.

It was early evening when we met with Phil Webb and his buddies and, although he had already had more than enough to drink, the men found it necessary to hit about four more bars before sitting down to a delicious Chinese dinner. By the time dinner was over, just after ten o'clock, we had missed the last train back to Abbeywood and the safety of our campground. We tried to get close and Paul felt we could probably walk the last few miles. We took the subway out to Tower Hill. Paul wanted to walk through the long, dirty, God-knows who could be living in there, tunnel to get to the other side and I would have followed him, of course, but I was terrified. Fortunately iron gates closed off the passageway. We took the last train back to the Embankment station. We were told by a uniformed guard at the station that we could get an all night bus to almost anywhere, including Abbeywood. We were grateful for the information.

The signpost for the bus read "exact change only." We didn't have it, but we waited anyway. When the bus marked Abbeywood pulled up, I was ready to beg, on my knees, if necessary, for transportation back to the safety and security of our camper. An enormous smiling bus driver greeted us with "where ya off to, Pet?"

"Abbeywood," I responded, "but we don't have the exact change, I'm afraid."

"That's all right, Darlin," as he handed me change from the ten pound note I had given him. "The campground then, Pet," he said, "upstairs, take a nap and I'll wake you when we get there."

Paul fell asleep instantly with his head resting on my shoulder. I put my arm around him and held him tightly so he wouldn't sway or fall off the bench seat when the bus rounded the corner. I stayed awake the entire trip and from my lofty perch looked out over the streets of inner core London. I was appalled at the number of doorways that were occupied by people covered with blankets, sleeping bags or cardboard boxes. This dark side of life corrupting every cosmopolitan city was completely foreign to me, although I know it exists.

From the chic, we descended upon the seedy and finally to the blackness of the outskirts, with only the occasional streetlight to illuminate the way. The bus driver not only called for us to come downstairs at Abbeywood, but stopped at the bottom of the street that the campground was on, not one of the regular stops, and kept the doors open, watching us until we were close to the gates. We waved goodbye. It was after three in the morning.

Late the next morning, we drove out to Bures-LaMarsh and had a pleasant few days visiting our friends, Cees and

Hedy. Once again we helped do some of the work in their exotic garden. We took in a flower show one day to see local flowers, plants and, my favorite, crafts. We dined at the Red Lion and while Hedy and I washed down a crunchy cod fish and chip with a shandy, a tasty lager and ginger ale combination, the men preferred sampling the various stout ales on tap. Dinner ended with Death By Chocolate, a dessert Paul and I had craved since the previous year. It was just as rich and delicious as we had remembered.

Once again in London, we went back to the Spanish Embassy and told some official looking person our story about the five hundred dollar ticket. We were advised "sorry, there is nothing we can do." "You should have refused to pay at the time," we were told. The Consular at the Spanish Embassy wanted to keep the ticket, but gripping the piece of paper for dear life, I told him that we would be taking it to the American Embassy to see if perhaps they could do something about it.

"If you want people to visit your country," Paul said, "you should not treat them this way."

A shrug of the shoulders told us all we needed to know.

We arrived at the American Embassy just in time for them to lock their doors for lunch. It was noon and we found a little pub close to the Embassy so we would be first in line when it reopened. Before ordering, Paul called Phil at work to let him know that we were back in town for a couple of days.

"I'm sorry Paul," said Phil. "We had a call from your friend Pat Thomas in Canada," he continued "your mum died last Friday." Phil suggested we come to his office and make all the necessary phone calls.

Before going to the office, we stopped at a British Airways counter. There would be no problem or cost involved in changing our ticket from April 9 to April 5. It took a couple of days to put our van in storage in Wales. Our friends, John and Elen Lewis, took care of arrangements. We just had to get there and John did the rest. We spent overnight at the Lewis' home in Radyr, just outside Cardiff. We took the train into London and flew back to Toronto.

This was not the homecoming we had prepared for. A family memorial service was delayed, waiting our arrival.

Chapter 39

Mother's home in Fonthill, Ontario had to be cleaned up, fixed up as best we could and sold. Since Paul and I were between homes, we moved in and immediately went to work. Lorna, the oldest sister, living in Kitchener, Ontario came by occasionally to help. Frances, from Montreal, Quebec visited once or twice. A third sister, Bobbi, was living in Jerusalem, Israel and we communicated with her by phone. Each family member put dibs on what they would prefer to keep. Everything else was to be sold in garage sales, donated to a worthy cause or thrown away. Much of it fell into the last category.

On the tenth of April, all by ourselves, in an area where we had no friends or family, Paul and I celebrated our fifteenth wedding anniversary with champagne and an elegant but quiet dinner.

"You know," I said, "you're mother promised us something special on this anniversary." "I really didn't think," I continued, "that this is what she had in mind."

"Very funny," was his only reply and we changed the subject.

We did the best we could with the cleaning. Paul fixed many of the obvious problems, which included painting and some touch up work. The screw driver that poked out of his back pocket became his constant companion. Keeping the place looking tidy but lived in, leaving all the lights on so the place wouldn't look so dark and having yard sales week after week, kept us busy. The house was listed at slightly below market value and the real estate agent, a family friend, had no trouble selling it quickly.

The family arrived in cars and trucks and carted away their new belongings. Bobbi's treasures were put in storage, awaiting her return. The proceeds from the estate, with Paul acting as executor, was split four ways. Our job was over.

One day, at the end of 1991, Paul and I loaded our little red Mazda pickup and a large U-Haul truck with all our worldly possessions and we headed south, in tandem, to Sarasota, Florida, The Sunshine State.

It was the beginning of another wonderful adventure and our quest for a home. We spent the first week in a hotel. It took no time at all finding a small apartment that we rented by the month with a six month lease. Although we had brought some furnishings with us, we purchased some new furniture for the apartment. The furniture was in the light colored Floridian style, so it would be appropriate for our new condo, when we found it.

We luxuriated in the sunshine. I took a golf lesson at Paul's insistence and we played at least twice a week. Paul played an extra game or two with the men each week. He volunteered at Mote Marine, a Marine Biology Lab and Aquarium and on those days he explained that he "had to go to work." They took him out fishing. His job was to catch and tag fish. He loved "the work."

I took weaving lessons for the first time and joined the Weaver's Guild. I exhibited my many crafts and demonstrated my skills in knitting, needlepoint, crewel and weaving at all the fairs. Everything I entered won Best of Show, first or second place. This was paradise.

Every free day, we went looking for a home and gradually narrowed our focus. Naples was too far and lacked things to do. Port Charlotte was too old population wise. Venice was interesting but still lacked something, we didn't know what. Bradenton, we just plain didn't like. Siesta Key was too expensive and too difficult to get on and off during tourist season. By a process of elimination, we settled on our original idea, Sarasota. With all of our exploring, it was still our favorite place by far. It was loaded with golf courses, museums and was the home of Ringling. The arts, with its many little theaters and its own opera house, had us fascinated. Although opera was not something that held our fancy, it was available in Sarasota and that's what was important. It also boasted a marine biology lab, botanical gardens, and a variety of schools and creative classes for the person so inclined. There was an endless list of positives and a mere handful of negatives.

With months of searching and investigating under our belt, we purchased a very large, two bedroom, two bathroom condo in what we thought was a convenient area, on the south side of town. Although we had been looking at some fixer-uppers, this one did not need much attention, just a little updating that we could do ourselves. We took possession on the first of April, 1992. We would start our move on the first of May. We were thrilled. We had a home. We had a place to put our feet up after the driving was done.

The beginning of May presented some unexpected health problems for me. We packed and moved a few boxes into our new home in our little pickup truck. During the move, I nicked my finger and thought no more of it until later that day when the cut became infected. With a little cleansing, the infection cleared up. We continued packing.

That same evening while brushing my teeth, a small area of my gums started to bleed and within an hour, it became infected. It cleared up a short while later. I went down hill rapidly from there but did not take too much time away from the move or to find out what was wrong. By the end of the week, I could no longer sleep laying down. I had a deep, throaty cough. I had no choice. I went to a doctor, was diagnosed with bronchitis and put on antibiotics. We continued moving and by the time everything was in our new home and put away, it was the fourteenth of May .

My health did not improve and on May 16, after a day of rest and sunshine, we headed back towards Canada. We stopped that night in Savanna, Georgia. After a bath and nap in the hotel room, we went into town for a mini tour and dinner. The next morning we walked down by the old harbor, checked out all the stores, looked through the window at what had been the head of the cotton processing plant and finally visited the museum before getting back on the road and driving about three hundred miles. I helped with the driving and it seemed to take my mind off my breathing problems and coughing spasms.

The following afternoon we were at our friends' house, Amy and Norman Prestup, in North Arlington, New Jersey. I took my last antibiotic. After a sleepless night, we left early the next morning and by the time we arrived in Montreal, I was gasping for air. That day I was diagnosed with double pneumonia, given appropriate antibiotics and told if I did not want to be admitted to the hospital, I had better rest. I did. When I could, which was not often.

Since it was not contagious, we had friends and family to visit. We had doctors to see and dental appointments that needed our attention. We had banking to do. We had the wedding party to attend for my nephew Stephen and his soon-to-be wife, Ruth. We did it all. I mended slowly.....but I mended.

In the midst of chaos, we planned our itinerary. During the hot weather, we would be in the north visiting Denmark, Sweden and Norway before heading south and into all the countries that had been behind the Iron Curtain when we left in 1989. We would also be visiting Rumania, home of my ancestors. I had maps and the location of where some relatives were buried. Our ultimate destination was Turkey. We would be gone a total of four months.

Against my physician's advice, we said goodbye to our friends and relatives on June 9, and arrived in London early morning June 10, 1992.

Chapter 40

The trip to London was totally uneventful. In two and a half years we had become seasoned travelers and things did not excite us like they did in the beginning. We arrived at Gatwick Airport at seven in the morning and knew exactly where to go to catch the train to Cardiff. We settled in quickly on the well padded seats and while Paul dozed intermittently, I stayed awake the entire journey, thanks to a cup of strong coffee. In Cardiff, we caught a local train to Radyr and received a pleasant, chatty welcome from John and Elen Lewis. When Paul and John left to retrieved our van from storage at the Barry docks, south of Cardiff, I took a short but much needed nap. My spirits lifted and the traveling bug hit, when I saw the van.

My diary for June 11, 1992 said "Something that never happens - I had to wake Paul at 10:45 A.M. He was exhausted." He slept so late and so soundly that I worried and checked on him often before awakening him.

After breakfast we went to Cardiff to take care of some business. We registered our van for the license sticker. We insured the vehicle. With essentials out of the way, we went to the Castle campground to meet our dear friends Don and Marjorie Jones. It was another pleasant and chatty get together. We were back in Radyr before the dinner hour.

We gave the camper a quick wash and readied it for the road. Before heading out the next day, Paul went shopping with

John for some necessities - several liters of oil, a filter and a gallon of windshield washing fluid. While they were gone, I unpacked our clothes and put them away, stowing the soft sided luggage in an unused compartment underneath the seats.

We hugged our friends, promising to write and waved to them as we backed out of their driveway. In less than an hour we were parked next to Don and Marjorie at the campground and within a matter of a few minutes were on our way again, in their van. We lunched at the Summer Palace in Llandaff before visiting the Cathedral Church of St. Peter and St. Paul located directly across the street from the restaurant. We enjoyed a walk and an ice cream at Penarth by the sea before shopping for groceries at a large, modern Tesco, that we never would have found on our own.

We were back at the campground by dinner time and enjoyed sandwiches, salad, melon and the company of Marjorie and Don until after ten o'clock. We went to bed while it was still light out.

After breakfast the next morning Paul and I walked to Cardiff Castle. Although we were camping on a dead end side street behind the castle, we took the long way around instead of fording the stream. This was my first major hike since the pneumonia. We had been to Cardiff Castle before but this time we took a guided tour and saw every inch that they were willing to show. Since several of the rooms in the castle are available for private parties, there was much to see and admire and the tour took a couple of hours, while a bit of a history lesson was given. After learning about the royal family that resided there, we walked the grounds. It was a glorious day full of sunshine and only a few wispy clouds.

We walked back to the campground via the arboretum. About half way between both bridges I realized I was rapidly running out of energy. We crossed the stream at its lowest point. I loved the coolness of the water, but the small sharp stones punctured the bottom of my feet. By the time we got to the opposite side and spitting distance to our camper, what wasn't pierced, was rubbed raw.

We rested that evening, spending much of the time studying our guidebooks and reviewing our itinerary. Before heading out the next morning, we breakfasted with Don,

Marjorie and Marjorie's son, Neil Roche, who lived in town.

Our first stop was Chepstow. We toured the outside of the castle and the inside of the local glass works. We drove to Oxford. After an hour or more of driving around the traffic choked University town, we could not find one parking spot large enough to accommodate our camper. Our tour, we decided, was in the van and that would have to satisfy us. That afternoon we drove to our favorite campground in Abbeywood. We arrived in time for a walking tour of the community, but it was late and most shops were closed. After a pub dinner, we returned to our camper.

Arriving in London by train the next day, we visited a flower show with our friends from Paradise Center, who were exhibiting some of their exotic plants. We peeked into every art gallery and craft store. We walked around every park until I could no longer stand up. While I rested on a bench and watched the queen's prized but nasty swans, Paul went through the War Museum, with much of it dedicated to Sir Winston Churchill. He thoroughly enjoyed the museum and I thoroughly enjoyed sitting and vegging. That evening, after the flower show closed, we met with Cees, Hedy and their daughter Monique for a pub dinner. We were back in our camper around midnight studying the ferry brochures and discovered that it would cost us about a hundred pounds sterling more than our previous crossing.

Although we had been there before, we could not resist another opportunity to walk around Canterbury before heading to Dover. We were on the evening ferry. Landing in Calais sometime in the middle of the night, we decided to stay on the dock with all the other campers that had arrived on our ferry and the previous ones of that day. We were tired and it was comfortable. It was very quiet the rest of the night and in the morning, we found spotlessly clean facilities available to us.

We loved being back in France and after a fast view of the Town Hall in Calais we found a Giant Mammoth (the French version of a enormous grocery, bakery, hardware, clothing store) and loaded our van with all the tasty niceties, including ten or more bottles of wine, that we had become accustomed to keeping on hand and only available or reasonably priced in France.

It was a short drive to the Cap Blanc Nez region with its chalk white hills and German bunkers scattered all over the area. We camped that evening in the city of canals, Bergues. While I prepared a terrific beef bourginone with lots of red wine in the sauce, Paul went for a walk. Needing a bit of the rest the next day, we walked Bergues just long enough to find a merchant selling fresh mussels and went back to the van. We spent the rest of the day reading, writing letters and generally taking care of my health, since I was still fluctuating between good and bad days.

Our first stop in Belgium, after shopping and banking, was in Ypres. I have all the brochures and flyers that show Ypres to be a lovely small town with shops, churches, a museum, a cathedral and movies. I don't remember any of them. All I saw were the cemeteries that dotted the gently rolling hills around the village. For as far as my eyes could see and in every direction, carved white headstones punctuated the green grass. This was the final resting place to thousands of fallen soldiers from distant parts of the world. We stopped at a Canadian cemetery to pay our respects. I was close to panic and my mind screamed to get out of that place. I never told Paul, I just clung to him. We left Ypres in the rain and I never again closed my eyes without seeing the leftover horror of World War II.

We stopped for a tour of Tournia, one of the oldest towns in Belgium. The cathedral was gorgeous and we walked slowly through the Folk Museum. We stopped at the chateau in Beloeil just in time for them to close their doors. Our guidebooks listed the gardens as a three star and we would have stayed until the next day had it been worth it, but everyone coming out said "nothing is in bloom yet." We left and camped that night in Mons, where the last shot of the Great War was fired.

We left late the next morning because of a misty rain and when we stopped in Binche, the heavens opened up. The old train station was lovely but the fruit and vegetable market was closing because there seemed to be no let up of the rain and few buyers or browsers were around. Although the rain had stopped temporarily, it had started again as soon as we arrived. We drove to the chateau and had a spectacular view of the town from atop the mountain. We checked into a campground early to wait out the inclement weather. Several games of scrabble took up most of the afternoon.

Our first stop the next day was the twelfth century abbey at Floreffe. The abbey was closed until after lunch but we walked the grounds and watched the peacocks, their magnificent plumage dragging on the ground behind them as they strolled around like they owned the place, which of course, they did. There was also a festival for the children going on with finger painting, coloring and clowns so we stayed and watched. We also took a quick tour of Namur, situated at the center of two rivers.

Dinant, even in the rain, was charming. The river rushed by on one side and a wall stood protectively on the other, leaving a narrow strip for the town itself. The road, in spots, had been carved out of the cliff.

Not far down the road stood another charmer, that we toured in the rain. Huy would have been a great walking town, had the cathedral not been closed. We tromped straight uphill to the fort before leaving. Our last stop for the day was Tongeren. It had a interesting one room little church but not much else.

We found nothing in our guidebook, neither signs nor symbols that indicated there was a campground anywhere in the area, so we drove to Antwerp. We found one campground, with just a few campers scattered about, in the heart of town. This alone was reason enough to stay awhile, however, I was again not up to par and felt congested. We both worried that my pneumonia was returning. The next morning we awoke to brilliant and welcomed sunshine. By noon, my health seemed to improve and we both looked forward to a stroll around town. Antwerp was not a big tourist city, much of it being dirty and busy, however, the grote market, St. Paulus Church and the Cathedral of Our Lady were worth a peek.

That evening we dined with Samantha and Adam from Australia, who were on a ten month tour that started in England, and with Anita and Bo Olssen, who insisted that we visit them at their home in Sweden. They gave us their address. Since we were headed to Denmark, Sweden and Norway, we promised we would stop in if we were anywhere close.

It was a short drive the next day to The Netherlands. We

stopped on the outskirts of Ultrecht for a picnic lunch before continuing to the delightful, walkabout town of Hoorn, just north of Amsterdam. The houses in the wharf section were built in the sixteen hundreds. Canals were everywhere. Lots of fascinating little gift shops lined the quaint streets.

We crossed the dike to get to Frieseland and were surprised at the hundreds of wild swans that made their home in these waters.

We arrived in Harlingen and set up in one of the many vacant spots of a huge campground. Fortunately we had not started dinner. Slowing making their way down one of the hiking trails, came Anita and Bo. They had seen the high top of our camper and came to fetch us and lead us back to where they were camping. We followed their motorcycles back into what seemed like bush country. It was more secluded and much quieter. The evening was spent "swapping lies" and sharing a barbecue dinner and wine.

After a long leisurely breakfast and goodbyes to the Olssen, we left. We stopped in the town of Harlingen for a walkabout. It had a small harbor with a few fishing boats tied to the dock and was a pretty little town, but there was not much else. We stopped late that afternoon in Weinshoten, spitting distance to the German border. We were not leaving Holland without another of their Indonesian Rijsttafel dinners. Sampling the food of each region had become a tradition of ours and an Indonesian Rijsttafel, when done properly, was one of the finest in culinary pleasures.

This one was done properly. Our table was filled with two portions of fried banana, pieces of broiled chicken, marinated beef in its own juices, stir fried vegetables, raw vegetables, something sweet, something bitter, sauces with various degrees of heat and more spices than you could shake a stick at. We had water, tea, coffee, desserts and all in mouthwatering little bites and tidbits. We ate until we could eat no more, piling up the dirty dishes at one corner of our table for easy removal. We waddled back to our camper well after dark.

We again had a long day. We left the campground mid morning, gassed up the van and picked up a few groceries with the last of our Dutch money and headed into Germany. We drove the coastline around Benserial and Esens and found the campgrounds littered with debris and loaded with people, crammed side by side. With such a short summer season, everyone wanted their tiny piece of the beach, and that's what they got.....a tiny piece.

We enjoyed a walking tour of the pedestrian section of Leer and withdrew sufficient deutchmarks to last us several days. We got back on the main road.

We thought we had had it this time. Paul passed a slow moving truck and was immediately flagged down by the police standing in the roadway. Shades of Spain popped into our minds. They spoke only German and wanted to see Paul's license and insurance. We did not understand the language, but they made it perfectly clear what our offense had been. Words and hand signals did the trick. Paul kept shrugging his shoulders indicating that he did not understand. When Paul said "ahhhhh" indicating that he finally understood, they gave him a verbal warning and we were off. We breathed a sigh of relief.

We camped that evening in a quiet spot just outside Oldenburg. We fell asleep that night, as every other night, with my arms wrapped around him, snuggling as close as I could and outlining his body with my own.

This ended my last complete day as a married woman, very much in love with the most wonderful person I have ever known.

Chapter 41

It started as such an ordinary day. We had slept in. We had breakfast. The morning chill had evaporated and was being replaced by sunshine. Morning life in the campground was hectic for many, so we waited before showering, dressing and getting back on the road. We were not going far.

The town of Bremen, spared devastation during World War II because the British refused to bomb the magnificent fifteenth century Town Hall and St. Petri's Dom, was our first stop. We walked in and out of all the old buildings, studying the architecture, admiring the stained glass, the paintings and the drawings. We stayed in Bremen most of the day because a street market was going on and we checked each table before choosing the fresh produce for our dinner that night. I bought giant mushrooms, green peppers, tomatoes and onions. I planned on making a vegetable spaghetti sauce and didn't need much since I always had olive oil and garlic in the van. Whatever vegetables, cooked or fresh that were left in the refrigerator, however small the portion, went into my sauce as its secret ingredient.

By the time the van was packed and everything put away in the cabinets so it wouldn't roll all over the floor as we drove, it was mid afternoon. We had had a wonderful full day in a beautiful old town and were off looking for a place to spend the night. By late afternoon we found a spot at a campground in

Zeven. The campground seemed lifeless. It was devoid of people, there were no trees or greenery and the office was deserted. A note taped to the window said that the office would be open in two hours.

Paul was impatient. He said he didn't like the place anyway and really wanted to be on the way. "Perhaps we'll camp in the woods," he said. "I really don't like this place," he continued. "Let's go."

Something about the campground left me with the same uneasy feeling. I didn't want to stay either, but wild camping that day, did not appeal to me. We got back on the road. We didn't drive far before I spotted another campground in the distance. It was up on a hill overlooking some pretty, gently rolling, countryside.

"I don't want to camp in the woods," I said pointing up the hill, "let's check out that one up there."

Paul reluctantly agreed.

As soon as we pulled in, we knew we would stay. The combination office, grocery store was open and an attractive, dark haired, woman, standing behind a desk, greeted us with a friendly smile. She told us, in German, to go find a spot we liked and to come back and tell her where we were parked. Although I speak no German, a few words were enough like Yiddish for me to know what she told us.

The spot we chose had lots of room. There were high bushes on both sides so we couldn't look into the windows of our next door neighbor's motorhome and, more importantly, they could not see into ours. It was a short walking distance to the swimming pool. It was clean and level and had its own water spigot. It was perfect. Paul parked, while I went back to the office to turn in our passports. The name, country of origin and passport number was filled in on their forms and both passports were returned to me.

While I rested, Paul went for a swim. A short time later, while I prepared dinner, Paul got the maps and guidebooks out and started charting our next few days' adventures. Since we had been to the bank the previous day, we still had plenty of German deutchmarks. We would spend the next day in Luebeck and on Sunday head towards the Danish border. We planned on camping on the German side and going into

239

Denmark early Monday morning when the banks would be open. We could get a fresh supply of money at that time and not have to worry about exchanging our deutchmarks.

Over dinner we talked about our Scandinavian holidays, knowing the region was closer in appearance to Canada than to Europe and we looked forward to the change. Paul found the town of Blekinge, Sweden on the map, home of Bo and Anita Olssen. Time permitting we would head that way. We clinked our wine glasses. We always rejoiced in our great fortune of being able to travel and loved the freedom and adventure.

After dinner Paul washed the dishes at one of the little outer buildings. He returned to the van and put everything away in the cupboards. Still full from dinner, he said he needed to go for a walk. I kissed him lightly on the lips.

I relaxed, putting my feet up on the extra chair. I opened my book, Sarum, to page one hundred and twenty-six and sipped at the glass of wine I had just poured. I was contented.

Chapter 42

He returned breathless. He did not look well. He put a cold cloth on his forehead. He tried to relax and listen to the radio. He knew something was wrong but said nothing to me.

"Are you OK, Baby?" I asked, "you look so pale."

"I'll be fine. I just ran too fast." he confessed.

"Why did you run, you just had a big meal?" I said, showing my annoyance while trying to make sense of what he had said.

"Because I felt wonderful," he responded.

"What happened?" I asked.

"I felt a sharp pain while I was running," he confessed.

"Did you stop running?" I asked.

"No, I ran harder," he said, "I thought I could outrun the pain."

Sitting in the van, he felt no pain. He just felt jittery. He was out of breath and perspiring. When it didn't clear up in a few minutes, I suggested we go to the hospital. He dismissed me with a wave of his hand, saying he would be OK in a few minutes. When he got sick to his stomach, I insisted we go to the hospital.

"Please, Baby, I know it's just indigestion, but let a doctor tell us."

He relented.

Although it was still light out, it was late in the day. I

ran up the hill to the campground office. It was closed. When I came across a group of campers, I asked if anyone knew where the hospital was located. When another camper offered to get his car and drive us there, I was relieved.

In minutes, Harry returned with his car. Still in his shorts and T-shirt, Paul put his shoes on, walked across the lawn, sat down in Harry's car, put his head back and started to snore. I climbed into the back seat and put my arms around him.

Harry's wife got into the back seat with me and just outside the campground gates started giving directions. All I remember was her voice saying recht (right) linx (left) at each turn. I remember the speed bumps on the road and wanting the car to fly over the bumps and not slow down. Paul was not moving, except for swaying with the turning of the car. I held him tighter and tighter.

"I love you, Baby." "Please, I love you, Baby," I kept repeating.

At the hospital, Harry jumped from the driver's seat, pounded on the emergency doors with one hand and slammed his palm on the buzzer over and over with the other hand. Hospital personnel rushed to Paul. His seat belt was ripped aside. He was dragged from the car and placed onto the gurney. In seconds all were running down the hall. I ran behind. A nurse stopped me. I was to wait in the hall.

It took only a minute or two and the doctor came down the hall. I was so relieved to see him. I was so sure he would say Paul burped or passed gas and that he was OK. I knew Paul was kidding. He had to be kidding.

The doctor said, "his heart had stopped and his brain was dead." The words made no sense.

"I'm sorry," said the doctor, more persistent, "his heart had stopped and his brain was dead." Again, I stared, not comprehending.

My God, what was this man saying. I stared at him. I stared at the closed door down the hall and then back at the doctor. It registered. I suddenly knew. I bolted for the emergency door. The doctor and a nurse both grabbed at my arms to try and stop me. They finally just ran with me. This could not be.

242

My beautiful Paul. He lay there on the bed, covered with a white sheet from the waist down. So still. His beautiful body. Wide shoulders. Blond curly hair on his chest that I touched so gently. My fingers ran down his arm and touched his chest. I caressed his face. His eyes were open part way. I tried to close them. They wouldn't stay closed. I stayed, both hands touching the man I loved more than anything or anyone on earth. I stayed until they led me away. I could not even cry.

They needed information. They needed to know what happened. When I told them he put his head back and snored. The doctor said "no, that is when he died." They knew what happened. The questions were few.

I called my friends, Joan and Cary Dressler, in Canada. Cary spoke fluent German and I knew he would come for me. They were not home.

I called Elizabeth McCreery in Toronto. Her telephone number was the only other one I knew by heart. I waited while her son, Conor, called for her. She had been in the tub. It seemed to take forever. I had no idea what time it was in Canada. I just had to talk to someone I knew. When the words were out, the tears started. She cried with me.

"Please feel my arms around you," she said.

It was too late. I felt nothing. There was no one.

The hospital bed that night was a lonely place. The nurses came in to see if the sleeping pills had taken affect. If they did, it was for a few minutes only. I stayed awake most of the night, lost. Too frightened to cry. Too confused to think about what I was going to do or where I would turn.

A German speaking nurse came for me early the following morning. Zombie-like, I showered and dressed. I was escorted to a small office with a desk and a telephone. They brought breakfast. I drank the coffee. I left the breakfast.

Owen McCreery called and advised me to call the Canadian Embassy. His words gave no comfort. No one was going to come for me. I was alone.

I don't know how long I waited for the Canadian Embassy, but no one returned my call. I called the American Embassy. The guard who took my telephone call said the Consular would call me back. He promised she would call within a few minutes. Lorraine Polik called within five minutes and I told her my husband died. "My husband is a Canadian but I'm American. Can you help me, please?" I asked, fighting to control every word.

"Let me start the paperwork," she said.

I had both passports with me. I gave her Paul's passport number, his full name and when I gave his date of birth as February 27, 1940, I heard a deep, sad sigh, "oh my dear," was all she said.

At the sound of her gentle sounding voice, I broke down. Then came the sweetest, kindest words I had heard since the beginning of my ordeal. "This is my weekend," she said, "would you like me to come stay with you?"

"Please yes," I begged.

Time stood still. I don't know how long I waited. I was still at the desk, the cold breakfast sitting in front of my unseeing eyes that were filled to the brim with tears, when the door opened.

"Mrs. Hossack," said the familiar voice in American English, "I'm Lorraine Polik."

"Thank you," was all I could say before the tears streamed down my cheeks. She let me cry.

Lorraine spent the day with me. She took me for a walk in the sunshine and we talked. She arrange with the staff to bring me something to eat, something cold that I eat in nibbles. She arranged for the cremation with a local funeral home. She arranged for the shipment of the ashes back to Canada. She arranged with the hospital to wait to be paid. Late in the afternoon, she drove me back to the campground. Lorraine explained to the owners what had happened. She stayed with me awhile longer and left me in their capable hands.

No one in the campground spoke more than a few words of English. I sat there, numb. They fed me. They tried to find someone who spoke more than a few words of English. In what little German I could understand, they told me that a couple would be arriving after church the next day, and that they would speak English. Someone found a sleeping pill for me. Someone brought me a glass of water and they watched as I swallowed it. Someone else walked me back to my camper. I put some music into a tape deck. I was drowning in a sea of people and no one to put their arms around me and tell me, in

244

my own language, that I will not go insane. I fell asleep before the tape ended.

By six o'clock in the morning, I was wandering around the campground, my mind in chaos. People looked, smiled and let me wander alone. Some knew. Most didn't. What could anyone say? What could anyone do? Someone from the office came for me while I was wandering and escorted me to the kitchen. Coffee and breakfast was put in front of me. The owners tried to speak slowly and I did understand a little. I just sat. I cried a little. I was so overwhelmed. So utterly alone. I needed my family desperately and had no idea how I was going to get home.

There was a telephone call for me. Somehow, at the bottom of the darkest pit imaginable, my brother Harry had found me. "Joei," he said, "please come home."
"Harry, how did you find me?" "Oh my God, Harry, what am I going to do without Paul," I cried.

"Leave everything, Joei, and come home," he begged.

"I can't, Harry, I can't leave Paul." "I can't leave my motorhome." "I'll get out of here, I just don't know how yet." "I'll be home soon."

"Joei, leave everything and come home." "I'll go back and get everything and take care of your motorhome." "Please just come home."

Harry had found me. Through Owen McCreery who had called my nephew Stephen, who called Harry. With the help of a neighbor who spoke German, who kept an International telephone operator on the line for hours, through the hospital, through the embassy, through the campground. He found me and the conversation just went around and around, over and over. I drew strength from the fact that Harry had found me.

"Oh my God, Harry, what am I going to do without Paul."

Harry kept repeating "don't think about tomorrow or next week or next year. Just come home. Forget about next week, just come home. Leave everything and come home now."

"OK, I'll come home. I don't know how yet. I can't leave everything. I'll come home soon." I hung up the

245

telephone repeating "I'll be home soon."

Later that Sunday morning, I saw a man walking around outside the camper, where the people were supposed to speak English. I approached, so sure that I could just make conversation. I asked if he spoke English and when he said "yes, a little" I started sobbing uncontrollably. His arm went around my shoulder protectively and he led me back to the side of his camper. His wife was sitting on a deck chair. She gave me her chair. I sat down and they let me cry. Gerda got a glass of water and a box of facial tissue for me. She held my hand and rubbed my arm. When I could speak, all I could say was "my husband died Friday night, here in the campground." That was the last moment I was alone.

"We will help you," was all Tony said.

My guardian angels were Tony and Gerda Jordaan from Apeldoorn, Holland. They tried to arrange for a driver from the NATO base where their son worked. I knew if I could get to the Hoek of Holland, I could sail back to England. They called the local automobile club to see what could be done. They checked my insurance policy to see if I could get a driver through the insurance company. They called a shipping line, but the office was closed.

In between trying to figure out some kind of solution, they fed me. They talked to me. They assured me they would help and they would do whatever necessary to get me out. They would not leave me alone. They did not know how, yet, but I was not to worry. They would handle it all.

Trying to rest in my camper late that afternoon, I studied a map and discovered a ship route that sailed from Hamburg to Harwich, England. Since my map was at least a year old, I worried that the route no long existed. Tony guaranteed he would get me on the first ship out. It was a very long Sunday and nothing concrete had been arranged. Again a sleeping pill was found for me and both Tony and Gerda escorted me to my camper. A hug from both.

By six o'clock Monday morning, I was back wandering the campground, not wanting to wake anyone. I passed the Jordaan camper only once. Gerda came after me dressed only in her robe. "Come, I have coffee for you," she said, holding my hand and leading me to their trailer.

246

By eight in the morning, Tony was on the phone talking to an agent at the shipping lines. I would be sailing at four that afternoon. I was on board as an emergency passenger, motorhome and all. Hamburg was approximately one hundred miles from Zeven, but I would soon be on my way. It had all been arranged.

There was another telephone call for me on that Monday morning. Her voice was so cool and deliberate, I knew that she had been crying all night. Joan Dressler, my friend and the liaison between myself and my family, was on the phone asking "Joei, what would you like us to do?" "We will do anything you ask, what would you like us to do?"

Without using the words, she was asking if I wanted them to come get me and I know they would have come, but "I'm sailing back to England this afternoon. Please call Harry and let him know I'm getting out of here," I said.

After lunch, although uncomfortable with the driving and vehicle conditions (steering wheel on the right), Tony drove my English van and Gerda drove their car to Hamburg. On my Visa card, I paid for the ticket that had been reserved for me. I called Lorraine at the American Embassy and told her that I would be sailing back to England that afternoon. She told her staff and I could hear a little cheer in the background. She wished me luck and told me her staff had been praying for me. I thanked her and told her I would write when I got home.

Tony and Gerda waited in line with me until I assured them that I could get the vehicle on the ship myself and that I would be all right. I knew they still had a long drive back to Zeven. Tony lifted my chin and looked into eyes brimming with tears, "if you look towards the heavens," he said, "you will one day see the sunshine." We hugged. A kiss goodbye to both.

The minute they left and were out of sight, I broke down. I waited in the queue for over an hour and when the crying subsided, I washed my face and dried my eyes so I would look reasonably presentable. I went to talk to the British people in the van ahead of mine. While we waited in line, I told them my story. They listened, saying nothing. Suddenly we were moving. I had to get back into my van and start the engine.

In the distance, I glimpsed a car with Canadian plates

and they had spotted my van, with big Canadian stickers on it, about the same time. The passenger, a woman, had waved. I had responded. We were moving like a caterpillar, each vehicle inching up a notch or two before the next could close ranks. My turn came. When they checked my papers before boarding, I was given a strange look and the ticket taker was shaking his head. Tony, it seems, had not been honest about the height of my van and I was ushered into another line, sandwiched between huge trucks. I was enormously relieved when I was parked in place and told to turn the key off.

Before leaving, I raided the refrigerator of a few perishables and some fruit and went on deck. The dining room was jam packed. There was one seat available at a table, occupied by a family of four. I asked if they would mind if I joined them and suddenly realized that with the hundreds of people in the room, I had met up with the Canadian couple. Again, I told my story.

Sheila was a nurse. After nibbling on my food, not tasting or caring to eat, Dan offered to care for their two children while she stayed with me. We walked and talked for several hours. She apologized for being so tired and offered to walk me back to my cabin. The thought of going to an empty room, particularly without the benefit of a handful of sleeping pills, did not appeal to me. I thanked her and went to the bar. I would listen to music all night if necessary. I could not stand to be alone.

Sitting right by the front door in the bar was the couple who had been in the van directly in front of mine. "Please sit with us," Mick insisted. They had been talking about me since I had told them my story on the dock. They did a lot of traveling together, mostly business, some pleasure and could not imagine the horror of my situation.

When I choked up, Mick had no trouble crying along with me since he had lost his mom a month before. Agnes and I shared our beer, since neither one of us could keep up to Mick and whatever hand was not holding a glass was held by either Agnes or Mick. The night passed and when the bar closed, they walked me back to my cabin. A kiss and a hug from both.

The next morning, I wandered the decks alone. When I sat, I cried. I didn't sit much.

My Welsh friend, John Lewis, had taken the train across England, met the ship in Harwich and I could see him standing just outside the fence as I went through customs. He drove me back to Cardiff. I cried or slept most of the way. Elen greeted me with a hug, her eyes, red from crying were filled with tears. Nothing was said. Dinner was on the table. We talked a little. I went to sleep physically exhausted, emotionally numb and mentally drained. I called the airlines the next morning and booked passage back to Canada. John would put the van in storage for me at the Barry docks and I was put on the train to London. My Canadian friend, Phil Webb, met me at the train terminal in London and took me home for the night. Phil and Andrea both spent a long night crying with me. Phil drove me to Gatwick Airport the next morning and waited while a ticket was prepared. It took one week to get from hell to home. My brother Harry, his girlfriend Sandra, my niece Rena and nephew Steven stood waiting for me at the Toronto Airport.
A NEW LIFE BEGINS.

Epilogue

It is unfair to end the book with "A new life begins." It was not a new life that began that day, a different one to be sure, but not a new one.

For the first two years my brothers, sister and their families maintained close communications. Our mutual friends kept in touch as best they could and frequently invited me to places that, under normal circumstances, I would have preferred to pass. I knew that if I passed too many invitations, they would stop coming my way. I went everywhere invited unless I had a previous engagement. I felt one minute of possible enjoyment was worth any amount of discomfort.

For the first two winters of living in the condo in Florida, I kept frantically busy. I took computer and writing classes. I volunteered at the opera and at the five little theaters in Sarasota. I demonstrated my craft skills at all the fairs. I joined singles' groups, exercise classes, hiking and biking groups. I made friends. I continued traveling, solo.

During the summer of 1993, I volunteered my services on three different archaeological digs in the south of England, something Paul and I had planned on doing together. I forced myself to learn to drive the van and I camped in it for short periods of time. In between the digs, many of the people mentioned in this book took wonderful care of me, Jean & Bill Higgs from Bristol, England, Marjorie and Don Jones from Welshpool, Wales, Phil and Andrea Webb from Otford, Kent, England, Brian and Ellen Nix from Creeting St. Mary, England, Dee and Dave Hunt from Norwich, England, Cees & Hedy Staple-Volk from Bures-LaMarsh, England. Bless them all.

During the summer of 1994, I spent a month visiting my friends in England and, while there, sold the motorhome that Paul and I had loved so much. With part of the money, I purchased a plane ticket to Turkey, prepared to spend two weeks close to the airport. I stayed three months in Turkey and another month touring a couple of Greek Islands and Cyprus. I made friends that I keep in touch with to this day. During the summer of 1995, I drove solo from Sarasota, Florida to Alaska in a small motorhome, camping all the way. That trip was definitely a love/hate relationship since I did not find the friendliness on the road that I had expected in campers and my VW Westphalia continually broke down. While the scenery in the state known as the Last Frontier was magnificient, the roads in the north country with their frost heaves, mud, gravel, lack of pavement were very intimidating. As much as I would love to redo that trip, I would not consider doing it solo.

At the end of 1994, after my trip to Turkey, my life changed dramatically and in a way I never dreamed possible. I wrote a travelogue on my trip and a local newspaper published it. I continued writing on travel and nostalgia and several of the local newspapers and magazines published my stories. Writing became a passion. Another talent I discovered buried under fifty years of living, was an ability to lecture. Since many women suddenly find themselves alone in later life, my lectures on solo world travel are well attended.

On the seventeen of February, 1998, with a blossoming career under my belt, I sold my condo in Sarasota, Florida and have, with a truck and fifth wheel trailer, resumed my gypsy life on a full time basis. Yes, I am still traveling solo.

On so many occasions, particularly in the early days of finding myself single, I heard "God does not close a door that he does not open a window." The secret is, when the window opens, you must be willing to crawl through it.

A new life begins every day.